LINDA YELLIN

has "the wit and verve of Susan Isaacs."
—*Publishers Weekly* on *Such a Lovely Couple*

PRAISE FOR

The Last Blind Date

"A laugh-out-loud-funny, nakedly revealing, kooky look at late, long-distance romance told with sweetness and soul. From the minute Linda picks up Randy at the airport with his fly accidentally unzipped, to their first New York date where he takes her to his friend's son's bar mitzvah and mistakenly calls her by his ex-wife's name, it's impossible not to root for their love."
—Susan Shapiro, author of
Five Men Who Broke My Heart and *Overexposed*

"With self-deprecating charm, Yellin takes her reader on a journey from Chicago to Manhattan, eviscerating New York City folkways with gentle yet biting wit. The author's voice is tender and authentic. You can see why Randy fell for Linda."
—Sally Koslow, author of *With Friends Like These*

"Linda Yellin's modern love story will leave you laughing 'til it hurts."
—Sam Apple, publisher and editor-in-chief of *The Faster Times*

"This memoir about love the second time around is romantic comedy at its very best. Breezy, fun, and worldly wise, it will put a never-ending smile on your face."
—Mindy Greenstein, author of *The House on Crash Corner*

"*The Last Blind Date* will have you rooting for Yellin as you eagerly turn the pages, hopeful that whatever the outcome she will just keep writing more."

—Laurie Graff, author of *You Have to Kiss a Lot of Frogs* and *The Shiksa Syndrome*

"I love this book. I couldn't stop reading."

—Nina DiSesa, author of *Seducing the Boys Club*

"The funny and touching truth about how a woman gets to happily-ever-after, a la Dorothy Parker."

—Susan Spano, former *New York Times* columnist

"A very funny book. Each page produces several giggles and at least one big belly laugh. . . . This is the kind of book that makes you glad that writers write."

—Sharyn Wolf, author of *Love Shrinks: A Memoir of a Marriage Counselor's Divorce*

The Last Blind Date and Such a Lovely Couple are also available as eBooks

THE LAST BLIND DATE

~~~~~~

LINDA YELLIN

G

GALLERY BOOKS

NEW YORK   LONDON   TORONTO   SYDNEY   NEW DELHI

Gallery Books
A Division of Simon & Schuster, Inc.
1230 Avenue of the Americas
New York, NY 10020

First Gallery Books trade paperback edition October 2011

GALLERY BOOKS and colophon are registered trademarks of Simon & Schuster, Inc.

For information about special discounts for bulk purchases, please contact Simon & Schuster Special Sales at 1-866-506-1949 or business@simonand-schuster.com.

The Simon & Schuster Speakers Bureau can bring authors to your live event. For more information or to book an event contact the Simon & Schuster Speakers Bureau at 1-866-248-3049 or visit our website at www.simonspeakers.com.

Designed by Jill Putorti

Manufactured in the United States of America

10 9 8 7 6 5 4 3 2 1

Library of Congress Cataloging-in-Publication Data is available.

ISBN 978-1-4516-2589-9
ISBN 978-1-4516-2591-2 (ebook)

For my mom
VIVIEN YELLIN
Thank you for your love, your salmon patties,
your wry humor, adorable good spirits, and for teaching me
to always look at the world through the *other* guy's point of view.
And thanks for marrying Dad, whom I miss very much.

Linda's Get-Out-of-Jail Card

In circumstances where I can't use a real person's name and can't make up just any name in case it *is* a real person's name, I'm using names of friends who don't care what anybody says about them. Or I'm scrambling details, maybe altering descriptions.

And if this makes sense, I'm hiring you as my lawyer.

Also, in the interest of not impugning any particular lecturer or getting Randy tossed out of his club, the actual Harvard Club topic in the "Out of My Ivy League" chapter was not on Frederick Law Olmsted. If there ever is a Harvard Club lecture on Olmsted, I'm sure we will attend. Assuming, of course, that Randy is still a member.

Contents

Some Pertinent Information You Should Know Up Front

~~~~~~~

When Randy Arthur of New York City separated from the first Mrs. Arthur, he left home with two suitcases, the stereo speakers, an agreement he'd get the children alternate weekends and every Tuesday and Thursday night, and a Five-Year Plan.

It broke his heart to leave the children, left him broke to leave Mrs. Arthur, but after years of feeling unappreciated by the woman he'd married twelve years earlier, it was a decision he felt compelled to make.

As Five-Year Plans go, Randy's wasn't up there with, say, Stalin's Five-Year Plans to industrialize the Soviet Union, but still, he felt a strong commitment to it. He'd focus on work, the children, pay the bills—and have lots of short-term, noncommittal, no-strings-attached relationships with a variety of beautiful women.

He was honest with the women he dated; told them right up front that he didn't want to get involved. But of course they never believed him. He was too attentive, too affectionate; in lieu of their names he called them "sweetheart" and "beautiful," leaving each woman under the impression that she was his beautiful sweetheart.

As soon as anyone got too close, attempted to buy theater tickets for shows months away, or suggested he redecorate the living room of his small one-bedroom apartment, maybe hang some pretty curtains, he said a gentle good-bye. His priority was the children, whom he never introduced to any of the beautiful sweethearts; he didn't want eight-year-old Phoebe and five-year-old Benjamin growing attached to women who would soon be moving on. It was a good plan, and because of his up-frontness with each succeeding participant, arguably an honorable plan, and should have been reasonably successful if he hadn't screwed it up in Year Two.

His best friend Dan who now lived in California suggested Randy call Linda who lived in Chicago and was the best friend of Dan's girlfriend Lynn. And if you failed to track that, ignore it, continue on, and go with the flow.

"What do I need with calling some woman who lives seven hundred miles away?" Randy asked Dan. In the interest of male bonding they spoke on the phone almost every week.

"My gut says you'll like her." Dan had a large gut so Randy tended to trust it. "She was here last year right before you were. She's tall. Dark hair. Decent body. She wrote a book. You should read her book. See what you think."

"What's her book about?"

"Her dead husband."

"Great. Already she sounds like fun."

"What have you got to lose?" Dan said.

"Airfare," Randy said.

But after Randy's current girlfriend started mumbling things about maybe leaving a toothbrush at his apartment, Randy began to think there might be certain advantages to dating someone out of town. Get together. Share a few laughs. Score some casy gratuitous sex, then escape on a plane. Talk about your no strings attached. The only thing better than a woman you don't plan to see again is a woman you'll never run into again.

So he called me.

Fifteen years ago I published a novel to no acclaim whatsoever. If by any chance you did happen to read it (and if you claim to have done so, I know you're lying unless you're my mother, one of my two sisters, or a handful of ex-boyfriends who were just making sure I didn't slander them)—well, if you *were* one of those six people, you'd already know the following:

Two weeks after college graduation I married a tall, handsome, damaged young man who'd spent three years in the Marines, one of them in Vietnam. He was sweet. He was confused. He was depressed. I was in over my head.

We had what was then called a whirlwind courtship, but I'd now call a what-the-hell-were-we-thinking courtship: engaged in six weeks. We met in college from different starting points. Small town—big city. Baptist—Jewish. He saw me as easygoing and uncomplicated. I saw him as strong and complex. The only other Vietnam vets I ever ran across were the ones I'd see on TV crime shows, their backgrounds always revealed during the big finish, right after they were arrested for hacking off a little old lady's head.

"Why did he do it?" someone would ask, and a detective with a somber voice and a bad brown suit would offer up the answer: "'Nam."

I loved that Teddy was a former Marine. What's sexier than a man who looks good in a uniform, fights for his country, and can wield an M16?

Okay, probably a lot of things. But when I was twenty-two years old, the Marine credential seemed like a good enough reason to get married. I just didn't know how to convince my new husband to maybe get a job. Or go back to school. To not stay in bed all day tormented and despondent.

In time he did rouse himself. He left me to drive to Alaska in his powder blue Volkswagen Bug with its oil leaks and broken heater. His plan was to find a job working on the pipeline. Seven weeks later he returned and announced he wanted to be a banker.

By then I was confused. *How'd he turn into a banker?*

He was hired by the First National Bank of Chicago to sit behind a desk on the main floor of their Erie Street branch opening new accounts and helping senior citizens balance their checkbooks. I worked in an advertising agency writing headlines for shampoo, a job he considered shallow.

We stopped talking, afraid to acknowledge the mistake that was us. We took separate vacations. One year Teddy went fly-fishing with his high school buddies while I visited my college roommate in Washington, D.C. Another year he went camping in Wisconsin with some guys he met at the bank while I visited a girlfriend who had moved to Boston.

After ten years of marriage, without ever really being *married,* we divorced. He moved to Oregon to learn carpentry and build furniture. I rearranged my closets and remained in Chicago. But we always stayed in touch, exchanging phone calls and letters.

He died of brain cancer four years later.

We were together his last nine months.

After the funeral I spent a year of sleepless nights blaming myself for every sad or lonely moment in his life—even the ones that took place *before* we met. I know it's self-centered to think I'd been the cause of someone else's every misery, but that's how bad off I was: too angry at myself to realize I was too involved with myself.

While the world slept, I agonized.

Why'd I stay on the pill when he wanted a baby?

Why'd I say no when he wanted to move to La Jolla and study oceanography?

Why wasn't I nicer to his mother?

I'd cry in the bathtub long past the water turning cold. I ignored my Bruce Springsteen tapes in favor of Billie Holiday. I felt so hopeless about the future that I didn't contribute to my IRA. People who once desired my company were more likely having conversations like this:

"Let's throw a party!"

"Swell idea."

"But do we have to invite *you-know*?"

"*Linda?* No way!" "Ugh." "She's a bummer!" "Miserable woman." "She'll bring down the whole night."

Even I wanted to avoid me.

I had always been one of those cheery, hopeful types. Half-full glasses. Silver linings. Lemonade out of lemons. Among my friends, I was considered the optimist. But for me, Teddy's death was the first time the words *everything will turn out fine*—turned out to be a lie.

At night I wrote in search of answers. During the day I dragged myself between my apartment and my job. Bus drivers admonished me, "Let's see a smile!"—these were Midwestern bus drivers. The truly unaware and insensitive would ask, "Hey, lady—who died?"

Friends eager to fix me tried fixing me up. And sometimes, just to get everyone off my back—particularly the friends of my mother with eligible sons, nephews, or wards of the state—I'd say yes.

There was germ-phobic George, who invited me to his apartment for our first date. He was afraid to go outside and breathe the air. He sat behind his big mahogany desk and motioned me to the seat on the opposite side.

"Is this a date or an interview?" I asked.

"I'm waiting for a call from my lawyer," he said, then proceeded to tell me about his previous home, the brownstone in the Gold Coast on State Street (which if you've never been to Chicago is code for: I'm rich) that turned out to be riddled with asbestos. Every nook. Every cranny. Just recounting the story was enough to make beads of sweat appear on George's forehead.

Keeping his words measured and precise, apparently surmising that I could only understand if he spoke s-l-o-w-l-y, George explained that he had just upped and walked away, leaving behind his Ralph Lauren Purple Label sport coats, his Thomasville furniture, his twenty-gallon freshwater fish tank built into the wall of his master bedroom—and moved to his current apartment with the excellent ventilation system.

I wasn't sympathetic sitting there on my side of the desk. I suggested that if he was so worried about creepy crawlers, maybe he should get his white carpets cleaned.

My dating skills needed some fine-tuning.

One week later, my friend Barbara wanted to fix me up with her depressed cousin, whose mother had just died of cancer.

"What do we have in common?" I asked. "Cancer and depression?"

My cousin Dolores fixed me up with a businessman friend of her husband's who cooked dinner for me: shrimp curry and something so exotic I still can't pronounce the name. After the strawberry parfaits—"made with *real* whipped cream, not Cool Whip," he was quick to point out—he leaned back in his chair and smiled at me. "I have terrific hands," he said. "Would you like me to crack your neck?"

Then there was Shish Ka-Bob, who took me to a Turkish restaurant and fancied himself a comedian. He'd say things like "May I be frank?" And when I said sure, he'd say: "Swell! Because my real name's Bob!"

I feel sorry for myself just remembering these dates.

The low point came when I let my friend Liz talk me into attending a Jewish Singles Super Bowl Party. A theme party for lovers of football and Moses held in the paneled basement of a synagogue. The guests were more determined than the football players.

Or maybe it was the guy who left his dog in the car while he fed me, and then left me in the car while he walked his dog. This was a man I knew had dog hairs on his bed linens.

And why did I let my mother's cleaning lady fix me up with one of her clients?

"I hear you're really neat," I said, when the client and I first spoke on the phone. His name was Martin. "I don't mean as in really cool, but as in—you pick your socks up off the floor."

There was a long pause.

"Well, I am rather tidy," he said.

The conversation never got more heated than that.

I was angry at every man I met. In the back of my heart I felt disloyal to Teddy, like I was cheating on him by moving forward with my life, by being alive when he no longer was. At least I wasn't cheating on him with anyone *good*.

I'd return home from dates and bury myself behind my computer.

Maybe my book didn't sell because it had the all-time worst cover design in the history of, well . . . cover designs: a photo of a pathetic-looking girl with a Mamie Eisenhower hairdo making cow eyes and clinging to the arm of a young man clearly too good for her. A perfect cover if the book were a primer for low self-esteem.

But even if people have no intention of ever reading your book, they generally think it's impressive that you're published. Of all the monikers a person can slap on themselves—abolitionist, abortionist, arsonist (I'm starting with the A's)—novelist is one of the better ones.

I was waiting for a box of free pencils at work one day when the man in charge of the office supplies closet said: "So, I heard you wrote a book."

"Uh, yeah. I did."

"What's the name of it?"

I told him, only to see his immediate disappointment when I didn't answer *Lonesome Dove* or *War and Peace*.

"Never heard of it," he said, in an accusatory voice, like if he hadn't heard of it, I wasn't a *real* writer. "But, hey, I think it's cool."

Strangers felt compelled to tell me their life stories so I could write about them. My landlord requested my autograph on something other than a rent check. While sharing an elevator, the stamp-collecting neighbor who lived next door said, "Gee, I'm afraid to say anything. It might end up in a book." While I thought: *You should only be so interesting.*

No one was prouder than my mother. The only thing that could have made her happier was if I found a new husband. She hated seeing me unattached. She was embarrassed that I wasn't married with three kids.

Five years after Teddy's death, even I admitted I was lonely. Not alone. But achingly lonely. Falling in love again didn't sound so terrible. I just didn't want to have to date to get there. I longed to skip the getting-to-know-you part and immediately jump to the rent-a-movie-and-order-in-some-Chinese part.

Which, in a way, is how I met Randy.

I flew to California the week of Valentine's Day to visit my friend Lynn and avoid Valentine's Day. California's an excellent place to ignore a holiday. Lynn was newly in love with

Dan, a Hollywood cameraman who once worked on a movie with Eddie Murphy.

"It's a good thing you weren't coming next week," she told me while fluffing the pillows on the bed in her guest room. Lynn's the nurturing type, a pillow fluffer and cookie baker. "Dan's friend Randy is coming out from New York, so the guest room is booked."

Months later I was home on a Sunday night watching a movie and eating Chinese when the phone rang.

"This is Randy Arthur," the voice on the other end said. "Do you know who I am?"

"Sure," I said. "You and I have slept in the same bed, only at different times."

"Well," he said, "timing is everything."

We spoke for forty-five minutes. A record for me. But the guy lived out of town. What could be less threatening? And halfway through the *Reader's Digest* versions of our life stories, it turned out to be one of those conversations where whatever either of you says, the other's responding:

"Oh yeah? Me, too."

"Really? Me, too."

We both loved *Gilligan's Island*. We both hated the musical *Cats*. We both preferred Swiss cheese over American. I found myself thinking: *At last, somebody understands me.*

I asked if he liked his mother and he said yes, he loved his mother, passing my *Do you have issues with women?* test.

He asked if I liked snakes, and I didn't exactly say I loved snakes or sought out their company, but told him, no, I'm not afraid of snakes and how in high school science class

I was the student who volunteered to wrap the visiting boa constrictor around my neck. Then he told me about Curly, his kids' pet red-tail boa constrictor kept in a glass tank in the living room, passing his *Do you have issues with cold-blooded animals?* test, while promptly flunking my *Good Taste in Living Rooms* test.

He said, "I read your book."

"Really? Me, too. That makes two of us now. How'd you end up reading it?"

"Dan insisted."

"I should hire him as my publicist. It's interesting waking up every day knowing you can be purchased used and new on Amazon for thirty-three cents."

"I liked you in it," Randy said.

"Really?"

"A lot."

"It's fiction," I said.

"Yes, of course. Fiction."

He kept calling. I wanted him to call. I know it sounds peculiar that I could break out of a depression after one good phone call, but by then I was looking for an excuse to be happy.

Leslie was a therapist and three-time divorcee. She tended to be a tad cynical about romance. "You should cut to the chase and go meet him," she said. We were stretched out on lawn chairs in her backyard, tanning our arms and legs while wearing huge sun hats to avoid wrinkling our faces. "Otherwise you'll start fantasizing about him, make him into some sort of Prince

Charming, and be disappointed when he turns out to be just another maniac who spent his childhood drowning kittens."

"What if he really is Prince Charming?"

"See. You're doing it already." She let out a long sigh. Everything about Leslie was long. Her legs. Her arms. Her wild, frizzy red hair spitting out from beneath her hat. Even her gold hoop earrings were long, practically grazing her shoulders.

Leslie had mixed a large pitcher of margaritas and we were each polishing off our second glasses.

"Randy's got a great voice," I told her. "Authoritative but sexy."

Leslie snorted. "Voices don't predict shit about a person. Visualize a radio DJ based on his voice and then get ahold of his photograph. It's always unbelievable—*that smooth, sultry voice belongs to* that *face?*" She refilled her glass, held the pitcher up at a slight tilt to offer me more; she looked like a mother in a Kool-Aid commercial. "Have you seen a photo?" she asked.

"Yes. He's cute. Owns a suit and tie."

"Cute doesn't mean diddly," she said. "The man could still have body odor. Meet him before you waste any more time."

In bed that night, listening to Springsteen's "Roll of the Dice," I phoned my friend Annabelle. She was planning to be in New York the following month for almost two weeks, on expense account, in a midtown hotel. Annabelle runs stress reduction seminars for top executives of large corporations. It's a lucrative profession because everybody has stress and nobody wants it. I asked Annabelle if I could stay with her, visit over the weekend, so I could check out if Randy was a kitty-drowning maniac with body odor.

"Good plan," she said. "The longer you wait to meet him, the more tension you may experience."

Annabelle hated tension. Everything about Annabelle was relaxed. Her minimal makeup. Her flowing cotton dresses. Her languid hand gestures. Even her curls were relaxed.

"Start with dinner," she advised. "Pay close attention to how he approaches dinner." After extended personal research on her part, Annabelle believed that a man makes love the same way that he eats a meal. "If he dives in without paying any real attention to the experience, if he's just focused on feeling full—he'll be the same way in bed. A man who shoves his food around his plate, who's not quite sure what to do with it, won't know a vagina from a hole in the wall. But a man who savors each part of his meal, pausing to sniff, taste, and admire every course—well, then you're heading toward dessert."

After we hung up and I spent several minutes thinking I might never eat with Annabelle again, I called Randy.

"If I happen to be in New York Columbus Day weekend, will you buy me dinner?"

"Sure," he said. "We can do more than dinner." He must have paused to consult his calendar before he asked, "Would you like to go to a bar mitzvah?"

That I didn't expect.

"For my friend's son," he added.

Okay. So it wasn't the sexiest offer I ever got, but I said, sure, why not? If Randy turned out to be a disappointment, at least there'd be a sweet table.

*   *   *

Two weeks later Randy invited himself to Chicago. He said that waiting over a month to meet me was too long. I could picture him in New York surrounded by his guy friends all egging him on to find out sooner rather than later if I was a maniac.

We exchanged descriptions so we'd recognize each other at the airport.

"I have a hunchback, hairy legs, and two missing teeth," I told him.

"My entire body's tattooed with Grateful Dead lyrics," he told me.

I wasn't sure what first impression I wanted to convey. Sexy and mysterious? Happy-go-lucky? Maybe blasé and nonchalant—like those rock stars who show up on *The Tonight Show* wearing old blue jeans and torn T-shirts. I opted for pert and optimistic: a yellow culottes dress with an orange belt, orange espadrilles, and L'Oréal Medium Ash Brown.

I borrowed my cousin Dolores's Lexus to pick him up.

Waiting for Randy at the gate, I started to have second thoughts, followed by third and fourth thoughts. What if we *hate* each other? This could be the longest, most painful blind date in *history.*

When the plane landed I watched the other passengers walk off and tried to guess which ones were the New Yorkers and which ones the Chicagoans. By the time a guy matching Randy's photograph finally emerged, I was wondering if I'd been stood up. The only other people getting off the plane were crew members.

He waved at me as he approached. I waved back.

He wasn't as tall as I expected, but tall enough; his hair more pepper than salt. The majority of the men I dated post-Teddy were bald, a circumstance I attributed to age and coincidence, not because I gravitated toward scalps. A head with hair earned definite brownie points along with the pressed khakis and the pin-striped shirt with the rolled sleeves. If I were writing a headline for his look, it would've been NATTY YET CLASSIC!

He walked closer with a big smile and an unzipped fly. I was too mortified for him to point it out.

He said, "Hello, sweetheart."

The First Part

Mama Said
There'd Be Men Like This

~~~~~~

On the drive from the airport to my apartment downtown, I made sure Randy knew the Lexus was on loan, not to go thinking I owned a fifty-thousand-dollar car; that I was a disaster in the kitchen, so he shouldn't be counting on any homemade meals; and that he'd be sleeping on the sofa.

I chatted nonstop. I felt like a seventh grader. "Cloudy sky," I said.

"Looks like rain," he said, peering up through the windshield.

"Sure does," I said.

He drummed his fingers along the armrest, kept tapping his foot on the car mat.

On the phone we'd talked about everything: his kids and how much he adored them; his new stockbroker career versus his old real estate career; Madonna's Blond Ambition tour; free will versus fate; chocolate versus strawberry; Pete Best versus

Ringo—and now we were discussing weather fronts. I struggled to connect the voice from the telephone with the real live man, sizing him up, checking him out, sneaking peeks during traffic stalls on the highway.

I caught him peeking at me while I was peeking at him.

"You're right," I said. "Could be quite a storm."

My apartment was in one of the tallest buildings in the city, on the fifty-eighth floor with an unobstructed western view. The straight avenues of the city stretched out into a panoramic grid. Walking into my living room at night felt like taking off on an airplane.

"Not what I expected," Randy said, setting down his canvas overnight bag next to the couch.

"Really? What did you expect?" I waited for him to say farmhouse, log cabin, moose lodge, one of those Midwest misconceptions typical of East Coasters.

"Well, it's higher up than I expected," he said, staring out the window, then scanning my white walls, white carpet, my white upholstered furniture, "and more virginal."

I served dinner out of cartons. General Tso's chicken. Black bean prawns. And something called Any Two Meats with Wonton.

We sat in the living room on adjoining white chairs, side by side, chopsticks in hand, passing cartons back and forth as we ate with our stocking feet on the windowsill. I poured champagne to class the meal up.

I noted that he ate with gusto. Annabelle would approve.

We watched the storm clouds roll toward us. Lightning slashed through the sky, whipping from one site to the next, a cosmic electric show followed by a rolling clap of thunder.

"If we're into signs, this could be the start of a major love affair," Randy said.

"Or a lot of flooded basements," I said.

Randy leaned over from his chair, bringing his face close to mine. He smelled like Dial soap. "Let's kiss," he said.

"Okay," I said.

Saturday morning Randy popped for breakfast at the Walker Bros. Original Pancake House. He ordered flapjacks and bacon and hash browns. I ordered a plain omelet, then left it untouched.

We spent the rest of the day doing the things couples do in those corny montage scenes in the movies, the series of clips that say: *We're getting to know each other! We like each other! Romance is in the air!*

We strolled past the shiny storefronts on Michigan Avenue, a street so idyllic, so pristine, a vision of such horticultural magnificence, that it feels like a movie set.

We watched the Michigan Avenue bridge rise and split for a high-masted sailboat on the river below.

We listened to the saxophonist who stands in front of Saks Fifth Avenue playing the *Flintstones* theme song.

Too bad it wasn't snowing so we could roll around and have a snowball fight, or hot enough to splash each other in Lake

Michigan, the two mandatory activities of every halfway decent montage.

Instead we walked along the lakefront and through Lincoln Park. Randy started rattling off the Latin names of trees until I told him that really wasn't necessary. I already thought he was smart.

He leaned over and kissed me beneath an *Aesculus hippocastanum*.

That night Randy was off the sofa and invited to sleep in my bed. "But no sex," I told him. "The rule is we keep all underwear on."

"What about bras?" he said. "What if nobody wears a bra?"

Before I could answer, his trousers were on the ground. I thought, *if there's ever a gold medal for Olympic pants removal, this guy'll be first on the podium.* Then I refocused on the situation at hand.

I believe underwear says a lot about a man.

White briefs: Practical. Reliable. Buys in bulk.

Thong: Weekend job at Chippendale's.

Nothing whatsoever: Everything's in the wash.

Randy wore colored briefs. Conservative in their own Fruit of the Loom kind of way, but with a promise of something extra.

I insisted we *take it slow.* No underpants were removed. We were warm and playful, we invented games in the dark; I traced words on his back with my fingertip and made him guess what they were; Randy whispered like he was a lech and I was the high school prude.

In the morning, I was first to wake. I made coffee, the lone item in my cooking repertoire, and after kissing Randy awake, we sat in bed, propped against the pillows. We sipped from matching white mugs. By then I was wearing an old Chicago Bulls shirt; I'd managed to comb my hair and splash water on my face, hoping I still looked desirable in daylight.

"Well, we made it to Sunday," I said. "Not many people plan a two-day date the first time they meet."

"You're fun," he said.

Fun. Was that a good thing? Or a polite thing? Like, *you have a pleasant personality.*

"What would you have done if you didn't like me?" I asked.

He didn't answer right away. His expression was serious and reflective. He said, "I'd have gone home early."

My coffee suddenly tasted cold. "We're still on for the bar mitzvah, right?"

"Of course," he said, then pretended to twirl a mustache like a lech.

For the next several weeks our phone conversations centered on erotic expectations. Randy elaborated on what he wanted to touch, lick, kiss, how often and why. How he couldn't wait to see me, hold me, study and explore me; he mentioned everything short of checking for body moles. I'd never known a man to be so communicative. I kept saying things like, that sounds interesting, that could be good, works for me.

I called Annabelle to explain that I would not be sharing her hotel room when I visited New York. She wished me luck, advised me not to stress out.

The taxi stopped in front of a neon sign. *P&G Café Bar.* I glanced down at the notepaper in my hand, read the address aloud once again.

"That's it," the driver said, aiming his thumb over his shoulder. "One door to the right."

As I exited the cab, carrying my weekender bag and a hostess gift of Frango mints, I spotted Randy walking down the street, all handsome and corporate-like in a dark gray suit and tan trench coat, carrying two wrapped bouquets of flowers. I'm a sucker for men in suits; they look solvent, responsible, like they've never bounced a check. This was before I learned Randy had spent two years as a hairy-faced hippie living in communes and hitchhiking around the country and not calling his worried-sick mother for months on end.

"Hello, beautiful," he said, kissing me, handing me the flowers and taking my bag. Men never called me beautiful. I couldn't help but feel, well, kind of thrilled.

He led me into the lobby of his building, which looked like a castle with its stone columns and arched stained glass windows.

He introduced me to Jerry, his elevator-combo-doorman, who complained about the Giants while the three of us rode to the thirteenth floor.

"I hope you enjoy the flowers," Randy said as he unlocked his front door. "One's roses and the other's lilies. I didn't know which you'd like better."

Once inside the doorway Randy set down my bag and emptied my hands of floral items, pulled me close, and kissed me again. I suppose he showed me his living room and kitchen and pet snake. And I suppose he put the lilies in a vase. And maybe I even unpacked. But the next thing I remember we were lying naked in his bed surrounded by lit candles with Van Morrison playing on the stereo.

Then all proceedings screeched to a romantic halt.

"I just want you to know I've had a blood test," Randy said.

"Wonderful. How's your cholesterol?"

"That's not the kind of blood test I mean."

"Really? Because if you've had sex with any other woman in the past six months, the test doesn't count and you still have to wear a condom."

"Well, I *have* had sex in the past six months." He sounded indignant. Like *of course* he'd had sex in the past six months.

He rolled over and with a practiced ease and grace slid open the drawer of his night table. I peeked over his shoulder.

"Geez," I said, "you've got your own Trojans concession stand in there. Have you had sex with every woman in New York in the past six months?"

"No, of course not. I just like to be prepared."

"For what? In case a cheerleading squad drops by?"

Randy closed the drawer after producing four foil packets. Mr. Great Expectations.

But he didn't overpromise.

*   *   *

Saturday morning, bar mitzvah day, we attended the Notre Dame of synagogues. Gold-leaf pillars. Vaulted ceiling. Park Avenue address. And such a crowd! Somehow my Chanel knockoff suit didn't quite cut it among the *real* Chanels.

The simple redbrick synagogue my parents attended, and forced their three daughters to attend back when we were still young and forcible, looked like its poor cousin. *This* synagogue, this God-blessed golden shrine to synagogues, glittered and gleamed. I wanted to run to the nearest pay phone to call my mother and report all the details. *The rabbis wear silver-trimmed robes. The floors are glass mosaic. You wouldn't believe the stained glass Moses.* I could imagine my father barking in the background, wanting particulars about the building fund, laughing at how those crazy New York *machers* must be up to their *tuchases* in third mortgages.

I sat with a prayer book open across my knees. Since I was in the neighborhood, I thanked God for sending Randy my way.

Jared the bar mitzvah boy looked like he'd outgrown his blue suit between the time it was purchased and the time he was standing before the congregants delivering a speech about Joseph and his coat of many colors. Some connection was being made between the weaving of threads and the weaving together of Jews around the world, but I missed the nuances, I couldn't quite follow Jared's point. Probably because of the Jewish boy sitting next to me.

During the three-hour service we were shushed twice, har-rumphed once, and clucked at three times by offended guests

surrounding us, most of them elderly ladies who evidently
didn't consider it proper for two people to paw each other during a religious ceremony.

After the remaining service rituals—songs, sermon, Torah—
the worshippers migrated to the Grand Hyatt Hotel on Forty-
Second Street for a reception.

An hors d'ocuvre table stretched down the entire length of
the ballroom, covered with trays of salmon mousse, popcorn
shrimp, and clams casino. The theme for the party was Hollywood. Flower arrangements replicated movie scenes. Marilyn
Monroe pushed down her white daisy dress as it billowed up
from a subway grate of ferns; Dorothy, Toto, and the Scare-
crow—bluebells, petunias, and clematis—marched through the
chopped liver; Scarlett O'Hara, all in red roses, graced a staircase of miniature egg rolls. Huge ice-carved letters, four feet
high, spanning the ballroom and table, spelled out JAREDWOOD.

The guests hit that table like it was 4 A.M. and last call at
the bar.

Randy and I elbowed our way through the stampede, homing in on the mini-crabcakes. A woman blocked my face as
she reached to pluck a melon ball. The rabbi shoved past me
to lunge for the halvah. The same people who'd found my behavior offensive in temple were certainly managing to offend
me at the hors d'oeuvres.

"Do you think anyone would mind if I wrap a few mushroom
caps in a napkin and stick them in my purse?" I asked Randy.

Twice he introduced me to other guests as Susan, as in—

the former *Randy and Susan*. I didn't correct him, didn't want
to embarrass him. I just pretended my name was Susan.

Guests rumbaed. Guests tangoed. A live orchestra played
Cole Porter, Sammy Cahn, and Hoagy Carmichael. I won-
dered if they'd brought the wrong playlist, the one labeled
"Debutante Ball."

I listened to toasts from aunts, uncles, cousins. A blessing
over the bread from Grandpa Harvey.

I discovered Randy danced with a skillful flair and open joy.

It was the longest bar mitzvah in the history of the Jews. I'd
known people who got married, threw a reception, and came
back from the honeymoon faster.

About the time I thought the party was over and we could
finally hightail it out of there, two long curtains were rolled
open and dinner was announced.

Sunday morning Randy suggested we go sailing. We were still
in bed. I thought we had just finished sailing. I was beginning
to believe the guy might actually run out of condoms.

"Sailing? Like on a boat?" I said.

"That's generally the way it's done. My father has a boat
docked in Staten Island. We can rent a car and drive out there.
Sleep on the boat. It's so romantic. I'd love to take you sailing."

We went sailing. It was a windy, beautiful afternoon with
large, constant waves. Scenic, if you like that sort of thing.
Randy maneuvered the boat out of port. Twenty minutes later
I barfed over the side of the boat. Three minutes after that,
Randy headed back into port.

*   *   *

I walked out of the marina bathroom chewing gum. Randy was rearranging the car trunk with backpacks, blankets, and a cooler containing uneaten salami sandwiches and unopened beers.

"I'm sorry," I said. "Boats and I aren't a good mix."

"Forget it." He didn't even bother to hide his disappointment. "It's just something I wanted to share with you." For the slightest moment I was afraid he was going to break up with me right there in the middle of the parking lot. He told me he'd been sailing since he was three years old.

I told him I'd been throwing up since I was three years old.

He slammed the trunk shut. *Did we just have a fight?*

"So, what else is there to do around here?" I asked, trying my best to sound upbeat, cheerful, like there was life after sailing.

Randy looked right past me, his eyes scanning the boatyard, probably searching for a woman with a stronger constitution, but he rallied, said, "Well, we've still got the rental car for the rest of the day. Do you want to drive to New Jersey and meet my parents?"

Meeting parents usually *meant* something. He's talked about me. They've asked about me. He's crazy about me. Then again, maybe it just meant he hated to waste a rental car.

I said, sure, of course, I'd love to meet your parents.

A more honest response would've been: *Meet your parents right after I heaved over their boat?*

*   *   *

We drove down a crowded turnpike past oil refineries, Newark Airport, a Budweiser brewing plant.

I said, "Hey—isn't this supposed to be the Garden State?"

Having gone from one moving vehicle to another, I was nervous. Either Randy didn't hear my stomach rumbling or he was too polite to comment. Or he didn't care what happened to the interior of a rental car. He did most of the talking; Benjamin this, Phoebe that. It was obvious he was nuts for them.

I slid across the seat wanting to sit closer and said what any woman would have said: "Your kids sound great. I'd like to meet them sometime."

Randy glanced over at me, then back at the road. "I never introduce my children to the women I date."

I slid back to my side.

He had a policy. "My kids have had enough disruption. I don't want them meeting someone, getting attached, and then she goes away."

Goes away? Goes where? My stomach hurt, but not from seasickness.

He said, "It'd be too confusing for them."

Randy's parents lived in a modest split-level in Clark, New Jersey, a town I had never been to, nor for that matter, heard of. The front of the house was fake stone on the first level with white aluminum siding on the second, and almost completely hidden by the tallest, fattest rhododendron bushes I'd ever seen, the redwood forest of rhododendrons, resulting in a blocked view and minimal natural light inside the living room.

Ruth was short and round, high-breasted and blond; she reminded me of Cinderella's fairy godmother. I kept expecting her to whip out a wand and say, *Bibbidi-Bobbidi-Boo!* Instead she whipped out crackers and orange juice.

Larry was also short, but all angular arms and legs, a wiry build and a jaunty gait. Bibbidi-Bobbidi-Boo married to Popeye.

They seemed delighted to have Randy in their midst. They fussed over him, circled around him, kept hugging him. They were warm and curious toward me.

Ruth gave me a tour of the house with its heavy dark furniture and bright red living room rug, which she promptly informed me they'd purchased in Turkey as a gift for Randy and Susan. *Only Susan hadn't liked it.*

Personally, I had to go with Susan on that one.

It was an eclectic, chaotic, friendly home. Cactus plants on the floor. Space heaters. Stacked folding tables. Teacup collections. Glass candy dishes. Larry's model boats. Dried flower arrangements. China figurines, most of them owls in oversized eyeglasses; Ruth collected owls. And just for good measure— big open plastic vitamin bottles lined up on the dining room table. About as nonchildproof an environment as possible. Randy either grew up learning not to touch anything or the second he shut the front door and took off for college Ruth unpacked the tchotchkes.

She showed me framed photos of Randy's Boy Scout picture (sweet), baby picture (pudgy), his high school graduation picture (sweet, pudgy, and dorky), his sister Andrea and her two daughters, and the real showstopper: a portrait of Randy, his kids, and a woman who looked *just like me.*

I tried telling myself, *some guys have a type,* Randy's apparently long thin face, long dark hair, and brown eyes—but seeing Susan's picture creeped me out. I wondered if I was some sort of sick attraction—like when Clark Gable kept marrying women who looked like Carole Lombard after Carole died.

"The Westfield diner or the Cranford diner?" Larry asked, interrupting the tour. "Which do you prefer?"

"I'm flexible," I said. "Never been to either one."

"Well, we'll fix that, young lady!"

After an intense family discussion over the Westfield roast chicken versus Cranford's lasagna, we ended up at the Rio Diner in Woodbridge, where Larry liked the cheeseburgers.

We sat on opposite sides of a high-gloss vinyl booth, Larry and Ruth on one side, Randy and me on the other. A dust-covered plastic flower arrangement lined the windowsill between us. Ruth beamed at me, beamed at her son. She looked ready to call the caterers.

Our waitress, Vera, her name tag posted in the middle of a fluffed-up hanky pinned to her uniform, flipped open her bill pad, all businesslike and efficient and said, "Ready, folks? Let's start with the girls."

I looked around. She meant Ruth and me.

While Vera waited, Ruth continued to study the menu as she shared her thinking process. "I had spaghetti on Tuesday so I don't want that again . . . eggs? Maybe eggs. No, I'm tired of eggs . . . is the salmon fresh?"

"Fresh frozen," Vera said.

Ruth made a face. "A Caesar salad," she said. "No anchovies. No croutons. Unless, Larry—do you want the anchovies?"

"I just want to order!" he said.

"No anchovies," Ruth said, closing her menu shut.

Randy and his father ordered cheeseburgers. I ordered dry toast and ginger ale.

Once Vera left, Randy and his dad chatted about the boat. Ruth conversed in charming non sequiturs. "So you're from Chicago? My cousin Lenore lived in Chicago. Died young." She broke off the top of a bread stick. "I never win the lottery because I never buy lottery tickets." Randy squeezed my knee under the table. Ruth held out her hand for inspection. "I don't like this nail color."

All of a sudden Larry dove his head into Ruth's chest, blubbering back and forth in her bosom, much to the chagrin of the other restaurant patrons. And me.

"I love my wife!" Larry announced when he came up for air.

"Oh, Larry, stop that," Ruth said, brushing him aside. "Anyone want a garlic stick?"

Larry wrapped his arm around a smiling Ruth. Randy was smiling, too.

I thought I was managing to join in on all the group smiling, be a part of the high spirits, but I kept thinking about my conversation with Randy in the car.

Ruth suddenly looked at me and asked, "Are you ill?"

CALL ME WHEN WE'RE MARRIED

～～～

Randy Arthur was not in the market for any long-term commitments. He'd been telling me this for over a year. He told me on the weekends I flew to New York to see him. He told me on the weekends he flew to Chicago to see me. He mentioned it on the telephone the weekends I stayed home and went to movies with my girlfriends while he stayed in New York with his kids.

A lot of women might not have tolerated so much ambivalence. But one, it took away any pressure on my end. And two, I didn't believe him. He'd call every morning before he left for work. At night, he'd call before falling asleep. We talked once or twice during the day. We were a couple with rituals.

"Talk. Talk. Talk," my mother said, calling from Florida. "Phone conversations is your idea of a boyfriend? You can't find one decent man in all of Chicago?"

How could I explain that a long-distance romance had certain advantages, not the least of which was a seven-hundred-mile emotional safety zone?

I *liked* that Randy lived a plane ride away. The possibility of a full-time relationship was far easier to handle than an actual relationship. I had already married a man I barely knew and couldn't save. A marriage that ended in heartbreak. What made me believe I had better judgment now? Age and maturity sure didn't count. My dating record was proof of that. Phone conversations were fine by me. You can't be afraid of a man going away if he's not there in the first place.

I should mention that I'm a lousy flyer. Airplanes and me are like sailboats and me. In fifth grade Stacy Dean, the class smarty-pants, told me her parents always flew on separate airplanes so in case one of the planes crashed, Stacy and her brothers wouldn't be left as orphans. My parents didn't do that. They weren't as thoughtful. But it's near impossible for me to set foot on an aircraft without focusing on barf bags, turbulence, wind shear, and death. So dating a man who *required* airplanes was not ideal.

And then there were those two other details:

Randy was still married.

And I still hadn't met his kids.

His divorce lawyer said it was no time for a girlfriend to show up. Randy said he couldn't risk the psychological damage my appearance might have on the children, but please don't take it personally.

So I didn't. I went from hurt to understanding, insulted

to complicit; I was willing to step onto flying objects for him. The last woman to trust a man so much was Mrs. Ulysses right before her husband said: "I'll just be a minute."

Until my own Greek chorus kicked in.

Leslie the three-time divorcée: *"Linda, do you really think this guy is sincere?"*

My older sister, Brenda, the pious, religious sister: *"You actually believe him?"*

My younger sister, Toby, the CPA: *"It doesn't add up."*

They insisted a red flag was flying at full mast.

My mother calling from Florida: *"If I were you, I'd tell him not to call back until his divorce is final."*

My father on the bedroom extension: *"And ask to see the paperwork!"*

Every time another Randy conversation began with *this-is-for-your-own-good*, often followed by theories involving eggs and a basket, my doubts ballooned.

I was in love with a man from the City That Never Sleeps— and I promptly stopped sleeping.

"Of course, you can't sleep. You smell a rat," Claudia said during one of our bed-to-bed 3 A.M. phone calls. Claudia also never slept; we were sisters in insomnia, in her case because she was constantly pissed at the Senate or Congress or some foreign dictator. Claudia hadn't had eight straight hours of sleep since the U.S. forces ousted Noriega in 1989. I could call her at any time of night and she'd pick up the telephone sounding wide awake and alert like she was in the middle of organizing a protest march. She was a political radical who looked like Sandra Dee. "Not meeting the kids yet is just plain abnormal," she said.

"He's got a policy."

"So did Mao Tse-tung." I could hear Claudia striking a match. "Did you read that article in *Newsweek* that insomnia can shorten your life?" she said. "I may die any minute now." I didn't mention how the three packs of cigarettes a day didn't help. "Tell him to cough up the kids or cut out."

I examined my legs for fuzz to see if I could go another day without shaving. "It's not like I don't *sort of* know the kids. I've seen videos of their birthday parties. Phoebe rides horses. Their goldfish are named Steve and Pete."

Claudia continued to insist that I confront Randy. Claudia sold airtime for a radio network—or as she liked to call it: *just air*—and could spin a powerful sales pitch. Claudia was tough on men; she had never married. She compared every guy she'd ever dated to her adoring father and eventually they all flunked.

"Ask for the order," she said, exhaling a long breath into the receiver.

I could hear a toilet flush, which meant Claudia had been smoking and peeing while we were talking. Maybe there was another reason Claudia had never married.

I called Annabelle from work the following morning. I asked if she thought I should ask for the order. She put me on speakerphone so she could talk and still meditate or perform downward dogs or burn incense or whatever it is antistress counselors do all day.

"Enjoy the happiness you're experiencing now," she said. "Release your attempts at controlling the future. Disappointment only occurs when you're attached to something being a certain way."

Annabelle's conversations often sounded like something somebody else would needlepoint on a pillow.

"Here's the scoop," she added, all her Zenness heading right out the door. "At your age—another bus doesn't show up five minutes later."

That evening Randy called while I was tracking a fly in my living room with a rolled-up *Time* magazine, Boris Yeltsin's nose partially revealed on the cover.

"What are you up to?" he asked.

I told him not to be alarmed if I suddenly dropped the receiver in pursuit of my prey.

"Why don't you open a window and wait for him to fly out?"

"What guarantee do I have that he'll fly out versus three hundred of his best friends flying in?" I watched the little bugger bounce from the ceiling fixture to the corner up over the television set. "You're calling early. Are you going to sleep early?"

He said, "Would you mind if we skip our next weekend together?"

I caught my breath. "Is that a trick question?"

"No, it's a real question. It's just that I haven't had a weekend—this will sound odd but, well—*off* between alternating weekends with you and the kids and it might be nice to have a chance to just hang out and catch up without any plans."

I'd been reduced to a plan?

"But you canceled our weekend two times ago."

"I was sick with the flu."

"And I volunteered to come play Nurse Linda."

"Then you'd have caught the flu."

"And we missed the weekend three weekends before that because of your college guys' reunion thing."

"That was different."

"Different how?"

"Turns out there's this family party I didn't know about. I must have erased my cousin's message before I heard it because she called again to ask if the kids and I were coming, and Susan said it's okay even though it's not my weekend."

Ah, the children; making me girlfriend non grata.

"Which cousin?" I asked, a stupid question because I'd never met any of his cousins.

"My mother's cousin Tula," he said. "She owns a stationery store in Queens."

"And she invites people to parties by leaving *phone messages?*"

"It's a last-minute thing. A surprise fiftieth-anniversary party for my aunt and uncle. I don't see them often, but I really like them."

I excused myself. "One moment, please."

There he was. Right in the center of the coffee table, just asking for it. Dropping the phone and using two hands to direct Boris's nose, I slammed the living daylights out of that buzzy little bastard. Retrieving the phone again I said, "Okay, honey, if that's what you want."

As soon as I hung up I called Claudia. She was going on about U.S. troops invading Haiti. I waited until she stopped, then I asked her if she thought another canceled weekend was a bad sign.

"Versus a *good* sign?" she said.

"Ever since I said *I love you*, he's been acting funny."

I could hear the news playing on the television behind her. My personal problems were competing with a military coup. I told her about Randy's phone call, the kids, the party-inviting cousin.

"When did you turn into a secret girlfriend?" she said. "You might as well be the guy's mistress. At least that way you'd get your rent paid."

I'd blurted out the *I love you* three visits earlier. It just happened. One of those in-the-moment blurts. When we were in bed. I could have said the words a million times by then, but with all due respect to Gloria Steinem, I was still rather hoping the *man* said them first.

But then I said something really stupid and pathetic: *Do you love meeee?*

Randy responded with this whole long speech about how if one person says I love you then the other person feels obligated to say I love you and people say it when they don't mean

it and that's why he hates to say it and how he'd said it in the
past when he thought he meant it but it turned out he didn't. I
believe he also threw in a few lines from Patrick Henry's "Give
Me Liberty or Give Me Death" speech along with a couple of
choice phrases from the Magna Carta.

After I killed the fly and Randy's phone call killed my evening,
I flipped between crazy-making thoughts and telling myself I
was being foolish, paranoid, ridiculous—basically delivering the
same pep talk women have been giving themselves for centuries,
usually right before they find out their husbands or boyfriends
are cheating. Sure, I could understand if Randy were bailing
for an important reason like *my mother's having a kidney trans-
plant*—but a last-minute surprise fiftieth-anniversary party?

I reviewed every male betrayal in my entire life, starting
in first grade when Dennis Berger gave every girl in class a
valentine, except me, because I wasn't pretty enough, past Ira
Chynsky in high school asking if I was free Saturday night and
when I excitedly said *yes!* asking if I could babysit his sister,
right through Kevin Toner excusing himself at a restaurant to
buy cigarettes and never returning.

But Randy was—well, Randy. Funny. Open. Available.

Except the following weekend.

Maybe I was asking too much. Maybe I shouldn't be hoping
somebody wanted me around all the time; that it was enough if
somebody at least wanted me now and then.

Even though marriage for me hadn't exactly been what you'd
call a huge success, I hated my single status, hated the *Are you*

married? question, followed by the glance to my left hand and look of glazed-over pity because obviously nobody considered me lovable enough to wed. When Randy showed up, invitations poured forth. Dinner parties. Cocktail parties. Double dates to the movies. I couldn't believe it. *Suddenly everyone's entertaining?* And then it hit me like a big fat social calendar aimed at my head: all these dinner parties and cocktail parties and movie double dates had been going on for years, only nobody was including me. I'd been socially undesirable and didn't even know it. I'd just assumed that everyone was staying home watching television. Like me.

Maybe *now and then* was better than *nothing.*

When the phone rang in the morning I was still in bed, half asleep. I picked up the receiver expecting to hear Randy.

"Hello," I said.

"What's wrong?"

It was my mother. That's all it takes. One little *hello* and she can sum up an entire diagnosis of my mental, physical, and emotional health.

"Nothing," I said.

"Liar," she said. "Problems with your telephone boyfriend?"

A wiser daughter might not have offered all the details, but if I hadn't, the Mothership would've eventually squeezed them out anyway.

"That's the problem with a phone relationship," she said. "You can't keep an eye on the man."

"Mom, you and I have a phone relationship."

"That's not the same. I carried you in my womb for nine months. Almost ten if you want to get technical." My mother had never forgiven me for arriving two weeks after her due date. "Maybe he has another girlfriend out there. Maybe he misses his wife. If he does, you can't stand in the way of a man returning to his children."

"I appreciate your pointing that out," I said. "I feel much better now."

Unable to concentrate at work, I spent the morning hoping my closed office door made me look industrious, not absent. I phoned Leslie at 12:50. I had ten minutes to talk to her between patients.

"Perhaps he's having commitment issues," she said.

"I don't know. I'm worried."

"And you're having anxiety issues."

In Leslie's world everyone has issues. Sometimes I had Leslie issues.

"Tell him how you feel. Express your feelings."

I could have mouthed the words as Leslie spoke them. That was her standard answer to everything. Feelings. Feelings. Feelings.

"Dating's like a cha-cha," she said. "One of you dances forward, the other dances back. Tell him his actions are creating insecurities within you. Be honest."

"Yeah, what guy wouldn't hop on a plane because he's so turned on by honesty like that?"

"Isn't the real issue here that if you end up with this man

you move to New York? You never want to talk about that, you avoid it. You're not just some twenty-year-old right out of school. You have an established life with relationships and responsibilities; people who care about you. People *you* care about. Maybe you're looking for problems to avoid the real problem. A move's a big deal," Leslie said. "Are you in denial?"

I was, but I denied it.

My first visit to New York I was twenty-two years old and off to produce a television commercial I'd written for Alberto VO5. All my expectations of the city were based on images from the movies. *Breakfast at Tiffany's. Miracle on 34th Street. Death Wish.* My boss was amused if not appalled that I had never traveled farther east than the Art Institute on Michigan Avenue, and told me to use my expense account to have a good time, which just goes to show how long ago we're talking here.

I liked New York, but it was never anyplace I wanted to *live*. Too chaotic. Too intense. Too *New York*. Maybe Leslie was on to something when she suggested I was ignoring the elephant in the room.

Woody Dolan was my role model for happily married men and the Fred Astaire to my Ginger Rogers; his visuals made my headlines dance. Woody was an advertising legend ever since his award-winning Eastern Airlines campaign in the sixties.

I liked partnering with Woody. Although I didn't go around broadcasting the information, I considered him a better writer than me, which made my job a breeze. Woody spoke with a lisp, so most people—other than the writers who'd worked with him—never gave him credit for being a wordsmith. And Woody considered his wife, Felicia, the be-all and end-all of womanhood; just listening to him carry on about the most mundane aspects of his home life gave me faith that everlasting love could actually last ever after. Felicia's meat loaves were sublime. What fun they had playing Scrabble. Her snoring was adorable. She could sing on key.

Woody perched on a metal stool at his drawing board, wearing his usual corduroy pants and flannel shirt, the same outfit I could picture him wearing for a weekend outing to Sears. I was sitting on a metal file cabinet, wearing my usual white shirt, jeans, and leather belt with statement-making silver buckle. A Chicago Bears pennant was tacked on the wall behind Woody's head right next to a Bulls poster and a big red and blue Cubs emblem. We worked with the door closed to discourage any account executives from dropping by with unsolicited nosiness.

I asked Woody how he'd react if Felicia canceled several weekends together, assuming they weren't married yet and assuming Woody lived in Chicago and Felicia lived in New York and Felicia had kids from a previous marriage and Woody couldn't meet the kids yet because Felicia was in the middle of a divorce.

He chewed on his pencil, a habit of his when he was thinking big thoughts. He said, "You've given me a lot of athumptions."

Woody proceeded to tell me about the first year he was dating Felicia and how she was seeing several other men at the time, including an ex-astronaut and a Mercedes dealership owner. But Woody was patient. He knew Felicia and he were meant to be together, and of course he was right.

Just then somebody knocked and entered without waiting for an invitation. Cari Cavendish was the account director on Glade air fresheners; she still wore blazers with padded shoulders and blouses with bow ties. Cari never got the memo that the eighties were over.

"How's it going?" she asked under the guise of friendliness, but in truth she wanted to know how it was going.

Cari spoke in corporate clichés. *Push the envelope, team! Seek windows of opportunity!*

We told her we were bursting with ideas and thrilled with our progress, feeding her fairy tales until she finally left, chirping *Think outside the box!*

. "Where were we?" I asked.

Woody then did what all Chicago men do: he resorted to sports metaphors, told me how Michael Jordan was famous for never thinking about the last game, only focusing on the next one, and how I shouldn't dump former losses onto some guy who had just shown up at halftime. "Think overall game plan," Woody said. He pointed his pencil at me for emphasis. "And keep your eye on the ball."

After returning to my office, I thought back on Woody saying how I shouldn't think back.

The last man I dated pre-Randy, a patent lawyer named Marshall, invited me to dinner at a steak restaurant—and then grilled me. *How often have you changed jobs? Do you sleep late on weekends? Are you allergic to cat hair?* I half expected him to subpoena my dental records. And we were only on the onion soup.

I hated that man. I hated his questions. I also hated the soup. I'd read all the articles and heard all the experts advise that you have to work at a relationship. I didn't want something that required work. I wanted something that felt inevitable, meant to be, that made me say, So *this* is what all those love songs and love poems are getting at!

I wanted someone who found me amusing, not confusing; charming, not alarming. I wanted somebody to know me, appreciate me, somebody who *got* me. I wanted Randy, so I would no longer need to explain me.

My office phone rang and I picked it up out of habit, not because I actually wanted to talk with anyone.

"Susan's going to the party," I heard Randy say.

"*Susan* Susan? Your Susan? The woman you're still married to but separated from Susan?" I doodled on a notepad, pictures of thunderbolts and big fat snarling lips.

"Tula invited her and Susan said yes. When I called Tula to ask what was going on, she said she still considered Susan a member of the family, what a wonderful mother Susan is, how everyone missed her—and she figured I wouldn't mind."

"What did you say?"

"I don't know. What could I say? I said I mind."

"Sounds like you really gave that cousin of yours hell. Did you tell *Susan* you mind?"

"Yes. I called her." He didn't elaborate further.

"Are you planning to do anything about this?" I asked.

"I suppose," he said. "We're negotiating."

I could feel myself retreating inside, my heart backing off. *No, do not make me love you and then hurt me. I can't do this. I refuse to do this. Hope followed by joy followed by scared to death. You want to hide behind anniversary parties and college buddy reunions and your ex-wife? Fine! But don't expect me to come looking for you. No, sir. No way. Teddy used up my quota in the heartache department. I'm done. Off duty. Not gonna happen.*

"Linda?"

My head hurt.

"Linda?"

My chest hurt.

I took a deep breath and said, "You two have been negotiating for almost three years. I'm no longer counting on any deals being struck."

Then I hung up.

That evening the telephone rang while I was scrubbing the grout around my tub.

"Susan's not going. The kids aren't going," Randy said first thing. "Phoebe's invited to a birthday party that day and Benjamin said he hates grown-up parties. I told my cousin I'm bringing my girlfriend."

"You never informed me you had a girlfriend."

"I miss you. I want you here." He wanted me there.

"What did Susan say?"

"Do you really want the details?"

"No, I don't."

He said it was all a misunderstanding.

I wondered, *between Susan and him*—or *me and him?* "What about your time off?" I asked. "Your weekend without plans?"

He started talking all over the place. "I've made a lot of mistakes, so many that I stopped trusting my judgment. I made commitments when I wasn't ready, stayed in relationships longer than I should have. I had this Five-Year Plan . . . don't get involved . . . focus on my kids . . . focus on my job. But . . ." He hesitated, sighed like an anguished asthmatic. His voice cracked, he sounded miserable. *"But I love you."*

And finally I could say, *I love you, too.*

The following weekend, riding to O'Hare in a taxi, I held my purse in my lap, a red nylon shoulder bag with three zipper sections, good for travel, a gift from my mother. Inside was an anniversary card for two people I didn't know but already admired for pulling off a fifty-year marriage.

When I got to New York I'd express my feelings, tell Randy the not-meeting-the-kids deal was giving me the willies. I'd be forthright, insistent, yet charming and compassionate. I'd keep my eye on the ball.

Someone's Acting Childish and It's Not the Children

After the busboy delivered the iced teas, I announced, "I'm meeting the kids this weekend." Joan gave me an a-okay sign, Karen a thumbs-up. Joan and Karen were both second wives and stepmom experts. They were also both blond and confident, except that Joan was straight-haired and confident and Karen was curly-haired and confident.

We were lunching at our favorite Michigan Avenue pseudo-bistro; noisy, crowded, the three of us seated at a round marble-topped table only big enough for two, so we could feel French.

If I was going to end up a stepmom, I needed advice. Not that anyone was booking any orchestras yet. Randy and I were still talking around the subject, each of us debating between taking a risk or running for the hills. My own history wasn't exactly reassuring. Let's see—a marriage that resulted in lone-

liness, divorce, death, and depression. But what were the odds
of that happening *twice*?

"It's time you got introduced to those kids," Karen said,
pouring Sweet'N Low into her drink.

Joan was slapping butter on a sourdough roll like she was
mad at it. "Why do you say that? The longer she waits, the better. The honeymoon's about to be over."

Maybe she was right. If ever there's a group that should
unionize and hire a good PR agent, it's stepmothers. Just
think of some of the famous ones running around out there.
Cinderella's. Snow White's. Hansel and Gretel's. Who can
stand these women? They were the start of second wives
getting a bad name. And my personal favorite—the Baron-
ess in *The Sound of Music*. I mean, really, twenty minutes
after she got that rock on her finger she was booking reser-
vations to ship those singing little Von Trapps off to board-
ing school.

"How long have you been dating Randy without meeting
his kids?" Karen asked.

"Close to two years," I said.

Joan stopped buttering. "You're either the most patient
woman in history or the most desperate."

A waitress deposited three matching tuna fish platters. "Anything else?" she asked, and left before waiting for an answer.

I removed a black olive off the top of my tuna mound and
handed it to Karen. "Just as I was about to meet them, Randy's divorce lawyer didn't want me showing up during final
negotiations."

"Lawyers suck," Joan said.

"He contended that bringing a girlfriend into the equation could cost Randy a lot of money."

"Yeah? Well not bringing you in could cost Randy his girlfriend." Karen was nibbling at her olive like it was a petit four. "This has been the slowest divorce in history."

I tried to put things into perspective. "New York doesn't have no-fault divorce. So it all made sense." How'd I end up defending Randy's divorce lawyer?

"New York sucks," Joan said.

"Wouldn't it be funny if it turned out Randy really didn't have kids?" Karen said, her curls bobbing along with her laugh.

"That would be hysterical," Joan said. "And suck."

"Okay, well I don't think that's the case," I said. "So let's skip the imaginary-kids discussion."

Karen looked like she'd just had the most exciting idea ever. "Hey—do you want a baby with Randy?" she asked.

"Who *me*? Yeah. Sure. Twins! And their names will be Medical and Miracle. But thanks for the compliment."

"You never know," Karen said.

"Have you ever read 'Can This Marriage Be Saved' in the *Ladies' Home Journal*?" I asked, steering the conversation away from my uterus. "Whenever it's a second marriage, the problem is always over the kids."

"Has Randy proposed?" Joan asked.

"Not yet. But what if he does?"

"So meeting them is a test?"

"Well, no, I didn't think of it that way, but gee, thanks."

"You read *Ladies' Home Journal*?" Karen said.

"Sometimes. At the beauty salon. It's not like I subscribe to it. I just like reading about *the wife's turn, the husband's turn, the counselor's turn*. I learn things."

"Linda's reading habits are not the point of this conversation," Joan said. "What matters is that she knows how to act around these kids so she can pass her test. There's a girl and a boy, right? How old?"

"Benjamin's seven. Phoebe's ten."

"The girl will be the challenge," Karen said.

"Yes," Joan said. "The girl will see you as a rival. Whenever you're all together, be sure to let her hold Randy's hand. Let her sit next to him. Don't kiss him in front of her."

"Wasn't it Rosie Braffman's fifteen-year-old stepdaughter who refused to talk to her?" Karen said to Joan. "The kid went on a total silence strike whenever Rosie walked into the same room." Karen looked at me and arched her brow. "The tension got to be so bad and Rosie's husband got so caught in the middle that eventually the marriage fell apart."

"Amanda used to spy on me," Joan said. "She'd search through my drawers, steal money from my handbag. I finally started leaving notes tucked behind my sweaters and underwear warning her to keep her grubby paws off other people's belongings. Once she knew I was on to her, she stopped. Now we get along famously."

I nodded. "Threatening notes. I'll remember that."

"Bonnie Suarez's boyfriend promised he'd leave his wife after his daughter graduated high school," Karen said, "but after the graduation he said he didn't want his daughter's college grades affected by her parents' splitting up so then—"

"That's not a stepmom," Joan said. "That's a woman dating a married man."

"Well, these are all inspiring examples," I said, pushing my salad plate away. I'd lost my appetite.

"Whatever you do," Karen said, "never get between a little girl and her daddy."

"It's like being in a love triangle with a ten-year-old," Joan said. "Got it."

"And remember," Karen said, "you're their friend."

"Friend. I'm the friend."

"And accept the fact that a man will always put his kids first."

"First. Kids first."

"I can't believe this guy hasn't proposed yet," Joan said.

"He can't," Karen said. "The kids might hate her."

The master plan went like this: Friday night I'd fly into Newark, take a cab to Randy's parents, and sleep at their house. On Saturday I'd go bowling with Randy and the kids.

I'll whip through the New Jersey part. Ruth and Larry greeted me at their front door. Larry took my overnight case. Ruth offered me chicken salad, discovered Larry had polished off the chicken salad, and made me a grilled cheese sandwich. The three of us sat at the kitchen table while I ate. Larry poured me a glass of milk. Then Larry stroked Ruth's arm while she chatted about the kids and Susan; what an excellent mother Susan was, how she was always volunteering for school field trips, making organic meals, sewing costumes for school plays.

I knew Susan was the mother of Randy's children, but I had no idea she was also Mother Teresa, June Cleaver, and Calvin Klein all rolled into one.

After Ruth and Larry said their good-nights and hurried off to bed, I changed into the nightgown I considered the most appropriate for wearing in the home of my boyfriend's parents — ankle-length heavy cotton along the lines of a young novitiate.

I slept in the den. As sofa beds go, it was tolerable. Only one metal bar dug across my spine instead of the usual two. I arranged myself in the position least likely to cut off all feeling in my lower body and called Randy from an old-fashioned rotary phone sitting on an end table covered with alabaster owls. We spoke in hushed voices; Randy so he wouldn't wake his kids, me so I wouldn't wake his parents.

"How's my sweetheart?" Randy said.

"Good. I'm good." I don't know why I expected him to believe me. I wouldn't have believed me. I told him about my flight and the cheese sandwich and visiting with his parents. I skipped over the part about Susan the Übermother.

In the morning I folded up the sofa bed and washed the breakfast dishes and cleaned the bathroom sink and wiped down the shower door. I did everything but offer to repave the driveway. Ruth and Larry drove me to the station. I thanked them for their hospitality. Larry kissed me good-bye on the cheek. Ruth thanked me for washing the dishes.

On the train into Manhattan, the conversations never let up, all of them taking place in my head. *My sisters' kids love me; why shouldn't these kids love me?* Good point. *What's the worst that can happen?* Nothing. *The silent treatment? Money stolen from my purse?* Ridiculous! *Who can't survive one lousy bowling game?*

Uh-oh.

I've been known to drop bowling balls on the backswing; get my fingers stuck in holes; once I broke a toe. Somebody else's.

Apparently when Randy told his kids that a friend was coming over to go bowling and that the friend was a really lousy bowler, they skipped around the living room. They'd be meeting a grown-up they could actually beat!

I arrived right on schedule, train to subway to Randy's, master plan still in place, proud of myself for not getting on the wrong line and ending up in Staten Island.

I ducked out of Randy's enthusiastic welcome hug. *"Not now,"* I whispered, remembering my marching orders from Karen and Joan.

"This is my friend," Randy said, introducing me. "Linda."

I squatted to be closer to the kids' eye level. For so long they'd been photographs and anecdotes and suddenly they were two actual people.

Benjamin was a three-foot-tall pudgy version of Randy. Same dark eyes. Same sweet smile. Same round head and creamy white skin. Only without the five-o'clock shadow.

Phoebe looked like she could be my daughter. Not that I pointed out the resemblance. Only a fool would have pointed it out. *Hey, kid! We're like carbon copies! Except I'm years older and you have legs like a Vegas chorus girl.*

As soon as I met Phoebe I realized Susan must have gorgeous legs. Mine were best described with words like: *descended from peasant stock.*

After all the drama in my head, meeting the kids felt oddly anticlimactic. Nobody keeled over. No crops failed. No water turned to blood. Phoebe and I stared at each other, something I knew children did unself-consciously, but as a grown-up made me uncomfortable. I stood up.

"It's nice to meet you," I said, shaking her hand.

"Yeah," she said, her eyes narrowing, her expression saying: *What's the real story here?*

"Nice meeting you. Really nice. Couldn't be one bit nicer!" I sounded like Kathie Lee Gifford hawking a Carnival cruise. I glanced over to see Randy mouth the word: *Relax.* "I'm Dad's friend. Just a friend. That's me all righty!"

What was my alternative? Tell them, *Hi, kids. You know all your fantasies about Mom and Dad getting back together? Well, I'm here to demolish them.*

"Do you like horses?" Phoebe asked.

"Horses? Sure. Horses are swell."

"Do you ride?"

"Personally? On the back of one? No, can't say I do."

"Oh." That was it for Phoebe. I'd flunked.

"I hear your bowling stinks," Benjamin said.

"Benjamin, that's not nice," Randy said.

"That's what you told us."

"Your dad's right," I said. "My bowling stinks big-time."

"Well, I'm going to beat you," Phoebe said, now enthused.

"Yeah, well I'm gonna beat everyone!" Benjamin jumped up and high-fived the air.

The conversation dissolved into several minutes of squabbling on the subject of who was gonna beat me worse until Randy broke up the debate by directing everyone to put on their coats. The next discussion took place in the elevator.

"How are we getting there?" Phoebe asked.

"The subway," Randy said.

"The subway's dirty and disgusting. Let's take a cab," Benjamin said.

"The subway's not dirty," Randy said. "I take it to work every day."

"It's gross," Phoebe said.

"A cab's better," Benjamin said.

My parents would have grounded me for suggesting a cab.

"Linda wants to take a cab," Benjamin said.

"I do?"

"Sure." He elbowed me in the thigh.

Randy whispered to me that Benjamin hated walking to the subway, that he avoided any activity requiring more energy than Donkey Kong.

"No secrets!" Phoebe said to her dad.

"You're right, sweetheart. No secrets," Randy said.

Sweetheart? That was my name!

"Do you kids want to pay for a cab with your allowance money?" Randy said.

"No way!" they said.

At the subway station, Randy instructed Benjamin to duck under the turnstile. Phoebe and Randy squeezed through together on one token.

From my side of the turnstile I said to Randy, "I'd like to pay retail."

*   *   *

If a bowling alley could double as a dungeon, Leisure Time would qualify. It's located in the Port Authority Bus Terminal, the city's central bus depot and numero uno paean to depressing architecture.

The Family Arthur and friend walked past the incessant click-click-dings of neon-lit pinball machines and the bumps and slaps of cheaters banging their hips into the machines, and around the corner to the low-ceilinged bowling lanes. The constant cracking sounds of strikes and spares, balls smashing against pins hitting the floor, group cheers, reminded me why I prefer quiet sports—like reading a book.

First we rented shoes. I hate bowling shoes. What's scuzzier than public domain shoes? After a thorough discussion on sizes of feet and when was the last time Benjamin changed his socks and whose feet were smellier, Randy helped the kids tie their shoes. I watched him, happy and pink-cheeked, horsing around with his children, rocking against each other, laughing and making faces. I loved how he loved his kids.

And hated feeling like an intruder.

A man behind the counter, with a neck tattooed in a florid script that read *Lisa,* held up a pair of beige and green eight-and-a-halfs for me. "Try these."

I flinched. They looked like they hadn't been polished since the Eisenhower years.

By the time all of us were decked out in shoes and had picked bowling balls, and Randy had set up the automated scoring monitor, and we had discussed if we should go in order of youngest first (Benjamin's opinion), girls first (Phoebe's opinion), or Daddy first (compromise position), I was afraid I'd miss my plane home. Every decision developed into a UN Security Council meeting with everyone having a voice and a vote. I was impressed with how Randy listened to his children's opinions, how he valued their points of view. I was raised in a household where family discussions boiled down to: *Because I'm your mother and I say so.*

Somehow, and I really have no idea how it happened, it was decided that I should go first. "Okay, let's start," Randy said. "Everybody wish everybody else luck."

"Good luck, Daddy!" both kids said.

"And you, too," Phoebe said to me, halfheartedly.

"Yeah. You're gonna need it," Benjamin said, snickering.

I walked up to the foul line, stared down the alley, lifted the ball in two hands, and eyed the seven little arrows in the floor that were supposed to help me aim, praying I wouldn't end up the world's biggest fool, praying Randy wasn't focusing on my butt and thinking it was ten times bigger than Susan's and asking himself, *Why'd I trade in Susan for this big-assed peasant girl?*

Then I threw.

I turned back to Randy and the kids, not even bothering to watch the ball bounce into the gutter, when I heard a strange and mysterious sound: a ball hitting pins in *my* lane.

I spun around in disbelief. For the first time in my life the stars aligned in my House of Bowling. I threw a strike then hit six pins on the first frame of my next turn, which turned into a spare. On my third turn I knocked down the eight center pins, then threw a perfect split shot for another spare. "Brilliant!" "Genius!" "Way to go, champ!" The praise was all from me.

I wondered if it was the shoes. They were filthy and repugnant, but maybe they were lucky. I considered buying them, making an offer to Lisa's boyfriend up there behind the counter. My confidence was unbounded. I approached the foul line for my next throw, announcing to my opponents, "I'm creaming you!"

I must admit it took a while before I noticed that nobody else was sharing my excitement. My score was up to sixty-five, more than the total of all previous scores in my entire lifetime, when Randy sidled up to me and whispered: "Throw the game."

"What?"

"Throw the game. The kids are getting upset."

"But I'm winning."

"You're supposed to be losing. I promised them. You told us you were terrible."

"I was terrible. But now I'm good."

He nodded his head in the direction of Phoebe and Benjamin, who were sitting at the scoring table glaring at me like I'd just announced Santa was a fraud.

"Fine," I said to Randy. "Just fine." *I'd known his kids forty-five minutes and already I was making sacrifices?*

I lofted the ball like a shot put, arching my wrist directly for the gutter and threw. As the ball landed with a smashing thud and rolled to the extreme left, a cheer burst out behind me.

I waited for the ball to travel back down the ball return and spit out for my next attempt. Again, I let it rip into the gutter.

I turned to Randy and smiled, *Happy?*

"Yaaaay!" Benjamin headed up for his next turn. "Nice going—heh heh."

"Better luck next time," a revived and cheerful Phoebe said.

We played two games. Benjamin won the first one. Phoebe won the second. I bottomed out both times.

"Who's up for pizza?" Randy asked his delighted children.

Phoebe raised her hand. "Me!"

"Me, too!" Benjamin raised his hand. "But I get to pick what kind 'cause I won the game."

"I won, too," Phoebe said.

"But I won first!"

"So what?"

"Everyone can pick," Randy said. "We'll order a half-and-half pizza."

We handed in our shoes and Randy paid for the alley time.

We strolled down Ninth Avenue, Phoebe skipping along-side Randy, the two of them holding hands. Benjamin and I followed.

"Congratulations on winning," I said.

"You're not that crummy," he said. "You started out okay."

"Thank you."

"Until you choked. Ha!"

"Eeewww!" Phoebe said. Randy and she had screeched to a standstill, viewing splattered vomit in the middle of the sidewalk.

"Double gross!" Benjamin leaned over to check out the main attraction, his hands resting on his knees.

"Why does puke always look like rice, beans, and chicken?" Phoebe asked.

Randy examined the specimen more closely. "Because it *is* rice, beans, and chicken."

I joined the conversation. "Somebody definitely spewed chunks."

Benjamin laughed. "What did you call it?

"Spewing chunks."

"I never heard that."

"Me, either," Phoebe said.

As my audience giggled I rolled out my repertoire. Up-chucked. Hurling. Pizza pavement. Heaved. The kids laughed hysterically, making me feel like I was Jackie Mason playing Carnegie Hall. I thought, *I like these kids, they're fun these kids.*

I'd spent so much time wondering if they'd like me, that I'd neglected to wonder if I'd like them. I began picturing myself as the next Maria von Trapp only without the singing act.

I added, "Ralphing. Cookie tossing. Launching lunch."

"Speaking of lunch, let's get that pizza," Randy said, leading his happy troops onward. The man has an iron stomach.

The kids were walking on either side of me now.

"You're good at puke words," Benjamin said.

"Yeah, not too bad," Phoebe said.

Emboldened, I took her hand in mine.

Randy was walking ahead of us. He looked over his shoulder and smiled at me. This was months before we knew my bowling outing would cost him an additional three years of alimony. "Linda comes up with all sorts of fun things," he said.

"Make up a game," Phoebe said. Did she find me amusing—or was she challenging me?

"Yeah, let's play a game," Benjamin said.

I whipped through my memory to come up with a clever sidewalk game that didn't require chalk. Something impressive. "Hey—ever play 'Step on a crack—break your mother's back'?"

Benjamin stopped, looked up at me in dismay. Phoebe released my hand.

I remembered a Superman movie where Lois Lane died and Superman reversed the earth's rotation to turn back time. I wished I knew how Superman did that.

"No, wait," I said, looking from Phoebe to Benjamin back to Phoebe. "That's a stupid game. Forget I ever said that. It was a joke. A joke."

ONE OF US PROPOSES,
I THINK IT WAS ME

~~~~~~~

We were sitting on a bench along a triangle of grass bordered by Seventy-Second, Broadway, and Amsterdam. Randy called it a park. In Chicago we'd call it a dog run. Earsplitting construction battled deafening traffic congestion. Twenty years earlier, *The Panic in Needle Park* was filmed there, a love story between heroin addicts. Across the street the Ansonia apartment building loomed overhead, a seventeen-story Parisian wedding cake with turrets and domes and iron fretwork, and the former location of Plato's Retreat, a seventies sex club.

We had just passed our two-year, four-month, one-week anniversary, not that I kept track.

I said, "I have three and a half reasons why we should get married instead of just live together."

A woman wearing a silver down vest stopped in front of us holding a plastic bag in one hand and her Yorkshire terrier's leash in the other. She waited for the dog to do its business. I waited. Randy waited. The woman finally bent over to retrieve the dog's droppings and left.

Randy took my hand. Just not in marriage. He was trying to explain so I wouldn't get the wrong idea, that it wasn't that he didn't care about me, *love* me, it was just the whole what-if-it-doesn't-work-out thing. "Divorce is terrible," he said. "The anger. The accusations. And the lawyers just make it worse. I never want to go through one again. I can't. And the surest way to not get divorced is to never get married."

I charged onward. "Reason one is—if I'm going to give up my friends and family and home and job, basically my *everything,* you should, well, you know—*want* to marry me."

No response.

"Two is—I've always felt ambivalent in relationships. Every one I've ever had. Joey Baba, sophomore year in high school. Jimmy Trowell, junior year in high school. Greg Nardi—" I stopped myself, realizing it was quite possibly an inappropriate time to relay the name of every guy I'd ever dated. "Well, you get the idea," I said. "This is the first time that I'm not ambivalent. And just *living* together is an ambivalent thing to do."

Randy nodded. Not an *I agree* nod, more of an *I'm listening* nod.

A man in a nylon Jets jacket interrupted, wanting to sell us batteries. I politely told him no thank you, that I had plenty at home in my refrigerator, maybe next time. The man left and I continued. "Reason three is, if I'm your wife, the kids will know I'm sticking around. That I'm permanent. Here to stay. The real McCoy. If I'm just a *girlfriend*"—I pronounced *girlfriend* the way someone else might pronounce *pesticide*— "they'll always be hoping you get back with their mom."

Randy nodded again, a serious, thoughtful nod. "What's the half reason?" he asked.

"If you marry me, I'll have a relative in New York."

Two weeks later airfares jumped and Randy proposed. I wish I could say it was one of those violins and moonlight sonata proposals but it didn't even include a Hallmark card. Randy called me at work and said, okay, fine, let's do it. My first husband proposed while we were walking across the parking lot of a Sinclair gas station discussing how gasoline was really cheap and we could afford to buy a car so we might as well get married. What was it about me and travel bargains that brought out marriage proposals?

Randy and I were visiting Florida for the weekend, staying in a hotel room so my parents could pretend we didn't have sex. My mother cooked a special dinner in honor of our presence. Brisket, creamed spinach, twice-baked potatoes, and Parker House dinner rolls. I can never tell the difference between once-baked or twice-baked, but my mother makes twice-baked for company and I was no longer just a daughter. I was company. The dining table was set with the *good* china.

She was wearing her dressy jewelry, not her everyday jewelry; her pearl-and-diamond earrings, and had gone to the beauty parlor, but that was in honor of Randy, not me. She looked younger than most of my friends' mothers, the only one of her own friends to not go old-lady blond. Her hair was dark and curled with bangs like Gina Lollobrigida.

"More potatoes?" she kept asking Randy. "Can you manage more brisket?"

My father was eating in his usual flurry with bread crumbs landing on his belly and flecks of spinach sticking in his mustache, which my mother just reached over and removed on automatic pilot. I noticed that his gray-streaked hair was shinier than usual, like maybe he'd added an extra dab of Brylcreem for the occasion, but he was more relaxed, more at ease than my mother, less startled that I'd finally brought home a man.

After crème de menthe brownies, Randy and my father strolled off into the television room behind closed doors. Suddenly, Randy was Mr. Traditional. I should have warned him the three things my father hated most in the world were: stockbrokers, New Yorkers, and men who touched his daughters. Randy was asking permission to hand me over to all three.

In the kitchen, my mother rinsed while I loaded. "What do you think the two of them are talking about?" she said, winking once, then again, in case I missed the first wink. She wanted to eavesdrop as much as I did.

I said, "Eighteenth-century French porcelain?"

I don't know why I was so anxious. I mean, really. *What more could these people want?* Randy was employed, a Harvard grad. *Jewish.* From age fifteen on, when I first started dating, all my boyfriends were Christian. My mother lived in fear of one day receiving an invitation to a grandchild's baptism. My parents were probably so happy to see me land a second husband that they wouldn't have cared if I'd brought home a sherpa. It's not like my father was going to say no. Or that I'd split up with Randy if my father did say no. But I felt like a high school student waiting to learn my SAT scores.

My mother swirled a sponge on the surface of a bread plate. "Beautiful faces are easy to find," she said dreamily, "but a lovable face, one that makes you smile first thing in the morning— then you know you're lucky." For a moment I thought she was saying that Randy wasn't handsome, but she passed me the bread plate and winked again. "I have a strong feeling that Randy will be worth the sacrifice."

"Sacrifice?"

"Moving to that place."

New York was *that place*.

"Mom, it's not the dangerous cesspool you think it is."

"Well, thank God you'll have a husband."

"A husband, Mom. Not a bodyguard."

She sprinkled Ajax inside the sink. "You know, the other day I heard your father talking up the Dolphins like a real fan. Go figure." Before moving to Florida, my dad's greatest source of pride in life, next to my mother and his Sansabelt pants collection, were his Chicago Bears season tickets on the thirty-five-yard line at Soldier Field. I'm sure he'd have held on to those tickets and arranged to be buried with them if he wasn't convinced that half his relatives would be digging through his casket. Instead he sold them to a member of his country club for big bucks, trading in his love of the Bears for warm winters and no state income tax. "People adjust," my mother said.

People do adjust. Hopefully even people with daughters moving to New York.

"They seem to be taking an awfully long time," I said.

My mother giggled as she attacked the sink with a scrubbie. "Yes, isn't this romantic? Start the dishwasher."

By the time the two men emerged they were laughing and shaking hands, like they'd just concluded a transaction over the sale of a cow.

Randy told the kids we were getting married. I was not in attendance. That would have been unfair in case they wanted to complain to the Department of Child Welfare. I heard the telephone version.

They were all feeding Curly the snake at the time. I will skip over the details. Especially the part about the doomed mouse. "Hey—remember Linda?" he said. "My friend we've gone bowling with and skating with and saw *Babe* with?"

"You mean your friend who keeps a bathrobe and sanitary napkins hidden in the back of your closet?" Phoebe said.

"Stupid pig movie," Benjamin said.

"What were you doing in the back of my closet?" Randy asked. Phoebe shrugged. Randy continued. "Well, how would you feel if Linda and I got married?"

Benjamin was more interested in Curly than his father's question, but Phoebe, all pie-eyed and concerned, asked: "What about Mom?"

Randy said, "Your Mom and I can't be married anymore."
Silence.

"But we're your parents. We'll always love you. And we'll be friends."

"Like *Linda's* your friend?"

Randy knew sarcasm when he heard it. He also knew not to debate semantics with a child.

Phoebe excused herself to the bathroom, where she stayed until Randy knocked on the door. When she came out she said, "It's not fair to Mom. What if she's mad at me?"

"For what?" Randy asked. "Your mom will always be your mom. Nobody else. And nothing you do could ever keep either of us from loving you."

Phoebe stared at Randy like *you better be right about this,* then spun around toward her brother and said, "It's my turn to play with Curly."

Benjamin was only three when Randy left home and didn't remember his parents as a couple. His best friend in second grade had a stepmother who had already informed Benjamin that stepmoms meant extra gifts. That was all Benjamin needed to hear. When Randy asked how he felt about my being his stepmom, he said: "No problemo."

"Does Phoebe hate me?" I asked Randy over the telephone.

"Not consciously," he said.

"*Un*consciously? Like it'll be my fault when she needs years of therapy?"

"None of this will really impact the kids until you actually move here."

"Why don't I find that comforting?"

"Be patient," Randy said. "Who could resist falling in love with you?"

I could have answered with a full litany of men's names.

My last weeks in Chicago, I worried.

Will my nieces and nephews forget who I am? Will my friendships survive long-distance rates? What'll happen to my self-image as a Chicago career woman who owns a condominium if I'm no longer a Chicago career woman who owns a condominium? What if I get polio and Randy's the only person in New York who'll visit me in my iron lung?

Leaving home was a lot easier when it was just theoretical.

"I keep waiting for the other shoe to drop," I told Annabelle one day. We were eating lunch together except that Annabelle was at her desk chewing on a tofu burger and I was at my desk wolfing down potato chips. "You know how it goes," I said, cradling the phone between my shoulder and chin. "Things are good. You're happy. And boom! A pogrom shows up. I'm scared I'll marry Randy and something *bad* will happen; that I'll have to pay a price for my happiness."

"Like what?"

I hesitated. I could feel the words catching in my throat. "Like something awful. Like my parents will die."

"Oh, honey," she said. Her voice was warm and kind. "Someday your parents will die. But at least you'll have Randy."

*   *   *

I'd switch my focus from leaving—to the wedding. I wanted something simple, small, but enough of a wedding to feel like a wedding. And a good-bye party.

"Do whatever makes you happy," Randy said.

Did he mean do what makes you happy because he didn't care about our wedding, and if he didn't care about our wedding, did that mean he didn't care about our marriage?

I'd tell myself to buck up, calm down. My worries alternated with pep talks.

What kind of a weenie can't live in another town? So you change hairdressers! How terrible is it to live a cab ride from the Guggenheim? Won't it be nice to be in Times Square New Year's Eve?

The pep talks transformed into panic: *What if I screw up this marriage, too?*

Teddy and I had owned an apartment in Chicago. We purchased it to save our marriage, to set down physical roots to compensate for our lack of emotional ones. I picked out paint chips and furniture while he complained about my choices. They were always too this or not enough that. I showed him a photo of two chairs I liked—white linen with brass legs. He told me he'd give them some thought, maybe in a month or two we'd reconsider, let's not rush into anything.

I ordered them anyway, paying for them out of my own checking account. I'd always kept a separate account, a consequence of my having attended a feminist lecture in college.

"What are those doing here?" Teddy asked the day the chairs were delivered.

"They're mine," I said. "I bought them for us."

My marriage to Teddy was fashioned on observations I made growing up: my parents' own traditional wife-as-home-maker-husband-as-breadwinner household; that, and the family sitcoms I watched on TV.

The women's movement offered me a different perspective—that I didn't *need* a man. *A woman without a man is like a goldfish without a bicycle.* I married Teddy primed to put a husband's needs first, while never fully devoted on an emotional level. Vulnerable was not for me! *Get a career. Don't be financially dependent. Open your own bank account.* All of them good lessons—but the subtext I heard was: Keep one foot in the marriage, the other ready to leave.

When we divorced I paid Teddy for his half of the apartment; there was no question as to who would keep the linen chairs. But I never quite enjoyed them, and I didn't want them in New York. I sold them to a neighbor.

When Randy assured me that we'd have a good marriage, I'd find myself apologizing to Teddy in my head. *I don't know if I'll finally get this wife thing right—but if I do, if I don't mess up, I wish I'd done it sooner, that during our years together, I wish I'd made you happier.*

With every item that didn't make it into the packing cartons—journals filled with gloomy jottings masquerading as poetry; books about life after death; the black suit I wore to Teddy's funeral—I realized that aside from the many good parts—my girlfriends, my sister Toby and her kids, jobs in which I'd flourished—Chicago also represented heartbreak.

I wanted to move forward into a bigger life, to move on and love Randy.

Like Scarlett O'Hara on the hill, fist to the air—minus the turnips—I found myself saying: *I can do this.*

We married in one of Chicago's finest Mexican restaurants. Not the kind with serapes and bad straw hats hanging on the walls, but a pretty restaurant, white, gold, and sunny. Stepping into my wedding dress, a white, unadorned sheath appropriate for the *older* bride, I felt ready to throw myself into the second half of my life with my best foot forward and my man by my side.

Randy, wearing a simple dark suit and tie, walked down the short aisle flanked by Phoebe and Benjamin. Phoebe held sweetheart roses. Benjamin held Randy's hand. The three adult sisters, his, mine, and mine, wore corsages. Nieces and nephews fidgeted. Dan and Lynn of California, our fixer-uppers, witnessed. Parents sat within spitting distance, the mothers' dresses fancier than mine. And Claudia, tough, cynical Claudia, cried throughout the ceremony.

My dad had asked to walk me down the aisle. I told him, you gave me away once and I came back.

I stood alone at the top of the white silk runner, waiting for the groom to turn around. Randy was standing under the marriage canopy, facing the rabbi, his back to me. My mother leaned forward and tapped him on the shoulder.

Our vows were in Hebrew, so neither of us can be exactly certain what we promised, but I believe the translation goes something like this:

Rabbi: Do you, Randy, take Linda to love, honor, and cherish till death do you part?

Randy: Of course.

Rabbi: And do you, Linda, take Randy, his children and New York, to love, honor and cherish till death do you part?

Linda: I do.

And then I kissed my old life good-bye.

THE MIDDLE PART

Transported

~~~~

Randy seemed surprised when I unpacked my flannel sleep-wear.

"What are those?" he asked, as I shoved his business suits into the far corner of the closet to make room for my nightshirts.

"I sleep in these."

"No, you don't. You sleep naked," he said.

"Not really." I stood back from the closet, assessing the situation. "That was just because we were dating."

I gave up on closets and attacked another carton, unearthing glassware buried in crumpled layers of the *Chicago Tribune*—now my *former* newspaper. Randy busied himself with wiping out the inner recesses of our kitchen cabinets, sponging away the previous renter's dead flies and bread crumbs, and making room for our dead flies and bread crumbs.

Our new home was charming in a chopped-up, worn-down way. A ridiculously big old apartment had been reconfigured into three simply ridiculous apartments, one of which was ours. The leasing agent described our layout as "rambling." I described it as illogical. Hallways to nowhere. A triangle-shaped shower stall. A refrigerator that blocked a window. But there were freshly sanded floors, decent closets, and even though the rooms were small, the ceilings were fifteen feet high. It would have been an amazing apartment if we could have turned it sideways.

Curly the snake, having outgrown his cage, and as far as I was personally concerned, his welcome, had been relocated to a pet store on Broadway. Randy's divorced-guy black leather sofa had been relocated to a newly divorced guy.

It was good to be setting up our own place. More than good. A relief.

"Maybe we should take a break, oh husband of mine," I said. "We need groceries. We can take a walk and buy groceries."

"I'm on a mission," he said, wringing out a soapy sponge over a bucket of gray water. "Do you want to wait until I finish the pantry or go yourself?"

"I want to go together but go now, before cabin fever sets in."

Randy stuck his head into the cupboard beneath the sink. I admired his blue-jeaned butt as it wiggled with his efforts. "Well, you go while I focus here," he said. "I think the marriage can survive a thirty-minute separation."

I looked around at all the partially unpacked, half-abandoned, unorganized chaos of my life's possessions. "It might take me that long to find my handbag."

"Take cash from my wallet," I heard a voice say from inside the cabinet.

How incredibly romantic, I thought. *Take cash from my wallet.*

Randy's head popped out again. "There's a long list by the phone. Have them deliver it."

"Sure," I said, counting out a handful of bills. "Anything my husband's heart desires."

"Your husband's heart desires beer," he said, as I walked around a pile of balled-up newspaper sheets to open the front door. "Bring back beer."

The closest grocery to the apartment building was microscopic compared to my Chicago neighborhood store, where the aisles were wide and inviting, the selection of items paralyzing in their possibilities. Shopping in New York was more efficient. If I wanted pineapple there was one brand, one size, one type. Take it or leave it. No agonizing over tidbits versus chunks, syrup versus juice. Cheese was another matter. New Yorkers are wacky for cheese. Even the smallest bodega offered piled-high tables of exotic selections, coolers overflowing with mysterious varieties. My idea of cheese was anything yellow labeled with the word *Velveeta*. But I loaded up my cart, checking items off Randy's list—anchovies, capers, hearts of palm, Camembert, Stilton, Fontina—then added my own favorites: peanut butter, chewing gum, iceberg lettuce.

"It's a delivery," I said, as I pulled the groceries from the cart, placing them on the checkout counter for the cashier, a heavyset girl who looked congenitally bored. A tattooed young man at the end of the counter was stuffing plastic bags like he had a bus to catch. "Except for the beer," I said. "I'll take the beer. Let me give you the address." I wrote it out, my letters thick, bold, and proud. "That's in New York City."

"No shit," the cashier said.

It seemed like as soon as I showed up, the romantic New York of *An Affair to Remember* turned into *Mean Streets*. I was in a town filled with eight million citizens, all in touch with their feelings, and eager to express them. I tried to think of role models who'd adjusted to new environments, but the only ones I could come up with was that Swiss girl, Heidi, calling *Grandfather! Grandfather!* and Sigourney Weaver in *Alien*.

So instead I set goals to develop new skill sets, studied New Yorkers to pick up pointers:

1. Do not wait at a crowded deli counter saying things like: "Am I next or are you next? I think you were next." You will never get served.
2. When you see somebody walking down the street with a smile, do not smile in return. They will ask you for money.
3. Everything's negotiable.

Struggling with a zipper in the dressing room of a Madison Avenue boutique one day, I overheard the conversation between a saleslady and customer in the adjoining dressing room. "You are so right," the customer said. "Nobody else but me could wear this, but it's so expensive." Then, without missing a beat: "Can I have a discount?"

I'd be too embarrassed to ask for a discount on a pound of butter, let alone a pantsuit.

For his fortieth birthday, I bought Randy's cousin Joel something called a Ye Olde Fashioned Ice Cream Maker complete with hand crank and recipes requiring dry ice. Joel unwrapped his present, studied the box for all of five minutes, and said, "Why would I bother with this when I live half a block from Häagen-Dazs?"

I could learn a few things from these New Yorkers who never minced words, never beat around bushes. I appreciated how Joel and I would not be spending the next several years engaging in pretend conversations when I asked: "How's that ice cream maker working out?"

And I hoped Joel appreciated it when, on his next birthday, he'd just be getting a card.

The children were the only two New Yorkers I couldn't count on for a straight answer. One Saturday afternoon they were sitting at the dining table designing birthday cards for Larry while Randy was running around the Central Park reservoir (a short-lived jogging phase) and I was running around the apartment trying to find my reading glasses.

"How's this?" Phoebe said, holding up a drawing of a horse.

"Whoa!" I practically skidded to a halt.

"I knew you'd like it," she said.

Benjamin dumped the crayon box onto the table. He was drawing bugs.

"Whoa *this*." I pointed to red scribbles on one of the white dining chairs, the chair between the two of them.

The children both resumed drawing with renewed speed and conviction.

"Who did this?" I asked, still pointing.

"Not me," Phoebe said.

"Not me," Benjamin said.

"Well, that just leaves Daddy," I said. "Are you telling me Daddy did this?"

Phoebe shrugged.

Benjamin shrugged.

"No, I'm saying I didn't do it." Phoebe turned and glared at her brother.

"Not me." Benjamin glared back at Phoebe.

I didn't know what to say after that. Randy was in charge of discipline, not me. I was in charge of keeping the kids from resenting me. *But I loved my white dining chairs.* I spun around and left the room. "Fine," I said, "just *fine*."

Why couldn't we have a nice honest conversation? Why couldn't they say something straightforward and direct like: *You're not my mother. You can't tell me what to do.*

When I wasn't trying to navigate the children, I was trying to navigate New York. I had ended up employed in a rather hurried, unexpected fashion and was expected to show up at work five days a week, necessitating one of my other new goals—

figuring out the subway system. I tried to feel a kinship with my fellow riders: the bongo players, the seat hoggers, the dozers and elbow jabbers and Juilliard violinists. I practiced my Spanish on the bilingual posters advertising ruthless divorce attorneys and life-changing vocational schools and the dermatologist whose sign listed so many skin disorders, I was afraid to breathe near it. Every time I boarded the train, I'd pretend I was balancing on a surfboard, feet apart, arms held stiff and to my sides, anything to avoid contact with the germy handrail. I watched in horror as mothers used their baby strollers to block closing doors. I did my best to learn the map and keep everything straight; the A-C-E lines and the J-L-M lines and the where-the-hell-am-I-now lines.

My mother called. She liked talking to me while she cooked my father's dinner. I liked talking to her while I was shuffling through takeout menus for Randy's dinner. "So how's my New York daughter?" she asked.

"Fine," I told her. "I'm learning the subway system."

"How do you know it's safe?"

"How do you know it's not?"

"I'll send you money for a taxi."

"How many taxis?"

She stopped talking. I heard water running, a pot lid clink. "You're happy, right?" she finally said. "Randy's good to you?"

"Of course he's good to me."

"Good," she said before hanging up. "Stay off the subway."

My mother-in-law called with a few tips of her own. "Randy

tells me you're learning the subway system." Randy and Ruth talked all the time. He was a good son.

"I'm trying my best," I said.

"Stand by the black shoe scuffs on the platform," she said. "That's where the doors open when the train arrives."

"Scuffs. Okay. I'll look for scuffs."

"And watch out for pickpockets," she said.

The following day I was riding south on a packed 9 train down the west side, feeling lucky to be positioned near the door, my escape hatch. The train stopped at Fifty-Ninth Street with its gum-studded floors and water-stained walls. A swarm of people waited to enter the train while riders on my car jostled to get off.

The doors opened and in the interest of efficiency and common sense, I stepped out onto the platform to allow room for my fellow passengers to exit and the newcomers to join us.

Two minutes later I was standing on the platform, watching my train rumble off into the distance, after fifty New Yorkers had just shoved past me.

"You'd think they were giving away free Buicks inside those subway cars," I said to Randy that night.

We were in the kitchen snacking before bedtime, both of us in our sleepwear, which meant the red silk nightie Randy had recently bought me, and a pair of purple briefs and not much else for him. I was standing in front of an open cupboard mowing my way though a box of Lorna Doones while frowning at my subway map. Randy was sitting and eating an Oreo, like a well-mannered human being. Whatever cautions and emotional roadblocks tripped him up before our marriage, he now seemed so at ease. Maybe because he was on his home turf. Or maybe because he'd read those statistics that married men live longer.

He said, "Remember the time I offered that woman my seat and she got insulted because I made her feel old?"

"No."

"Sure you do. We—" He blinked at the memory. "Oh, wait."

I waited, then said, "Wrong *we*?"

He concentrated on his Oreo.

"Okay, well, back to this marriage—" I slid open our junk drawer, the one that held loose stamps, rubber bands, plastic knives, and discount coupons for car companies with Israeli names. I shoved in the map. "I don't think this subway thing is going to work out," I said.

Randy reached over and slid the drawer open again. He dug around and pulled out a second, smaller, folded-over map. He said, "Study this."

The bus system wasn't half bad. Buses came with windows that actually looked out onto daylight and real humans to announce the stops.

The only problem was it took three days to get anywhere.

"Call a car service," my new neighbor Stefanie advised me. We were waiting for the elevator together. Conversations with Stefanie only lasted as long as it took for the elevator to arrive. "A car service is the only way to get around the city."

Stefanie was a senior partner at a top litigation firm. She had perfect posture and a jaw that seemed perpetually clenched; she wore crisp Donna Karan suits and carried an overstuffed accordion-style leather briefcase. She kept pressing the down button like it was an irritating opponent. Stefanie scared me.

"I can't take a car service every day," I said. "It would seem . . . pretentious."

"To whom?" she asked, coolly.

"Well . . . to *me*."

In my family, the only time you rode in the backseat of a long black car was when you were following a hearse.

The next day I splurged on a cab between my office and home, eager to put as much distance as quickly as possible between me and my job.

New York cabs were promoting seat belt safety. As soon as the driver flipped the flag on the meter, a celebrity recording reminded the passenger to buckle up for safety, buckle up. Elmo was tolerable. Dr. Ruth unintelligible. But Eartha Kitt was insufferable. She growled like a tiger.

"How can you stand listening to that all day?" I asked the back of the head in the seat in front of me. I glanced at the identification license. JULIO.

Julio shrugged. "I don't even hear it anymore."

"That's a real talent," I said, "tuning things out."

Julio patted the top of his meter. "This is the only sound I care about."

I wanted to be Julio. I wanted to stop hearing things I didn't want to hear. Hissing buses. Clattering trucks. Squeaky brakes. Pounding construction.

The neighbors' bedroom television through my apartment walls.

Or worse, their lovemaking, after they turned the television off.

The city's decibel levels seemed to rocket now that I couldn't leave. I marveled at New Yorkers standing near jack-hammer crews, chatting away like attendees at a tea party; felt inspired by pedestrians strolling into the paths of speeding police cars, oblivious to blaring sirens; watched in awe as babies slept while subways roared past.

I'd escape to Central Park, sit quietly on a bench, and promise myself I'd adjust. Everyone who passed me seemed to be heading somewhere else with an urgent sense of purpose. All I wanted to do was get out of my own way, and feel comfortable exactly where I was.

Our bedroom had two windows, offering twice the opportunities to not hear myself think. Randy tried to help me sleep by purchasing a CD collection of nature sounds. One featured Hawaiian breezes, although I still don't know what makes a breeze sound Hawaiian. Another was called "Mystic Waterfalls," but that one just made me want to pee all night. Randy orchestrated a mix of the nature noises, laying them out on his CD platter, pushing the "random" button to skip from ocean waves to tweeting birds with a little Van Morrison thrown in.

The moment Van started singing for one more moon dance, Randy fell asleep.

I'd prop myself up and gaze at my husband's face. I adored all the scents and sounds he emitted, even the dreadful ones. I found them endearing. I'd repeat a mantra to calm myself, *Home is where the heart is,* and wonder if I'd ever feel at home. When the mantra and bird sounds and stuffing pillows over my head didn't thwart the dump trucks and car horns and chattering in my head, I'd sneak into the living room and dial my fellow insomniac.

"How long before a sleepless person starts hallucinating?" I asked Claudia.

"With or without drugs?" she said.

"If I don't get some sleep soon I'll start going crazy and if I go crazy I'll have to be institutionalized and if I'm institutionalized—" I never got past the institution part. My voice was drowned out by motorcycle revving, sidewalk drilling, and the staccato squeal of a car alarm. Nobody protested. Nobody cursed out windows. The consensus seemed to be that if you were lucky enough to find a parking spot on a New York street, who could blame you for bragging?

"What's going on in that town?" Claudia asked. "It sounds like a barroom brawl."

I told her about my conversation with my cabdriver, how he blocked out noise. "Who are these people who just pick up and move to New York and feel fine?"

"They're twenty-year-olds," Claudia said.

*   *   *

Thursday night I was eating canned tuna in the kitchen and reading a magazine article about surprising uses for coffee filters. Randy would be at the kids' mom's place until after he put them to bed. My mother called from Florida complaining of heart palpitations and shortness of breath.

"Maybe you should go to the emergency room," I said, my hand clenching the receiver. "Have you contacted the doctor?"

"No, no, no," she said. "All the doctors down here hate older people. They only live here so they can golf year-round."

I could hear her sucking in a big gulp of air and releasing it in one long dramatic wave of frustration.

"Mom, if you promise to call the doctor right away, I'll come down right away. Do you promise you'll call?"

"I'll see if I can find the number," she said, "not that it will do any good. He's probably dining at his country club."

"Put Dad on the phone."

"He's at *his* country club. Sitting on the toilet."

"Mom, call the doctor."

I booked myself on the first available flight to West Palm the next morning. My older sister, Brenda, my observant religious sister, can't fly on a Friday. The plane might be late and the sun could set and flying on Sabbath is a sin. My younger sister, Toby, had gone from being a CPA to working with suicidal teenagers and troubled high school students. Asking her to take a day off was like inviting someone to die. So I knew any emergency trip to Florida was up to me. I had no business taking time off from work, but mothers were harder to come by than jobs.

"I'll go with you," Randy said as soon as he got home.

"You don't have to. You stay here. Let's see what's doing." It was a kids' weekend and I didn't want him missing his weekend with the kids.

I ran around our bedroom yanking clothes off hangers, pulling open drawers, packing like I was on a game show.

Palm Beach Airport is all pink and sunny with blond wood benches, more like a pool cabana than an airport. My mother had arranged for a driver to meet me in the baggage department. I found him standing at the bottom of the escalator, a short, gray-haired little man, probably a retiree with a part-time job. He was holding a cardboard sign with my name in big letters.

Highway traffic was sparse, it being the off season. I stared out the window at the flat, sun-washed landscape, anxious about my mother's health, concocting all sorts of terrible scenarios in my head. Her brother had died from a heart attack; her father had died from a heart attack.

We pulled into the entrance area of my parents' building; half the balconies were closed off by storm shutters, indicating the snowbirds had retreated north. "How much do I owe you?" I asked my driver. I counted out twenties while he unloaded my suitcase from the trunk.

The doorman, a short, gray-haired little man, probably a retiree with a part-time job, nodded and waved me in. I'm sure my mother was buzzing downstairs for hours to remind him her daughter would be arriving any minute now. She was standing in her open doorway as I stepped off the elevator. Either the doorman had called her with a heads-up or she'd been waiting there since I last spoke to her from New York.

"Mom, how are you?" I said, hurrying down the hallway, lugging my bag.

"Your father's getting on my nerves," she said. "All day long with the Court TV. He thinks he's the jury foreman." She opened her arms to hug me.

"Better now that you're here," she said. "Go kiss your father hello. He's watching the cross-examination." She tried to pick up my overnight bag.

"I'll take it, Mom. It's heavy."

"What've you got in here? Rocks?"

"New York bagels."

"Who needs New York bagels? They're heavy as rocks."

By the time we ate dinner a far less charitable daughter might have accused her mother of luring her nine hundred miles south under false pretenses. My mother seemed perfectly healthy. After a meal of the house specialties—chilled beet soup, salmon patties, and Costco vanilla-frosted cupcakes for dessert—her theory was that before I arrived she had been on the verge of a heart attack, but seeing me safe and sound despite my moving to that Sodom and Gomorrah of a filthy, dirty city turned out to be a miracle cure.

My theory was that she worried about me, but of course she couldn't just spit the words out, be direct and say so; it's not like the woman had been raised in New York. I was beginning to see the advantages of more direct communication.

"Mom, you've got to quit watching those *Law & Order* re-runs. New York's much safer now." In reassuring her, I realized I was reassuring myself. "I know you think I'm being mugged on a daily basis, but I live on a well-lit street with dozens of po-licemen, dogs, law-abiding citizens. Aren't you excited to have a daughter living in New York?"

My father said, "Half the retirees down here are from New York. The half she doesn't like." He was slicing a cupcake down the middle, even though we all knew he'd eat the second por-tion, too. "It's a good thing we like Randy so much."

"I'm glad you're married," my mother sighed.

On Sunday, a taxi picked me up three hours before my flight, which was one hour sooner than necessary, but my mother hates for any of her blood relations to miss a plane. My father asked if I needed extra money for the cab and even after I said *no,* he gave it to me anyway. My mother asked if my suitcase was locked. She handed me a tinfoil package. "Salmon pat-ties," she said. "For Randy."

I feel wistful and uneasy every time I hug my parents good-bye.

As the taxi drove off I watched the two of them, arm in arm and still waving, grow smaller through the rearview window.

"So where we heading?" the driver asked. His brown hair was cut close to the scalp like an army recruit's; the skin on his neck looked thick and creased, raw from too much sun.

I spoke to his reflection in the rearview mirror. "New York," I said. "I live in New York."

"Oh." The driver clicked on the radio, some call-in talk show about golf.

After listening to a snore-inducing discourse on chippers, I said, "Actually,. I'm kind of new to New York."

His eyes narrowed and met mine in the mirror. "How long have you lived there?"

"Just over two months."

"Two months? Where are you really from?" He seemed to relax; his voice became friendlier.

"Chicago."

"Chicago? What do you want with New York?"

"I got married."

He twisted around to check me out. "And you couldn't find a guy in Chicago?"

I shook my head no. "It didn't work out that way."

He pulled onto the exit for Southern Boulevard and the airport. I felt good about seeing my parents, grateful they were fine; eager to return to Randy, less eager to return to New York.

"So why didn't you make your husband move?" the driver asked. He was looking at me in the mirror again.

I said, "He's got kids."

"Too bad," he said. "Sounds like you're stuck."

MY FIRST JOB IN NEW YORK
(THIS WON'T TAKE LONG.)

~~~~~~~

One Saturday afternoon, two months before moving to New York, I was sorting through my bathroom medicine chest. Claudia was sitting Indian-style on the floor, her back against the bathtub, eating a Granny Smith apple and smoking a cigarette.

"I have so much to look forward to," I said. "Love. Marriage. *Unemployment.*" I read the prescription name on an old, crinkled-up metal tube. "What's fluocinonide cream for? Why do I own this?"

Claudia pointed to the garbage pail. "You'll find a job," she said. "New York's got a million ad agencies. They can squeeze in one more worker bee."

"What's the expiration date on nose spray?"

"The day after you first use it."

I tossed out insect repellent, a Band-Aid box with one Band-

Aid, an old toothbrush. "I wish I weren't so nervous about this work stuff. People know me in Chicago. I have a reputation."

"So what? A school slut has a reputation." Claudia stubbed her cigarette into the Lenox saucer she was using as an ashtray. Claudia has little respect for other people's china patterns. "I think it's exciting," she said. "You can reinvent yourself. Be a whole new person. Like you're going into the Federal Witness Protection Program."

"I got a call from a headhunter. There's a vice president's job at that ladies' TV channel."

"The one with all the weird movies? Where the heroine's life is always a train wreck?"

"Yeah. That one. The job's for managing their creative services department. I don't even know what a creative service department does. But they're considering advertising people because branding's involved."

"You can brand," Claudia said. "Interview. It's New York. If you can make it there, you can make it anywhere."

I closed the medicine chest door and said, "What if I can't make it there?"

Claudia chewed on a big bite of her apple before she answered. "I don't know," she said. "Nobody ever talks about that."

I faxed my résumé to the headhunter, who called me back the next day for a "telephone interview." I told her about my Kraft Macaroni & Cheese campaigns and my Glade air freshener campaigns, neither of which had anything to do with television other than that they'd both run on television. She told me how her mother was born in Chicago and that she had several cousins in Chicago.

Two weeks later I was flown out to New York for a real live interview with the telephone interviewer's boss. This was fine by me because it meant a free trip to see Randy. I never mentioned that I had a fiancé in New York, just a friend I'd be staying with. I didn't want anyone questioning my motives. I was instructed to meet the Interviewer Boss at a hotel room in the Peninsula hotel. Already, it felt like one fishy interview.

"What if he's just some guy waiting to attack me?" I asked Randy, while I was rifling through my handbag to make sure I had my wallet.

"Then he would have picked a cheaper hotel." Randy watched me juggle my comb and keys and lip gloss. "And why would he cough up airfare to attack someone from out of town?"

"Who knows? I haven't been reimbursed yet."

"You're just nervous."

"Fine. Okay. But if my body's found on Fifth Avenue later today, I just want you to know that my dying words were: *I told you so.*"

"Thank you. I'll keep that in mind," Randy said, kissing me good-bye for luck. Or forever.

The Interviewer Boss turned out to be a great guy who explained he lived in California where he ran a consulting firm, but the president of the TV station and he were old friends and that's why he was interviewing New York candidates out of a New York hotel room. He talked about how I'd be responsible for all of the network's branding and promotions and interstitials, along with my department's budget and the twenty-two people reporting to me. And how his wife grew up in Chicago.

"Normally you'd meet Owen next, the VP of marketing. But Owen's away this weekend, and since you're already in New York, let's arrange for you to meet Jeff."

The president. He wanted me to meet the president.

"Okay," I said, figuring it's a practice interview. Just for practice. But wondering when should I mention: *I'm totally unqualified for this job.*

On my way back to Randy's apartment I stopped at a bookstore. I needed a crash television course. What's the difference between cable TV versus network and syndication? What the hell are interstitials! What do you call that little symbol in the bottom corner of the screen besides *annoying?*

I asked a prim, bookish salesperson behind the information desk, "Do you have something like a *Television for Dummies?*"

The woman peered at me over her eyeglass frames and informed me, "Television *is* for dummies."

"Yes. Of course. I'm sure you're right. But I thought maybe there'd be a book by that name."

"I'll check." She scanned her computer while I stood there thinking, *Hey, this is Borders, lady—not the Library of Congress.* She started rattling off titles. "I have *Reincarnation for Dummies. Rottweilers for Dummies. Reflux and Heartburn for Dummies.*"

"Maybe we can jump ahead to the T's," I said.

"I presume so." She continued studying her screen while

I waited; she was probably reading her e-mails. Finally she pointed me to the back of the store and a sign hanging overhead that read MEDIA. "I believe that's what you're looking for," she said.

"Thank you," I said. "I appreciate it. Right next to where I usually pick up my Tolstoy and Proust."

Aside from five books that sounded like they might teach me something about the TV industry, I also bought *Accounting for Dummies* and *The Seven-Minute Manager,* which was about all the time I had to learn management. I was just sorry I couldn't find anything on the order of *The Idiot's Guide to Bullshitting Your Way Through a TV Job Interview.*

I met Jeff the President at the Stanhope Hotel. These television people sure liked meeting in hotels. At least this time we were meeting in the restaurant.

I showed up early and scanned the room looking for someone looking for me. The hostess informed me that my other party had yet to arrive and asked would I like a table?

I must have looked like a hooker as I sat there making meaningful eye contact with every man who walked in. But I could tell right away which one was Jeff the President. He strode in with the presence of a quarterback and the jaw of a Ken doll; the man effused authority. Everything about him said *president,* although not necessarily the president of a woman's television network.

The hostess directed him to our table. "I'm Jeff," he said to my "I'm Linda," sticking his hand out. He also had the hands of a quarterback. I didn't know if I should stand up or keep sitting. Jeff was still standing. What would a man do? And what difference did it make what a man would do? I was interviewing for a ladies' channel.

While I was still debating sitting versus standing, Jeff pulled out the chair across from mine and sat.

"Good to meet you," he said. "Sounds like you have a cold."

I shook my head no.

Within minutes he ordered a roast beef sandwich and a Diet Coke. I claimed to be unable to eat, hoping maybe Jeff would think I'd lost my appetite because I was so excited to meet him, when really I never eat during interviews. Instead of concentrating on my answers, I end up obsessing over whether something's stuck in my teeth.

"So, what channel are we on?" Jeff asked, getting right down to business.

"Twelve," I said. Then asked, "Was that a trick question?"

"No. But one woman I interviewed didn't know. It was a short interview."

Thank goodness I knew. Maybe I'd last through Jeff's roast beef.

Jeff talked about the job's long hours; the terrible pressure, the fast pace, making it all sound wildly unappealing. He spent the rest of the time justifying why a man could be president of a ladies' television network, offering up all sorts of reasons, none of which sounded logical, but at least I was smart enough to keep my mouth shut.

By the time we stood outside in front of the Stanhope, my puny hand shaking good-bye with his quarterback hand, I could tell he liked me. I just didn't know why.

"It's been good talking with you," he said. "We'll be in touch."
I'd hardly said two words the entire time.   ·

The original telephone interviewer called to tell me they
wanted to fly me out to spend a day at the network meeting
people and seeing how I fit in.

"Okay. Sure," I said. "Why not?" Even though I could
think of a dozen reasons why not. But free airfare was free
airfare.

I flew in the night before my meet-and-greet so I could
ravage Randy's body and get a good night's sleep, not realizing
that the two plans were incompatible. I was tired when I arrived at the network's reception lobby. I'd been instructed to
ask for Owen, the man who'd be my boss if I were offered a job
and decided to be his employee.

Owen was the yin to Jeff's yang. Slight build. Thin face.
More of a locker room attendant than a quarterback. But he
sported flattering eyeglasses and a dark trim beard and had the
kind of eyes I'd think of as warm and soulful if I were on a date
with him instead of an interview.

He also talked about the job's long hours, the terrible pressure, the fast pace, then showed me photographs of his son,
who fortunately was adorable, so I didn't have to lie when I
said, "He's adorable."

"It's time for you to meet Victoria," Owen said, checking
his watch. He walked me down the hall to Victoria's office,
where I spent the next half hour listening to her tell me about
the job's long hours, the terrible pressure, the fast pace. For

a business with terrible pressure and a fast pace, all anyone seemed to do was sit around and talk.

Victoria passed me along to Chip, who passed me along to Sheila. Nobody told me what specific jobs the people I met did, and it seemed rude to ask. *"Gee, Sheila—what do you do for a living?"*

Instead, I kept dropping the word *interstitial* into my conversation to make sure I sounded professional.

The Interviewer Boss called me from California when I was back in Chicago. "They liked you," he said. "You're still in the running."

"Really?"

"I'll know in a day or two if you're getting an offer."

"An offer for the job? Gee. Okay. Thanks."

I wanted it but I didn't want it. I felt like I was standing on the stage in Atlantic City when it was down to the last two contestants before the crowning of Miss America, me and the *other* girl. I'd be up there thinking, *I want to win! I want to win!*—all the time knowing that if I did I'd be stuck spending a year touring old people's homes and cutting ribbons at grand openings for shopping centers.

Before we said good-bye, Interviewer Boss added, "You're up against someone from HBO."

"Why would they consider someone with no TV background when they can have an HBO person?" I asked.

He said, "The HBO candidate is a man."

Two days later they made me an offer. Estrogen won out over experience. And ego won out over common sense.

*   *   *

I'd had a well-laid-out timeline for my move. When I'd give no-tice at my Chicago job. When I'd hire the moving van. When I'd start looking for an advertising job in New York. And now I was on speed dial, everything happening earlier than I'd planned.

"You can do it," Claudia said, as we ran around my apart-ment tossing books and frying pans and photo albums into packing cartons, all of the cartons labeled *miscellaneous.* "Think of yourself as resilient."

I laughed.

"Or crazy," she said. "Think of yourself as crazy."

At night I'd get phone calls from Randy telling me how excited he was that I'd be there even sooner. While he talked romance, I wrapped juice glasses in newspaper.

During the day I'd get phone calls from Sheila and Chip and Gigi asking for sign-offs and opinions on projects. Appar-ently, I'd already started the job.

"Trust your gut," I'd tell them. "You can do it!"

The production department sent me a videotape of my twenty-two employees introducing themselves along with their job titles. I studied the tape, rerunning it over and over, trying to memorize names and faces and make sense of their job descriptions.

As my plane to New York took off, I peeked out the window, a truck with my life's belongings somewhere en route below me, and watched my safe, comfortable hometown fade away.

*   *   *

Randy sent me off to work my first day with encouraging words about how much faith he had in me and how great I'd do, really great. We were standing in the hallway outside our apartment, waiting for a down elevator. I was hugging him like I was clinging to a life raft.

"Maybe I should just broom this whole TV job thing and stay home and have sex all day," I said, after glancing about to make sure none of the neighbors were around.

"Well, if you want to stay home and have sex today, go crazy," Randy said. "But I have to finish getting dressed and go to work."

The elevator arrived. Randy patted me on the butt as I stepped inside. As the doors closed, I heard him call after me: "Pretend you're Diane Sawyer."

Twenty minutes and one subway ride later, standing outside the double, ceiling-high doors leading into the headquarters of my new employer, I squared my shoulders, lifted my chin, wished myself luck, and headed in.

I spotted my first familiar face from the videotape. I smiled and said, "Good morning, Kathy!"

"Joyce," the woman said, her expression saying, *and I already hate you.*

I should have known right then to turn around, walk straight to HR, and hand in my resignation. But just at that moment a thin, angular woman, with the kind of hunched shoulders girls develop when they're too tall in junior high, introduced herself.

"I'm Fern," she said. "Your personal assistant."

I had my own personal assistant?

"Nice meeting you, Joyce," I called over my shoulder, as I followed my own personal assistant to my new office.

Within ten minutes, I could tell Fern was the epitome of crisp and efficient. "You have a meeting at four today to discuss what furniture you want to order and how you'll want to decorate," she said.

I could decorate my own office?

"You'll need to spend about an hour in Human Resources this morning signing papers, going through procedures. I'm sure you know the drill. After that I have you scheduled for meetings with Owen, production, finance, and design. Will you be going out to lunch, or should I order something in for you?"

Fern would order in lunch for me?

"In," I said.

"Fine," she said. "I'll bring you menus."

I wanted to pinch myself.

By late afternoon I knew I'd made a terrible mistake. I'd gone from meeting to meeting in a blur. I called Randy at his office and whispered into the phone, "How am I supposed to tell people what to do if I don't know what they do?"

"It's only your first day," he said. "Fake it."

I tried to lower my voice into something sounding sexy. "Ever since I met you, big boy, I never have to fake it."

I looked up and saw Fern standing in front of me with an armful of office supplies.

"Oh, hi Fern," I said.

"Next time I'll knock," she said, frowning, as she deposited pens and tape and pads of paper on my desk.

At the end of my second week the vice president of promotions suggested we go to lunch. I was grateful for the invitation. The thrill of Fern handing me a tuna sandwich every day was wearing off.

Natalie's department was smaller than mine but so tight-knit they were the office's version of a high school clique. All the women seemed to be self-assured, good-looking, and smug. They produced the network's public events and parties, things like 10K races for important causes.

Natalie was dark-haired, short, and energetic, in three-inch heels that made her medium-height and energetic.

"There've been eight people in your job in the last eleven years," she said, while picking at a pear and goat cheese salad. "Some people just never fit in."

"Oh." Nobody had mentioned that before. I was the new vice president of a revolving door. "Thanks for the—what exactly was that? Advice or a warning?"

"Neither," Natalie said, her smile sweet enough to induce cavities. "I'm just making conversation." Natalie had run her department for years. No turnover in Natalie-land. "There hasn't been anyone in charge of Creative Services for almost seven months. Until you, that is. Until you showed up."

"So the department's gone from lots of bosses to no boss to now me? That must mean a lot of unhappy people."

"Well, of course they're all still miserable about Mindy."

"Mindy?"

"Yes, when Mindy was here . . ."

That was the first time I heard the words that would come to haunt me on a regular basis. *When Mindy was here . . .* Mindy was my department's beloved predecessor, who, Natalie was delighted to inform me, was the most beloved woman to ever grace the television world. Mindy was talented. Wise. Encouraging. Kind. Charismatic and compelling. A dynamo who could do no wrong.

"Her assistant Fern—I mean, your assistant Fern—took Mindy's leaving especially hard. She worshipped Mindy."

"I'm up against *worship*? Why did Mindy leave?"

Natalie clicked open her purse and pulled out a lipstick and a small mirror. She freshened her lips before saying, "She got married and wanted some time away with her new husband. She's best friends with Chip and Sheila and—well, half the people in your department. I'm sure they talk to her almost every day."

Which meant Mindy was getting reports on *me* every day. At least now I had a reason to be paranoid.

After approving of herself in her mirror, Natalie blessed me with her sweet smile again. "Which department should we write this lunch off to?" she said. "How about yours?"

A big part of my new job was to oversee the advertising of the network's original movies, which should have been right up my alley. Only I had a hard time telling the movies apart. *Woman marries abusive husband. Woman throws coats over kids' pajamas in middle of night and sneaks away. Husband finds her. Husband hits her. Woman shoots him dead. Handsome cop arrives. Feminist lawyer gets woman acquitted. Woman and handsome cop get married.* Sometimes the star was Markie Post. Other times the star was Cheryl Ladd. But whoever the star was, she hadn't appeared on television in ages, except in one of our original movies.

"What do you think of this poster?" Sven, a graphic designer and one of the few males in my department, asked one day. Sven was buff and blond and smelled like cigarettes.

I tried my best to be diplomatic, build morale, even though I knew he was perpetually mad at the world because he worked at a ladies' network instead of ESPN. "Well, it's very nice and all," I said. "Good typeface. Nice colors. But it looks like the posters we did the last two months, except with Jaclyn Smith's head."

Sven closed his eyes and let out a pained sigh. "So what's wrong?"

I smiled, struggling to be a good cheerleader. "Well, maybe we can mix things up a bit. How about this time you put Jaclyn in the back and the prescription pill bottles in the front?"

"Jaclyn will split a gut if you do that. Get stuck behind pill bottles? When Mindy was here—"

I know I should have said something really tough, like, "Well, Sven, there's a new sheriff in town," but instead I thought, maybe Mindy was right and Jaclyn should stay front and center. "Okay," I said. "Use your good judgment."

*   *   *

Never in my life have I made more bad decisions, been a bigger fool, or hemorrhaged more self-esteem. But at least the benefits package was good.

The network was packed with women in their forties all going through their menopausal worst on the same day: throwing tantrums, screaming in hallways, slamming doors. I felt like I was in a women's prison movie except instead of a cell I had a corner office.

Fern hated me. I could feel disdain oozing from her pores. She didn't hand me messages; she slapped them on my desk.

"Arlene's upset with the support for her Golden Girls marathon and Michele needs a response on the Susan B. Komen cancer dinner. And are you going to the Crystal Awards? Jeff expects you there."

"I'll talk to Arlene. Yes to Marianne. And yes to the Crystals."

Fern wrote notes on the pad that was a constant extension of her hand.

"And have you thought about the party you'll be hosting in L.A.?" she asked.

"I'm hosting a party?"

"Yes. On the opening night of the conference. I'll arrange for a hotel suite. Cocktails. Hors d'oeuvres. The department head always throws a party. You can invite your friends in the industry."

"I don't have any friends in the industry."

"The party's three weeks away," she said, scribbling on her notepad. "Make some."

*   *   *

The one part of the job description nobody had mentioned up front was all the awards dinners. Television people like to reward themselves, usually in hotel ballrooms while eating chicken breasts. Almost weekly, sometimes twice a week, I'd find myself applauding for another icon of the cable industry being honored for this, that, or the other thing. The better dinners honored celebrities, people I'd actually seen on television. It wasn't until I showed up at one with Randy in tow and in tux that I realized the *spouse* part of the invitation was just a formality. During the cocktailing and hobnobbing Randy shook hands with Jeff in one of those men-sizing-each-other-up glaredowns, pleasant on the outside with an undercurrent of caveman. No other spouses were present. No other spouses dozed off and started snoring while some network president was extolling Marlo Thomas up there on the dais. Even Marlo knew not to bring Phil Donahue.

And now Jeff was casting an evil eye in the direction of the audible ruffled breathing while Chip and Sheila and a few hundred strangers snickered into their napkins. I kicked Randy under the table.

"I can't believe you did that," I said on the cab ride home from the Hilton.

"It wasn't on purpose. It just happened. I must have drunk too much."

"I noticed."

"How do you sit through all those speeches?"

"Awake. I sit through them awake."

The next day I could feel the whispering in the hallways. *She brought her husband. And he fell asleep.*

The network headquarters were located in the same building as an advertising agency. The two companies shared a lobby. Every morning I'd find myself looking longingly at the agency elevator bank, envious of the happy souls being whisked upstairs to create commercials for Hershey bars and American Express cards. I was stuck with the angry women and the catfights.

Claudia called from Chicago regularly to see how I was surviving.

I told her how I couldn't believe all the backstabbing, conniving, and betrayals.

"Yeah, those movies can be pretty cheesy," she said.

"Forget the movies," I said. "I'm talking about the office."

I tried to speak with Owen, man to woman, mano-a-womano, about the corporate culture, hoping he might have some helpful insight that I'd overlooked. We'd just been through my weekly status report, and on paper, things seemed to be going fairly well.

"Did you ever notice how, despite all the high heels and perfume, this place is a little rough around the edges?" I said.

"Sure," he said, shrugging. "It's a den of snakes."

I liked Owen. He was soft-spoken, shy, a below-the-radar kind of guy who could drag down any conversation within minutes by unloading a barrage of statistics. When Owen walked into a meeting, everyone else in the room suddenly remembered important phone calls they had to return, conferences they promised to attend, grandmothers' funerals they'd hate to miss. I was in the middle of a conference with my production manager one day when she spotted Owen heading down the hall and promptly said, "Gee, I'd love to keep talking, but I have a chemo session."

"Gail," I said, concerned and alarmed, "are you ill?"

"Oh, no, not really," she said, backing out of the door; "it's just preventive."

I tried inviting Owen to department meetings, hoping he could build a stronger connection with the group, be better appreciated. After the usual stampeding retreat, I'd be left with Owen, just him and me, while I mumbled to the empty chairs, "Well, I guess we'll finish this discussion some other time." I'd turn to him. "I'm sorry nobody could stick around. We're all just so busy."

"Yes, I see," he would say. "Ninety-six point three percent of the participants just left with only forty-two percent of the workday hours remaining."

Every Friday afternoon, at the end of the day, Owen would walk into my office and tell me something to upset me. One week: "I hear everyone in your department has their résumés out on the street. You might want to think about that. Have a good weekend." Then he'd leave.

Another Friday: "I hear everyone in your department doesn't think you know what you're doing. You might want to think about that. Have a good weekend."

My goal became to leave the office on Fridays before Owen could give me something to think about.

"Gotta go!" I called out to Fern as I whipped past her desk. "Chemo session."

Natalie invited me to a meeting with her department, where I found myself surrounded by five of her intense Natalieniks all insisting that my department didn't waste one more New York minute getting our panty-hosed butts moving on creating TV spots for the network's new sponsorship of the WNBA.

"Fine," I said. "I understand the urgency."

Two days later Natalie and I were called to President Jeff's office. "I see on my status report that we're moving forward on promoting the WNBA," he said. "What's the rush? We haven't finalized the details yet."

"I am of the same mind, sir," Natalie said. She turned to me and I wondered if she stayed home at night perfecting withering glances in the mirror. "But Linda just jumped ahead. I couldn't stop her."

I didn't defend myself, mainly because it was impossible to talk with my jaw on the floor and because it would have been unprofessional to call Natalie a lying sleazeball out to save her own skinny ass. Instead I told Jeff I would put a hold on the project and slunk out of the office alongside a smirking Natalie.

"I don't get it," I said as soon as we were out of Jeff's earshot. "The other day you were all in a big rush to get going and today it's like you never heard of the project."

"Really?" she said. "I must have forgotten."

*   *   *

I'd try to remind myself that whining was generally considered unattractive behavior. But some nights I just couldn't help myself. As soon as I walked in the door, before I even got my coat off, I'd unload on Randy. "These people detest me and wish me dead."

"Nobody detests you."

"They all do. I always make the wrong decision. I fire the wrong people. Hire the wrong people. My assistant hates me because I told her she doesn't have to tip fifteen percent of the entire bill for a food delivery. She hates me for being cheap. I'm in charge of the department budget—aren't I supposed to be cheap? If I felt any more pathetic around there, I could star in all their movies. Except then Jaclyn Smith would be pissed at me, too. Today Sheila said to me, 'Oh, Linda, you're so nice.'"

"See. That's nice. You are nice." Randy managed to remove my coat while I remained in high-tizzy mode.

"*Nice* is code for 'you are weak and spineless and I'm gonna chop you up, make mincemeat of your soul, and eat your young for breakfast.'"

"Okay, so maybe that's not so nice," he said, getting me to sit next to him on the sofa, "but is there any remote possibility that you might be exaggerating here? Being overly negative?"

"I don't know. What would you think if every day you walked into work and found a thumbtack on your chair? Sheila said to me: *Watch out for Carol*—Carol's the head of West Coast TV development—*she's out to get you.* When did I become a person whom other people are *out to get*?"

*   *   *

Jeff took me to lunch at a small Italian restaurant two blocks from the office. The place was dimly lit so I didn't have to worry about food stuck in my teeth. We both ordered the fish special. Pan-roasted monkfish with Roma tomatoes.

"You have a Midwest management style," he said to me, not quite looking at me, only squinting, like he was wearing contact lenses and both had slipped.

I said, "I'm from the Midwest."

"You're a consensus builder instead of a decision maker."

"Asking other people's opinions makes them feel valued and part of the process."

"This is television," Jeff said. "Things move faster here." Then he went on to talk about *when Mindy was here* and *back when Mindy was here—*

I said, "If everyone loves her so much, why isn't she here?"

Four weeks later, Mindy was back. I was moved out of my office, sans assistant, and reporting to Mindy. Or what's known in corporate America as *Please quit so we don't have to pay out your contract.* It was a showdown of mean versus tough and I was supposed to be the tough one.

The end of her first week, Mindy walked into my new office, located about three time zones away from the rest of the department, and said, "This weekend, let's both spend at least six hours watching our lineup and writing a log of every commercial that runs and time how many minutes between commercials. Then on Monday, we'll go over our notes together."

She sounded giddy with excitement, like we were two best friends about to embark on the time of our lives.

"Okay, sure," I said.

I couldn't think of any practical reason for logging commercials all weekend, but I also couldn't refuse. Saying no would be a breach of contract and grounds for dismissal empty-handed.

Saturday afternoon I sat with a stopwatch, clicking and timing, clicking and timing, asking Randy to cover for me when I ran to the bathroom.

"Can't you take a break?" he finally asked.

"No," I said. "I have two more episodes of *Golden Girls* to cover."

On Monday morning I handed my notes in to Fern, Mindy's assistant, just as Mindy went whizzing by.

"Gee, I never got to take my notes," she said, stopping for a moment and sounding all light and breezy, like we were exchanging recipes. "But you save yours and someday soon I'm sure we can discuss them." She dashed off while Fern handed back my notes without even looking up.

I called Claudia from my desk in the diaspora.

"Am I the only person who knows that the most beloved woman in television has a dark side?"

"Why are you whispering?"

"They can fire me for making personal calls."

"Pretend I'm a woman in distress and you're researching the plot for a new movie."

"Good idea. Do you mind flying to New York and showing up here with a black eye?"

I wasn't invited to meetings. I wasn't included in conferences. Nobody talked to me. Not Jeff. Not Owen. Even the few people who at one time talked to me no longer talked to me. I was miserable, waiting around to see who blinked first. I sat in my office all day writing lists with titles like: *Things I'd Rather Be Doing Instead of What I'm Doing*:

1. Be burned at the stake.
2. Eaten alive by red ants.
3. Attacked by sharks.

Oh, wait. I'd already been attacked by sharks.

After three more of the longest weeks in anyone's careerdom, Mindy called me into my former office, her current office.

"I've been studying your time sheets and all your hours seem to be attributed to 'miscellaneous,'" she said. "I find that curious."

And then for some reason I still don't understand, the toggle bolt finally flipped. I looked my darling boss in the eye. "Listen, America's TV sweetheart, we both know you would have never hired me and I can sure as hell say—I would have never signed on to work for you—*but I'm not quitting.*"

That afternoon she fired me.

I know I was supposed to pull myself up by the bootstraps, dust myself off, get back on the horse; all those equestrian-type comebacks, along with making lemons out of lemonade, making network out of cable. Instead I hid at home feeling sorry for myself and watching television—except for channel 12.

My blood money arrived six weeks later. By then I was back in the saddle, sending out résumés to advertising agencies. I stood next to Randy in our building mailroom, having ripped open the envelope like it was a pardon from the governor.

"Aren't you proud that you toughed it out and got this?" Randy said, admiring my check.

I was unable to latch on to any feeling of gratification.

Failure. Embarrassment. Fiasco. Those feelings I could muster.

DATING FOR GIRLFRIENDS

My ego pummeling at the television job made me realize how dearly I needed a support system. And not just the kind made of spandex.

I'd never given much thought to the prospect of living in a town with no girlfriends—or at least none of *my* girlfriends. I was so excited to be married and no longer dating in search of love, that it never occurred to me that I would soon find myself dating in search of someone capable of recommending a decent hairdresser or a competent gynecologist. Back in Chicago there were plenty of supportive souls to cheer me on between jobs, point me in the right direction when I was dating a psychopath (this was a more time-consuming activity than you might expect), or attend endless Saturday matinees together under no pressure to wear makeup or even be in a good mood.

Janet and I traveled to Italy together and declared ourselves to be so compatible that we often lamented one of us wasn't a guy.

Adele would read my tarot cards, while reading a book on how to read tarot cards, and always predict a rosy future.

Patty and I would disco in front of her bedroom mirror while blasting the stereo and singing along with Sister Sledge.

That's not the sort of thing you can do with a *stranger*.

The year *Newsweek* magazine ran a cover article stating women over forty stood a better chance of getting struck by lightning or kidnapped by a terrorist than getting married, we all made a pact to find husbands before the deadly deadline. We bolstered our prospects by arranging a frenzy of blind dates for each other, usually with our own castoffs or third-rate third cousins.

I told myself: *This is all I need.* Sisterhood. Support. Companionship. Okay, no sex, maybe that was a drawback. But I was happy. I was fine. I was woman. Hear me roar.

I had girlfriends.

When I was first dating Randy, I met several of his friends and often their wives or girlfriends, most of whom felt compelled to tell me how much I looked like his first wife. His friend Bill's wife seemed incapable of calling me by my own name, just *Susan*. This particular woman was ruled out as a potential girlfriend.

I reconnected with Mark, a former coworker from Chicago, who had moved to New York several years before I did. We double-dated. Randy and me. Mark and his girlfriend Laurie.

I liked Laurie immediately. Maybe because she didn't know Randy's first wife. So when the opportunity presented itself, I asked Former Coworker Mark how Laurie felt about *me*.

"Do you think Laurie would ever like to get together with me alone?" I asked. "You know, just the two of us—for like girlfriend kinda talk."

We were standing on Seventy-Third and Third, having just had breakfast at EJ's Luncheonette. Mark only liked to eat on his side of town.

"Girlfriend kinda talk?" he said.

"You know—anything that doesn't involve automobile parts or a third and down."

Mark studied two girls in matching plaid skirts and matching navy blue knee socks walking past us arms linked. Then he turned his attention back to me.

"Well, she does like you and all. She told me so, so I know she means it. But Laurie doesn't even have time for the girlfriends she already has."

I rode the crosstown bus home to the west side, staring out at my new hometown, my forehead pressed against the window, too depressed to worry about germs. Apparently, I'd have to wait for one of Laurie's friends to *die* before there'd be an opening for a new friend.

Ginger Gillette was in town from Chicago for her ad agency's board meeting. Ginger was famous for being the one female member of the board. I sat sideways, my legs draped over the arm of the one chair in her undersized room at the Royalton hotel, watching Ginger rearrange her suitcase to make room for the leather boots she'd purchased that morning.

"You have to be patient," she said. "It's supposed to take two or three years to feel at home in a new city."

"Says who?"

Ginger didn't look up from her task. She was focused on folding a sweater in half, then half again, trying to make it smaller. "Says everyone."

"Have you heard of any hard-core cases?" I asked. "The more difficult ones who take maybe ten or twenty years?" I didn't want her to leave, go home, abandon me in a girlfriend-less town.

"You'll do fine," she said, turning to me and offering up a reassuring smile. "It's not like you have an annoying personality."

What scared me was that I might not have a lasting personality. Chicago girlfriends whom I considered my psychic twins, women who swore we'd grow old together, who promised they'd take a bullet for me—began to fade away. Leslie seemed unable to forgive me for being happy. Annabelle disappeared into a hot affair with a hot stone massage therapist. Phone calls with disco-dancing Patty grew awkward and forced and eventually just stopped. Even if those friendships had lasted, I longed for some female heart-to-hearts within state borders.

I attended a book signing at Barnes & Noble, and wormed my way into a discussion between the two women waiting for autographs ahead of me. They declined my suggestion that we all go for coffee.

I looked for empty bus seats next to women with interesting faces and made myself start conversations. Clever, engaging banter like: *"Does this bus stop at Fifty-Second?"*

Most of the time I was told to check the map or ask the driver. But that's how I ended up lunching with Dee Dee.

Over fruit cups and cinnamon toast Dee Dee eagerly told me about her boyfriend. How rich he was. How handsome he was. Halfway through a melon ball it became clear that she was no longer actually dating her boyfriend. That he had broken up with her over a year ago. Mid-watermelon, I realized she was stalking him.

I, too, decided to break up with her.

A dinner with Pam, the daughter of a friend of my mother's, quickly ended when Pam scolded the waiter for delivering a sorry version of a margarita—which she'd insisted on ordering in a Thai restaurant.

And then there was Marisa, a sales rep for a graphic design firm, with whom I was developing a telephone friendship leading to a potential Barneys and Bloomingdale's shopping friendship, who spent half an hour complaining how her bastard of a husband didn't listen to her.

When I finally apologized that I had to cut the conversation short and get back to work, she screamed, "You never listen to me!" and slammed down the phone.

I'd have to find other ways to make friends. Other places to search.

The one place I never thought I'd find myself—as soon as I reached an age of free will and personal choice—was in a gym.

Gyms and I, we never hit it off. Last to be picked for the softball team. Last to be picked for the relay team. Last to be picked for the basketball team—despite being the tallest girl in the class. I've never had an athletic inclination in my entire life.

The only reason I passed eight semesters of high school phys ed was thanks to my ever-vigilant mother, the mortal enemy of dirt and scum everywhere. She starched my gym suits. Once a month, on clean gym suit day, I would be asked to stand and demonstrate what a laundered gym suit should look like. I made crackling sounds as I rose up, my freshly washed sneakers now also on view, a paragon of clean hygiene, and an object of scorn for my schoolmates.

Gym class picked up where grade school playgrounds left off, with a caste system and pecking order that slid from cool to hopeless. I envied the with-it girls, who were inevitably also the athletic and popular girls, the ones who were able to run around the bases without ruining their hairdos, or able to kick a soccer ball in a direction they actually wanted it to go. They radiated entitlement. They left towels on the locker room floor.

Cool but inappropriate were the greasers and delinquents who were only in attendance because if they didn't show up and get that one last gym credit, they wouldn't graduate. Their uniforms were never washed, not once, the entire year. They groaned for each other's amusement during toe touches, mocked whatever perky gym instructor was unfortunate enough to turn her back at the wrong time. They were the first to volunteer for the outfield or end zones where it was easy to sneak a cigarette, the ultimate sign of contempt.

Next moving down the PE food chain were the natural athletes, the girls not pretty enough to be cheerleaders but who actually liked gym class. These were the same girls who wrote for the school newspaper, held bake sales to raise money for the marching band, and hung crepe paper streamers in that same steamy gym for school dances. In the future they'd join women's studies groups and run for city council.

After them came the girls coordinated enough to avoid making fools of themselves, followed by the klutzes, and the one überklutz in the starched gym suit.

"Mom—can you write me a note to get me out of gym?"

Every week I asked. Every week she challenged me. Other girls brought notes from home with claims of cramps, headaches, torn ligaments. I wondered what leverage they held over their parents, what it took to sway those mothers into written conspiracies.

"What's wrong with gym?" my mother asked.

"I'm wrong with gym. I'm a moron in gym."

"That's because we aren't athletes in our family. We're intellectuals." By intellectuals she meant we listened to Broadway show tunes on the hi-fi and my parents watched Jack Paar at night. She looked me straight in the eye with the pride of a woman who knew her way around an ironing board and a can of spray starch. "But we're not quitters."

Actually we descended from a long line of quitters. Uncle Leo, who went AWOL from the army during the Second World War as soon as he realized danger was involved. Cousin Irwin, who skipped the country rather than face jail time for insurance fraud. My aunt Blossom, who left a groom standing at the altar while all the relatives rushed to the gift table to reclaim their punch bowls and chafing dishes. But my mother was in no mood to hear about it.

In college, my gym grades counted toward my overall average. My tennis teacher told me I swung the racket like the Good Witch Glinda.

"Well, aren't you supposed to teach me how not to do that?" I said.

"Who do I look like?" she said. "Billie Jean King?"

My subsequent D kept me from graduating magna cum laude instead of regular cum laude.

After that, it was good-bye, gymnasiums.

So it was with only the greatest reluctance that during a marathon phone call, a "four-cigarette-er" as she called it, I considered Claudia's advice to join a gym "in the interest of making New York friends." Claudia painted a pastoral picture of intimate chitchats shared over adjoining butt blasters, heartfelt bonding taking place on side-by-side thigh abductors, lifelong friendships forged during funk aerobics.

"If gyms are such a great place to meet people, why haven't you ever joined one?" I asked her.

I could have heard her response travel across Ohio and Pennsylvania even if she weren't holding a telephone. "Don't be ridiculous," she said. "I hate humanity."

There is no point in time, Greenwich mean or otherwise, when a New York gym is not offering a promotion. But I didn't care about thirty days free this or that. I joined the gym closest to home. I didn't want to expend one extra calorie commuting between my apartment and a locker room.

Randy, no big fan of indoor exercise, or any exercise for that matter, offered to also sign up, become a member for moral support. He stretched out on the sofa, one arm crooked behind his head, and watched me practice toe touching in the middle of our living room.

"Your coming with me would defeat the purpose," I said, looking at him and looking at my toes, looking at him and looking at my toes. "I have to put myself out there. Be open to meeting new people. If I went to the gym with you, I'd only talk to you."

That, plus, somehow I didn't want to recruit my husband to help me meet women.

After spending a considerable amount of time shopping for a friendly, flattering gym outfit—black stretch pants, black tank top, turbo-sports bra—I forced myself to actually walk into the gym on a Saturday afternoon. Half of Manhattan must have been there that day. The energy was palpable. The music unbearable.

The beefcake behind the counter showed me how to swipe my membership card and directed me around the corner to the ladies' locker room. *What better place to meet women?*

I plastered a big smile on my face and threw open the two swinging doors like I was waltzing out onto a Broadway stage to greet my new girlfriends—all of whom were running around naked or wrapped in towels. This particular circumstance left me stymied for a conversation opener. *Nice shave! What razor do you use?* Or—*are those real!*

Actually, nobody seemed to be talking. Two women in all their less-than-firm glory were stationed in front of a mirror, each bending over with a fat round brush in one hand and a humming blow-dryer in the other. Another woman was sitting on a bench, one airborne leg extended, tugging on panty hose. Several had their heads in their lockers, pulling things out or stuffing things in. Showers were running, locker doors slammed, music flowed out of a speaker overhead, the kind of nonthreatening tune usually heard in an elevator. But no tête-à-têtes or girly banter. Just communal silence. Until I plopped my gym bag on the floor and sat on one of the benches.

"That's my space." A towel-wrapped woman with dripping wet red curls—who still managed to look like she belonged on the cover of *Vogue*—loomed over me. I looked down the rest of the empty bench and back up at her.

"How's that?"

"I sit there," she said.

"But you aren't sitting here now."

"That's where I sit."

I slid down the bench, making room for her. She glared at me like I'd just stuck a wad of gum on her spot. I slid down farther.

"Good," she said, as she dropped her towel on the floor and sashayed off to a counter with moisturizer bottles, tampons, and cheap plastic combs. That was some body she was showing off. I unzipped my gym bag.

"Isn't she a piece of work?" I heard a woman say. I looked up at a heavyset middle-aged woman wearing a thick terry-cloth robe and a pink shower cap. Her eyes were rimmed with dark liner. She nodded her head in the direction of Ms. That's-My-Spot, who was now busy slapping lotion on her legs, one foot propped on the edge of the counter in a position only her gynecologist could appreciate. "She thinks she's still homecoming queen." The woman pulled off her shower cap, revealing jet-black, cropped hair.

"This is my first time here," I said.

"Oh, yeah?" the woman said. "I can't stand the place. It's packed with out-of-work actors and struggling writers. Narcissist Central." She opened a locker and loaded up her arms with dark hose, a leather skirt, and a black silk blouse—then shut the locker door with a swing of her butt. "I'm only here because my doctor said I had to choose between a treadmill and a heart attack. I'm beginning to think I'll take the heart attack."

I held out my hand and said, "Hi, I'm Linda."

She looked at my open palm and said, "I don't want to catch your cold," and waddled off to the shower area, disappearing behind a plastic curtain.

Just as I finished wiggling into my stretch pants, a woman in a knit sweater coat and black ankle-high stiletto boots hurried into the locker room and whipped past me like she was ticked off and didn't want to be there. The smell of stale cigarette smoke followed in her wake. She threw her silver metallic hobo bag onto a bench and yanked at a locker door handle. When the door stuck she pounded it with her fist, cursing until the door popped open.

I couldn't believe it. The same personalities from my high school gym class had grown up and joined my gym.

The workout rooms were on five different floors—not five big floors, but five barely medium-sized ones, the brownstone version of a gym. There was an aerobic floor, a cardio floor, a dump-off-the-children floor while mom's taking yoga on another floor. The weight room was on the top floor. Taking an elevator seemed hypocritical, even for me.

I started up the back staircase with a cheerful determination, ducking around a couple in matching Yankees T-shirts, engaged in their own athletic activity: tonsil hockey. By the time I hit the top floor and the last dozen steps, I felt ready to drop dead from an asthma attack. Maybe I could start a friendship with someone while they administered oxygen.

The weight room was filled with strange intimidating machines and equally strange intimidating weight lifters. I saw shoulders the size of Mack trucks. Forearms thick as fire hydrants. Rippled bodies and calves bigger than my thighs. *How much time did these people spend in the gym?*

I would have asked, but nobody's ears were available for questions. Everyone was plugged up and tuned in with Walkmans, headphones, earbuds; each pumping away in their own musical world.

I knocked out a few five-pound curls just to say I did. My form was off and I dropped a barbell, but at least I was exercising.

I rode the elevator to the yoga floor, took one look at all those meditative souls, and knew they didn't want me interrupting their inner peace.

That left the cardio floor, an area I'd equate with all the joy of a visit to the motor vehicle department. Cardio floors baffle me. If I wanted to ride a bicycle or row a boat, I'd find a park with a pond. The same goes for treadmills. I hate that going-nowhere-fast feeling. And I'd already done enough stair climbing that day to kill myself. So I opted for the elliptical machines. My cousin Delaine swears that ellipticals get rid of cellulite, they tone things that normally don't get toned. And watch out hips, she likes to say. Ellipticals are hell on hips.

Who can argue with a machine like that?

It was an excellent plan and might have worked if a dozen other Delaines hadn't beaten me to it. An entire chorus line of elliptical lovers were striding away, each on her own machine, each with a wire trailing between an eardrum and a personal television set perched above her handlebars.

Only two machines were available and it didn't take me long to figure out why. The one lone male in the lineup—I guess he was worried about his hips—was flanked by two empty machines. Enough sweat was pouring out of this guy to run a dishwasher. His TV was tuned to a wrestling match. He was the one person in the gym who'd probably be willing to start a friendship.

I walked home the out-of-my-way way, through Central Park. I loved how it felt both peaceful and chaotic at the same time.

Like me.

I considered the park my personal hiding place, not that I was creeping behind bushes. It was where I could sit and observe while feeling anonymous. Of course, lately I was always feeling anonymous. I watched people flying kites, rowing boats, riding bikes; sharing music, laughter, and drugs; big happy groups of friends, and I longed to be part of them.

I'd felt lonelier in Chicago than I was willing to admit, a painful visceral loneliness. I remembered returning from a business trip to Cincinnati, getting off my plane at O'Hare and envying the passengers who had someone waiting at the gate for them, eager to welcome them home. Randy was supposed to fix that feeling, and in so many ways he did. But I was still the loner on the bench. I saw a man across the pathway who reminded me of Teddy. Same thick dark hair. Same elegant stride. Same Marine Corps posture. I told myself, it's a sign. Teddy was telling me to hang in there. His spirit's here for moral support. Then I told myself I was seeing things and it was time to go home.

As I unlocked the front door to our apartment, I heard running water.

"Did you have a good time?" Randy called out from the kitchen.

Should I tell him that I had failed at making one decent connection? That friendships with me seemed to be in low demand? I stuffed my jacket into the closet, called down the hall. "Honey, we'll need extra place settings at the table tonight. For all my new friends."

Standing in the kitchen doorway, I flexed my bicep. "Whaddya think? Did it pay off?"

He said, "Remind me not to pick a bar fight with you." He was slicing romaine, making a salad, wearing the apron in the family.

"I think my biceps are big enough," I said. "I'm not going back."

"No fun?"

"No nothing. How will you feel if you're my only friend in New York?"

"Honored," he said. "Give it time."

He picked up a red onion. Started chopping.

I told him I didn't care if I never made one friend. I hated the health club.

"Not your thing?" he said.

"How do you feel being married to a quitter?"

He stopped chopping, handed me a cucumber and a scraper.

He said, "I'll write you a note."

NOSE TALKER

～～～

Sunday morning the telephone woke us. Without even bothering to look at the caller ID, Randy handed the receiver across
the bed. "It's for you," he said, and fell back asleep.

Every Sunday my mother calls by nine. If she were a de-
cade or two younger I'd ask her to wait until after she watched
Meet the Press, but with older parents, the last thing I need is
to discover my mother keeled over dead on a Sunday morning
and I didn't take her call.

"Did I wake you?"

"No, Mom."

"Oh. Then you sound stuffed. Are you catching something?"

"No, Mom."

The advantage of a Chicago accent is that people believe
you when you lie and say—out of politeness—that no, they
did not wake you nor are you coming down with a cold; it's just

the way you talk. Even my mother buys into it. She no longer talks through her nose. Since moving to Florida, everything about her has headed south. Her voice. Her height. And she would say her breasts and knees.

"What do you want for your birthday?" she asked.

"I don't need anything." I rubbed Randy's belly while he slept.

"You must need something. Can you use a blouse?"

"I don't need a new blouse."

"What about bathroom towels?"

"We're covered in that department."

"A new wallet?"

"No."

"House slippers?"

"Okay. Maybe some new house slippers. Size eight and a half."

"What color?"

"Blue."

"Blue?"

"Yes."

"Excellent. I'll send you a check. You can pick them out yourself."

No matter what answer my mother drags out of me, she always sends a check.

"I love you," she said before she hung up. "And take care of that cold."

I don't know how the whole Chicago nose thing got started. Maybe it began as a secret club—a way to identify fellow lovers of bad winters and good pizza. Or maybe it started with the first pioneers heading west. Anyone who spoke through their noses was tossed off the covered wagons by the time they hit Lake Michigan. The other passengers couldn't stand the thought of traveling two thousand more miles listening to those nasal accents.

After my disastrous foray in television, where I learned I was far better at watching TV than working in it, I signed on as a freelance copywriter at what was then one of New York's biggest advertising agencies, until four years later when it would be taken over by a conglomerate, lose two-thirds of its clients, and become one of New York's former biggest ad agencies. But at the time I thought of myself as returning to the comfort zone of advertising; the uncomfortable part was meeting new coworkers. Every morning felt like walking into a high school cafeteria and I was the new transfer student, scanning the room for a place to sit. I felt self-conscious on a good day; on a bad one, ill at ease and insecure. Beginning with a profound fresh awareness of my voice.

Sophomore year in high school, a lovely white-haired speech therapist named Mrs. Ylvasaker (lesson one was pronouncing her name) attempted to de-nasal me. All the kids in school had Chicago accents, but I was singled out, branded "in need of special attention."

For one hour every week Mrs. Ylvasaker made me repeat sentences with *m*'s, *n*'s, and *ng*'s—the only letters *supposed* to sound nasal.

She tried to teach me the difference between pronouncing the roof of a house and the ruff of a dog. I pronounced both the canine way.

She spent hours focusing on *hat, cat, fat*, desperate to fix my *hat*s, *cat*s, *fat*s with their elongated *a*'s.

Her main method of motivation was telling me stories of other nasal speakers and how people subconsciously hated them for talking through their noses.

"Have you considered surgery?" Mrs. Ylvasaker asked one day after I'd taxed her patience beyond its usual limits.

I looked down at my arms, stomach, legs. "On what?"

"Your septum. I'm positive it's deviated."

I didn't know I had a septum. Let alone a deviated one.

"No," I said. "I like my septum."

And hated knives.

I turned out to be Mrs. Ylvasaker's greatest failure, the type of student who made her question whether her entire life was a waste. By the end of the year she retired and moved to Arizona. But at least she left me scarred for life.

Over my lifetime I've spent inordinate chunks of energy attempting to *fix* myself: Lose weight. Straighten hair. Improve posture. Stop biting nails. Buy acne cream. Buy wrinkle cream. *If only I looked like Twiggy. If only I looked like Cheryl Tiegs.* Self-examine. Self-criticize. Self-doubt. *If only I looked like Audrey Hepburn.*

I was my own personal triage project, sorting out what might be improved versus all the lost causes. But if there's one halfway decent perk of getting, well, *older*, it's that some things just fade into the total package; they start mattering less.

My voice was never pretty. But it wasn't until New York that it felt like a stigma.

The first day I met JoAnn, the art director assigned to collaborate with me on Fisher-Price, she said, "I hear you're from Chicago."

We were brainstorming in her office, JoAnn behind her drafting board, me beneath a wall covered with layouts for something called Peek-a-Blocks. JoAnn radiated chic; she only wore haute Japanese, anything cut at odd angles with asymmetrical seams and weird hems.

I wondered if somebody had *told* JoAnn I was from Chicago—or if she just *heard* it.

I greeted the office receptionist with a simple "hello" and she immediately asked: "Do you have a cold?"

The man behind the office building newsstand said in his thick Russian accent, "You're not from around here, are you?"

My hats and roofs spoke volumes.

I felt branded by my Chicago background, apologetic. Convincing a New York ad agency to hire a Chicago writer was like cracking the Junior League. I was a second-class citizen from the Second City because my portfolio was filled with *packaged goods*: soaps, soups, and cereals. If it weren't for the billings, New York agencies would spit on packaged goods; they consider them a step below dog food, also a packaged goods account but at least a fun one. Airlines are cool. Hotels are cool. Soft drinks and cruise lines are cool. Toys are considered a pain in the ass, which is why I was hired for the Fisher-Price job. And if you're wondering why toys aren't cool, turn on any television set on a Saturday morning.

*   *   *

The following night, Randy was sitting up in bed watching *The X-Files*. I was curled against him, practicing *roof* versus *ruff*.

He looked at me and asked, "Is there some particular reason why you're barking?"

I sat up. "I'm working on my Chicago accent."

"Why?"

"I'm trying to sound like a New Yorker."

"Why?"

"People make assumptions based on accents. Southern equals charming. Italian equals sexy. Iranian equals please step out of line, sir, and show us your documents." I reached for a nail file off the top of my dresser without having to move from the bed. Our apartment was decorated in late-century overcrowded.

"What's so terrible if people know you're from Chicago? People like Chicagoans. Think of your accent as a banner of honor, a regional dialect from a big, proud city known for its hardworking citizens."

"Yeah," I said, attacking a rough spot on my thumbnail, "that and the St. Valentine's Day Massacre."

The phone rang. Randy answered it. Growing up, we were taught in my family that it's impolite to call anyone after ten o'clock. I guess we were the only family to learn that rule because people call after ten all the time.

"Hello," Randy said into the phone. "Hi! How are you? Oh, okay, she's right here."

That meant it was Claudia. She still treated Randy like he was my temporary boyfriend who'd soon go away so there was no point in bonding with him. I think on some super deeper than deep subconscious level she was pissed at Randy for actually marrying me and not living down to her expectations. He never seemed to notice, though. He just handed me the telephone and went back to watching his government alien conspiracies.

"Do you think my accent's bad?" I asked Claudia.

She said, "What accent?"

JoAnn and I created five different commercials for Fisher-Price Bubble Mowers, a plastic kid-sized lawn mower designed for spitting out bubbles instead of cutting grass. JoAnn called it the perfect toy for kids who wanted a future in landscaping.

The agency scheduled focus groups so housewives and mothers could criticize my copy and choose which commercial they hated the least. The spots needed to test well. If not for the agency's sake, then for mine.

The groups were held on a separate floor so the participants wouldn't be influenced by the agency's famous name. At least the participants too oblivious to notice they'd just walked into a building with the agency's famous name carved over the door. The research floor was even decorated differently. Pink walls and gray carpeting instead of what we were subjected to in the rest of the agency: walls painted a sickly shade of yellow that you swear can't look any worse—until somebody turns on the fluorescent lights; and brown carpets covered with mystery stains, most of them rumored to be from after-hour sexual encounters or murders.

It was a relief to spend a day on the research floor.

*   *   *

JoAnn had begged off from the focus groups, claiming her grandmother had been hit by a bus, but really because of an Issey Miyake sample sale. She wasn't afraid to dodge groups; JoAnn had a *staff* position.

While waiting on my side of a two-way mirror for the housewives and mothers to sit down, write out their name tags, and let their opinions rip, I stuffed my face with grapes and M&M's and Pepperidge Farm cookies. The main perk of attending focus groups is free snacks. I was supposed to be discussing demographics and audience response with Erin and Jean, two women from the agency's market research department, but instead I bounced my accent assumptions theory off of them. Erin and Jean each had one of those Ivy League voices that say *Rich! Educated! Elite!*

I asked, "What's your impression of Chicagoans?"

"In regards to television audiences?" Jean asked, picking through the grapes.

"No. In regards to in general."

"Not counting you?" Erin asked.

"Yes. Besides me."

Jean abandoned her grape grappling. She seemed to be giving my question serious thought.

Erin put down a handful of Cheetos, rapped her fingers on her chair arm. "Hard to say."

"It shouldn't be that difficult," I said. "Just tell me what comes to mind."

"Okay," Jean said. Both of them started calling out images.

"Brown shoes!"

"Unsophisticated!"

"Not stylish!"

"Polish sausage!"

"Drinks beer and watches sports."

"Dull."

"Friendly!"

"Drives a Ford Taurus."

"Eats a lot of corn and potatoes."

I knew I'd better stop things fast before I ended up hating both of them. I asked, "Anyone want an Oreo?"

JoAnn and I reported to Bettina, an executive creative director and the agency's full-time angry feminist. Bettina's signature look was black jeans, cowboy boots, and silk blouses with the top four buttons left undone to broadcast that she didn't wear a bra.

Bettina's best friend at the office was Martha, an account director with the biggest diamond and emerald wedding band I've ever set eyes on. I believe Martha was slim and blond and wore Armani suits but I can't be sure; I could never take my eyes off that ring. Martha spent every lunch hour at work sitting in Bettina's office, the two of them eating chopped salads, playing Scrabble, and gossiping about all the other employees.

I stood and waited while Bettina agonized and concentrated and chewed on her fist, finally plopping a letter on the board. It must have been a good one because Martha couldn't believe how *she* hadn't seen that spot and how she'd absolutely *kill* herself if it meant now she'd lose the game. Martha turned the board and studied it, her gigundo ring blinding me in the process.

"There's a casting session tomorrow for a Softer Side of Sears shoot that I'd like you to cover," Bettina said to me after adding up her score and dismissing my update on the focus groups. Creative people hate research. "We need someone pretty but, you know—*Midwest*."

"Not too sophisticated, friendly, drives a Ford Taurus?"

"Exactly. As if someone like you had a good-looking daughter."

I wasn't sure if I had just been complimented or insulted, but I said sure, no problem, my pleasure, at your service.

When you're freelance, you'll sweep the floors if it means getting paid your day rate.

The next morning JoAnn and I sat on a big white overstuffed couch, pens and pads in hand, as a parade of models batted their eyes, flashed their teeth, and strutted their stuff in hopes of being cast in a Sears Zip Front Cotton Velour Robes commercial. Each model handed us a Polaroid picture stapled to her head sheet.

The photos on the head sheets—aided by makeup artists, hair stylists, professional photographers, and airbrushing— never looked like the Polaroids taken five minutes earlier in the waiting room. But they did show a range of emotions: sultry; insouciant; or don't-mess-with-me-I-have-attitude.

The head sheets also listed acting credits and vital statistics. Height, weight, dress size, blouse size, pants size (always size two), and the really vital stuff like glove size. But never age. A model would rather tell you her bank balance than reveal her age.

Our handsome young casting director in low-slung jeans

THE LAST BLIND DATE

and a ripple-revealing T-shirt—who introduced himself as Call Me Lee; JoAnn called him Jail Bait—told each model where to stand and when to start talking. One line of copy was required: *Good morning, Sunshine!*

It was mind-boggling just how many ways there were to mangle three simple words. We'd be asked about motivation (sell robes); backstory (you just woke up and brushed your teeth); and how soon was the spot going to run, for how long, and was it national? (Soon. Short. No.)

After each model read the line, we'd smile, say thank you, and with a few simple check marks reject them right and left; for me, making up for every sixth-grade dance class where I stood alone on the sidelines, trying my painful best to keep smiling, while the pretty girls frugged. "These girls may have looks, but we have power," I said to JoAnn.

In the two minutes between the time one model left the room and the next walked in, JoAnn and I made comments.

"Nice knock-knees," JoAnn said.

"Crummy nose job," I said.

"Can you believe that frosted polish?"

I actually liked the frosted polish, but chose not to mention it.

I scanned the head sheet. "Says here she played 'Visiting Niece' in two episodes of *Guiding Light.*"

"Didn't last a week. And how 'bout that overbite?"

"You don't think *Guiding Light* is impressive?"

"Of course, not," JoAnn said. "But I'm not from Chicago."

Before I realized I'd just been patronized, Call Me Lee brought in the next model.

"This is Kendall," he said.

"Kendall what?" I asked.

"Just Kendall."

Many of the girls went by one name, emulating famous one-name people. Cher. Sting. Penn. Teller.

Tall and blond Kendall was so beautiful we instantly hated her and then so sweet we promptly forgave her.

Good *morning*, Sunshine! *Good* morning, Sunshine. She gave us several readings. I think Call Me Lee fell in love with her. As soon as she left JoAnn burst out laughing.

"Jesus," she said, "and I thought *your* voice was nasal."

The Sears clients flew in from Chicago for a preproduction meeting, the meeting that comes before the production meeting and after the prepreproduction meeting, just in case we don't have enough meetings.

Bettina invited me to present the casting tape of our model selections. "If the clients like you, I can assign you to some of their projects," she said, "and maybe you can keep working here."

I wanted to do a good job. Dazzle. Impress. Make 'em beg for more. I wanted to avoid job hunting.

The clients filed into the long, brown-carpeted conference room with its overpolished table and overhead movie screen. Introductions were made; bagels and sweet rolls offered.

"Good morning," the Sears assistant brand manager said through her nose.

"Pleasure to meet you," the Sears VP of marketing said through his nose.

"Same here," I said through my nose.

BLESS YOU MY PEOPLE

~~~~~

I'd been living in New York for over a year. The subway system finally made semi-sense. The pizza delivery guy recognized my face. And so far the kids hadn't short-sheeted my bed.

I was not particularly adept at understanding little boys, having never been one, grown up with one, or had one. Ask Benjamin not to blow milk through his nose and he'd reel off three hundred reasons why it was necessary, like an ace defense attorney. He was unable to recognize teasing, didn't know from nuance, and when he was interested in a topic his focus intensified; you had to break into his world. And don't even bother if he had a video game going. He could also wiggle his ears or roll his tongue should the need occur.

Phoebe liked to gossip and had numerous girlfriends, all of whom seemed to be named Ashley. She thumped instead of walked, slammed instead of closed. She was never short on opinions. Johnny Depp—cool. Harrison Ford—old. Winona Ryder—stupid. Phoebe introduced me to the music of the Spice Girls. Benjamin introduced me to the music of somebody named Ghostface Killah. Randy and I introduced each other to earplugs.

After interviewing three gynecologists three days in a row—every time I looked down at my knees another candidate was looking up—I found one I liked.

And even though the ad agency hadn't offered me a staff position, I was bringing home a paycheck for writing seductive descriptions of musical playmobiles, musical tea sets, and musical kitchens.

But I still felt like a tourist with a visa.

JoAnn and I were given another Sears project, a print campaign for drawstring capris. I was hoping that by now we could really be friends.

One day I broached the subject of our getting together after hours.

"For work?" she said.

"No, for fun."

JoAnn hesitated, looked confused. "I suppose. Maybe sometime. But don't you think we spend enough time with each other at the office?"

"Too bad you can't join a church," Claudia said, after I relayed my latest attempt at bonding. "You could meet people at choir practice and pancake breakfasts."

"Thank you, Miss You-Should-Join-a-Gym. Now you've got me becoming Christian."

I was holding the telephone in one hand and an open refrigerator door in the other, assessing a half-eaten burrito. Randy was at the kids' multiplying square roots with Phoebe and memorizing Chinese provinces with Benjamin.

"People have been meeting other people through religious affiliations for centuries," Claudia the atheist said.

"Yeah. I believe that's how my uncle Gershon met Hitler."

I closed the refrigerator door sans burrito.

Before Claudia hung up, she said, "I leave you in God's hands."

During Teddy's illness, anytime anyone talked about how his brain cancer was God's will or how God doesn't give you more than you can handle—"Okay, then let me get this straight. If he couldn't *handle* cancer, then he wouldn't *have* cancer?"— anything idiotic like that, I'd go nuts.

God lost his appeal those last few years in Chicago. Even Randy, appearing in the guise of a Jewish boyfriend, couldn't send me running to a synagogue. But protest though I might, I still *felt* Jewish. I wanted a rabbi when I married; I lit candles on Hanukkah; I appreciated a decent slice of Nova.

When I was eight years old my family moved from Chicago proper to Lincolnwood not so proper, a transition suburb for people who'd earned enough money to move out of the city but weren't quite ready to make the leap to the North Shore suburbs, where the *real* money hung out. Lincolnwood, though, had its own little status haven, Lincolnwood Towers, a mile-long pocket of *the better Lincolnwood homes*.

Taller split-levels.

Longer ranch houses.

Rec rooms with wet bars.

It was as fashionable as you could get while living on the wrong side of the Edens Expressway.

Before the sixties the reason for the Towers' exclusivity was somewhat questionable: No Jews. No dogs. No Negroes. And not necessarily in that order. Mexicans were also unwelcome, unless they were mowing the lawns, but a few Catholic families managed to squeeze in under the radar around the time the pope approved eating meat on Fridays. Then the law changed. A neighborhood could no longer be restricted. Just rude.

We were the second Jewish family to move into the Towers, although I still don't know who the first family was. We never met them, never knew which house they lived in. I don't know why my parents were willing to buy a house in the Towers. They never struck me as the social renegade types. But my mom loved the layout and my dad loved the backyard.

We lived across the street from the Marlings, Catholics who owned a dog. Between our two families, the property values on our street must have plummeted.

My mother informed her three daughters that we had to be on our best behavior at all times; that if we did anything wrong, the neighbors would blame it on our being Jews.

"Wrong like what?" I asked.

My mother considered the vast possibilities.

"Wrong like tracking mud in on the new carpets."

I was scared. Even my own mother might turn informer at a moment's notice. There she'd be chatting at the grocery store, making new Christ-loving friends: "My second daughter—

Linda, the one with the curly hair—didn't wipe her shoes when she walked in the house last night. Can you imagine?"

"Of course," the neighbors would say while standing in the checkout line, bending over their carts unloading their pork roasts and Spam cans and loaves of white Wonder Bread. Their voices would waver between empathy and abhorrence. "What do you expect? We hear she's *Jewish.*"

Every morning I'd walk to the school bus with Buddy Marling and see other kids whisper behind cupped hands. Or avert their eyes. Out of sheer survival instinct I would've made the sign of the cross if only I knew which direction my hand should move. I debated over what would be worse: getting crucified by my new neighbors or murdered by my parents.

People noticed me, knew my name; they probably believed I had horns and cloven hooves. For once, I was a somebody. A somebody who just wanted to blend in.

I was so used to not flaunting my Jewishness that when I moved to New York it surprised me to hear other people—regular, normal, everyday people, the kind you'd sit next to in a doctor's office—sprinkle their conversations with Yiddish phrases. *"That cabdriver was a mensch." "Our doorman is a schnook."*

On Friday nights the lobby of our building smelled like chicken soup; a rabbi's family lived in 1B.

I saw mezuzahs on doorways and spotted numerous Orthodox synagogues, almost as small as the mezuzahs. The names on our apartment building's mailboxes read like the membership roster from my mother's temple sisterhood.

I saw gold-chained stars worn with carefree pride. In Chicago, only black men wore gaudy Jewish stars and I always figured they didn't know what the hell they were doing.

On Kol Nidre, the holiest part of Yom Kippur, the holiest of Jewish holidays, I attended synagogue with my new acquaintance Debi, whom I met through my old Chicago friend Liz. (Yes, a potential girlfriend. One month later Debi was transferred to San Francisco by her computer sales firm.) Yom Kippur's when everybody gets to atone for their sins of the previous year. First Debi and her brother Zachary went in with their two tickets, then Debi came back outside and slipped me Zachary's ticket, so already I was sinning.

I wasn't committed enough to cough up my own two hundred bucks for a ticket. And Randy wasn't even committed enough to sneak in. (High Holiday ticket gouging is one of the charming quirks of Judaism. Rather than pass around a basket every week, tickets are sold for the three days a year even the least Jewish Jews go to temple, Randy being the exception.)

The temple was packed. So packed I found myself thinking there might not be enough seats—an observation confirmed by several tussles on the order of: *Hey, buddy—I was here first.*

Of course, I was in no position to criticize.

The temple, tall, simple, beige, was actually a church that turned into a temple on Friday nights and Saturday mornings. Sort of a religious time-share. Five rabbis in long white robes sat on velvet chairs lining the today-a-bimah-tomorrow-a-chancel; the Torah was on wheels—rolled out for the Jewish

services and rolled away for the Christian ones. Off to the
side a group of musicians—a cellist, a pianist, two violinists,
and a flautist—studied their sheet music and tuned their in-
struments. A draped red cloth was hanging overhead. Hiding
Jesus. I couldn't stop staring at that cloth; I was mesmerized
by it. *Do not pay attention to the man behind the curtain.*

One of the white-robed rabbis approached the pulpit, and in
a deep florid voice that made him sound like Spencer Tracy delivering his big *Inherit the Wind* summation, he offered up a few
blessings, getting us all in the mood to spend the next twenty-
four hours following the five rules of Yom Kippur: no eating, no
drinking, no fornicating, no anointing our bodies with oils, and
no leather shoes. After that list, the only thing left to do is pray.

The leather shoe ban goes back to when wearing them was a
sign of wealth. Showing off on Yom Kippur is a sin; it's wrong to
dress any wealthier than anyone else. The rabbis were all wearing
sneakers. Along with several congregants. Two-hundred-dollar
Air Jordans.

We recited some prayers.

Rabbi Two talked.

We recited more prayers.

The musicians played. The guitarist, a pasty-faced young man
who looked like he was dying for a cigarette, was really groovin'. A
Jewish Jimmy Page. Next to him the pianist, a plump woman with
a smile much too broad to be appropriate for a day honoring sin,
rippled her fingers across the piano keys with grace and elegance. A
frizzy-haired girl in Cleopatra eyeliner played the flute like a dream.

After a stirring instrumental number, the kind that inspires
you to not just *think* about God, but *experience* him, the musi-

cians were joined by a succession of singers. One after another they piped in, as I clutched at my heart and felt swept into an unexpected emotional pull. *These singers were descended from heaven!* Incredible, phenomenal, Barbra Streisand meets Frank Sinatra Hebrew-singing singers. I was no longer in synagogue. I was at *the world's greatest concert.*

I leaned over and whispered to Debi, "Where'd they find these people?"

She turned and smiled at me, a smile that said she found me amusing, in a pitiful kind of way. "Times Square," she said, "where there are fifteen musicals running on Broadway."

I considered this to be an amazing piece of information. It had never occurred to me that Broadway stars could be singing my holiday prayers.

"Are they Jewish?" I asked.

I couldn't wait to get home and tell Randy how remarkable the singers were and how easy it was to sit through services in New York, but by the time I got home he was asleep.

The next morning while we were still lying in bed purposely not having sex, I offered to cook him a big breakfast. That was my idea of humor since we were both fasting. Even though Randy doesn't go to work and doesn't attend temple on the holiday, he still fasts, which is doubly hard during all the food commercials he sees while watching TV all day.

"Y'know, I actually thought that if I ever had a Jewish husband I'd have a *date* for Yom Kippur," I said.

He put his hand on my breast.

I brushed it off. "Not today."

"Since when are you so religious?" he asked.

"It's the holiday," I said. "And I live in New York."

Even I was surprised by my sudden fervor. As a kid I'd always hated missing school on the holidays, not because I missed *school* but because I hated explaining why.

One year Dickie DeGallo cornered me at recess and asked why I was out the day before, if I was sick and full of germs.

"No," I said, "it was Rosh Hashanah."

"Rosh-a-what?"

"Rosh Hashanah. Jewish New Year."

Dickie looked at me like I was trying to pull a fast one. "Any moron knows New Year's is January first."

I looked around the noisy school courtyard, hoping a ball would bounce in our path and knock Dickie out.

I said, "We use a different calendar so the holiday's in September. Or October. It changes every year."

Dickie snorted. "What kind of a stupid holiday is *that*?"

I recognized this conversation was getting me nowhere. I was the last person I knew who should be trying to explain a six-thousand-year-old religion to Dickie DeGallo. If only I'd paid better attention in Sunday school. I tried to think up an answer I could give him that would be satisfactory enough to make him go away.

"We sacrifice animals," I said. "You own a dog, right?"

Every year the ad agency where I worked in Chicago alternated days off between Columbus Day and Martin Luther

King's birthday. That way the agency could give us one holiday off instead of two while still avoiding disenfranchising the African-Americans and the Italians.

But here I was, living in a city that *closed its schools* for the Jewish holidays.

Six months later, when Passover rolled around, the holiday that's famous for making the movie *The Ten Commandments* famous, I'd find myself at Randy's aunt Ev's for the Seder. I've never understood Seders. Everyone sits around a big table eating brown food, getting drunk, and thanking God for killing Egyptians. I'd miss my family. I'd hate being away from home. *What am I doing with these people? Why am I celebrating with them?*

But I'd realize that for the first time in my life there was a Seder taking place in the apartment next door, and the apartment next to that, and the apartment across the hall.

That, in itself, was a miracle.

Weeks later I'd be walking down Eighty-Fourth Street on a Saturday afternoon, the city feeling festive, the weather unseasonably warm. I'd pass two men in long dark coats and broad-brimmed hats in front of one of the tiny Orthodox shuls that dot the neighborhood, and happily think: *These are my people.*

"Good Sabbath!" I'd call out to the men.

They'd both glance at me in my shorts and tank top, the rubber flip-flops on my feet. Then they'd cup their hands and avert their eyes.

PRIVATE SCHOOL BENJAMIN

~~~~~~

While I was trying to find God, make friends, and keep myself employed, Phoebe and Benjamin were busy doing what kids do—getting educated. Randy did his best to teach me about Manhattan private schools, but frankly, I just didn't get it. For one thing, the kids never seemed to go to class. President's Day was a two-day holiday. Good Friday meant getting Thursday and Friday off. Teacher's Conference Day lasted a full week.

Between snow days and holidays Phoebe attended the prestigious all-girls Brearley School, known for spitting out famous prestigious girls like Caroline Kennedy. Benjamin attended Ethical Culture, a coed school on Central Park West known for teaching ethics and holding concerts.

"It sounds like something Daffy Duck would say," I told Randy when I first heard the name. "Ethical Culture. Ethical Culture. Really. Say it ten times fast."

"If it's all the same with you, I'd rather not."

"Geez. I guess you private school parents can't take a little joke."

One night he told me about all the schools Susan and he applied to for each of the kids, and how anxious they were about Phoebe and Benjamin ending up in good places. We were in bed watching *Goodbye, Mr. Chips*, the version with Petula Clark bursting into song every two minutes.

"Around here getting kids into the right schools is serious business," Randy said. "People coach their kids. Cultivate friendships with admissions directors. I heard of one family that went straight from the maternity ward to sign their kid up with a tutor."

"We did something like that in Chicago, too," I said. "As soon as a kid was born you'd get on the seven-year waiting list for Bozo tickets."

"You just keep your fingers crossed and hope your kid doesn't mess up on the interview."

"The *interview*? How do you interview a three-year-old?"

"The schools know how to do it. They draw together, play with blocks, check to see if the kid has a good disposition."

"And if he doesn't he probably needs a nap."

Petula was charming all the English schoolboys, inviting them to tea with Peter O'Toole. I was guzzling out of a beer bottle.

Randy continued my school lesson. "Some people think— and not necessarily me—that if your child doesn't get into a good preschool, he won't get into a good lower or middle school, will never be accepted to a top high school, and then has no chance of getting into an Ivy League college."

"All because he flunked *blocks*?"

"Yes."

"And were you ever married to any of the people who think this way?"

"Well, maybe." Randy reached over and took a swig of my beer. "Susan insisted.Benjamin didn't get into Horace Mann because he mangled his Play-Doh. And that it's my fault neither of the kids had a shot at Trinity after I yawned during Phoebe's interview."

"Why were you so tired?" I asked.

"I was up late the night before studying the school's year-books, in case they quizzed me. The interviews aren't just about the kids. They also size up the parents. You have to say things like *I'm a team player* and *we like to endow buildings*."

"Are you telling me we owe somebody a gymnasium?"

"Fortunately not. Phoebe got into Brearley because they were so impressed with how she verbalized."

"Does that mean 'talked'?"

"Yes. Excellent. Good job," Randy said. "With a little luck, I think we can get you into a decent New York kindergarten."

Phoebe had more homework in one night of seventh grade than I had in four years of college. Benjamin carried a book bag on his back that weighed more than he did. The first time I saw copies of the kids' report cards it was obvious that New York parents get a lot of bang for their tuition bucks. Along-side every grade the teachers wrote a progress report, an entire treatise making endless observations about study habits, at-titude, and class participation. Subject by subject there were comments on pop quiz results, behavior patterns, and contributions made during specific discussions on certain days. *"Benjamin's insights on Lewis and Clark's expedition across the Great Plains were well received by other class members during Explorers Day."*

The most any teacher ever wrote on my report card was: *Linda talks in class.*

I was trying to figure out the express buttons on the microwave when Benjamin walked into the kitchen and gave me a twenty-minute lecture on magnetron thermal fuses and interlock switches.

"Wonderful," I said. "But can you bake a potato in three minutes?"

Phoebe didn't simply write a paper on First Ladies; she hand-stitched replicas of all their inaugural gowns.

"Maybe I can quiz you on your homework," I said to her one Sunday. "What are you studying?"

"Latin."

"Latin, huh? That's quite a language. What else are you studying?"

"Calculus."

"Great. Sounds good." I patted her on the head. "Keep up the good work."

I was determined to become more knowledgeable about the kids' studies. Going to school was the biggest chunk of their waking lives. I saw my involvement as a way for us to share and grow closer, bond and connect, and for me to have something to talk about over Monopoly while Randy was off getting his teeth cleaned. The three of us were sitting on the living room floor with the Monopoly board spread open on the coffee table. We'd selected our tokens and drawn for our turns. Phoebe was the horseback rider; Benjamin was the race car; I was the old shoe and banker. After every turn Benjamin counted his money. That was his favorite part of the game. I seemed to be spending most of my time in jail. That was his second favorite part of the game. Phoebe liked playing with the little houses.

"So what are your teachers like?" I asked, tossing the dice.

"Mean," Benjamin said.

"Not bad," Phoebe said.

I landed on Marvin Gardens and doled out rent money to Benjamin for his two hotels while the little land baron gloated.

I told the stepfruit-of-my-loins how algebra class drove me batty what with all its crazy trains—the one that leaves the station at ten o'clock going thirty miles an hour followed by the one that leaves at ten-fifteen going thirty-five miles an hour and which one gets there first?

"Why doesn't everyone just look at the schedule?" I laughed.

They did not laugh.

I told them how I got in trouble in social studies when I asked what good it did me to know Luxembourg was approximately the same size as Delaware, how Miss Buchanan made me clean the erasers.

They did not relate.

I told them about everyone being scared of communism and hiding under our school desks so we wouldn't get hit in the head with bombs.

"Your teachers thought desks ward off bombs?" Phoebe said.

"What kind of bombs?" Benjamin asked.

"Big ones," I said. Benjamin bought Park Place. "I'm sure Dad did the same thing in New Jersey."

Phoebe leaned forward with the straight-backed authoritative air of a high school principal. "The communists wanted to bomb New Jersey?"

The kids looked at me like I didn't just come from another state or generation but from another planet, and had been taught by the world's stupidest teachers, then proceeded to chat pleasantly between themselves about Khrushchev's 1956 twenty-five-thousand-word speech denouncing the cult of personality.

I wanted the kids' approval. I wanted to be someone they could look up to. I didn't want them to know I'd never heard of Khrushchev's speech on the cult of personality.

"You're trying too hard," Randy told me that night.

"That's ironic," I said. "My grade school teachers said I didn't try hard enough."

In the morning, on my way to work, I observed parents walking hand in hand with their little uniformed children en route to school or a bus stop. It's a sweet sight, one that conjured up memories of my own school day mornings when my mom would yell from her bedroom: "Pour yourself a bowl of Rice Krispies! And don't slam the door on your way out!"

I found myself feeling defensive about my public school education. It's not like I didn't learn anything. I can balance a checkbook within 10 percent, build a volcano out of baking soda and vinegar, and name the four presidents on Mount

Rushmore. I never got the hang of New Math, but it no longer matters, since ten years later teaching arithmetic that way was considered a national disaster.

Even before the school year started, I ran into some neighbors in our building mailroom discussing their kids' private schools.

My upstairs neighbor Suzi chatted about her daughter at Spence.

My downstairs neighbor Colleen chatted about her son at Dalton.

Josephine Cummings from 6C ripped open an envelope. "Ohmygawd! I'm beside myself with joy. Our little Gary got accepted into preschool at Collegiate," she said with an excitement that in my family would be reserved for *"Our little Leonard won the Nobel Peace Prize."*

I learned that everyone is far less chatty *before* their little darlings are accepted to a school. Insider tips and conniving moves are kept under wraps, but because Phoebe and Benjamin were already enrolled in decent schools and any prospects I maintained of spawning my own future offspring would have made it into the history books, it was considered safe to confide in me.

I was talking myself out of head-butting a stubborn vending machine at the office one day, desperate for some Planters Peanuts, when a woman from the media department said to me in a hushed voice: "I hear that in the interest of diversification, Trevor Day is looking for Hispanic boys this year. Don't tell anyone."

I retrieved my quarters from the change slot and said, "But Tiffany, your son's not Hispanic."

"Shhhhh," she said. "We're working on it."

There was more talk in the building mailroom when word got out that the Malinicks in 9C were breaking their lease and moving to Scarsdale in the suburbs. But two days later we heard the Malinicks decided to stay.

"What happened?" I asked Keith the doorman.

"Their daughter *did* get into private school," Keith said. "Her acceptance letter was lost in the mail."

"All this fuss is confusing to me," I said to Randy that night while we stood over our bathroom sink together, brushing our teeth. "You went to public school in New Jersey but still managed to get into Harvard."

Randy leaned over and spit. "I told them I was Hispanic."

The only thing more distressing than not getting an interview slot with a school was getting a rejection from the school. I once saw a woman in the ice cream aisle at Gristedes loading up her cart with *Ben & Jerry's.*

"Is there a sale?" I asked the stock boy.

"No," he said. "I heard her son didn't get into Calhoun and she's going home to kill herself."

"Where'd you go to school?" I asked.

"Public school," he said.

"Me, too!"

We high-fived each other. Then he resumed stacking cans of Campbell's chicken soup.

BOO AND BOO HOO

~~~~~

It would be my first Halloween in New York, having missed what should have been my first Halloween in New York when I flew back to Chicago for my cousin Connie's Halloween baby shower. Randy and the kids and I were sitting around the kitchen table drawing jack-o'-lanterns. Mine was pathetic, resembling something closer to a human kidney.

"What kind of costumes will you be wearing?" I asked Phoebe and Benjamin, reaching across Randy for a green crayon.

"A mutant ninja turtle," Benjamin said. He was using blunt scissors to cut circles out of orange construction paper.

"I was going to be a horse trainer but decided to go as a teenager," Phoebe said. She was sketching an intricate pump-kin outline, appraising, erasing, and sketching again.

"How do you dress like a teenager?" Randy asked. He was

deeply involved in drawing a half-moon smile with jagged rect-angular teeth.

These people were pumpkin-drawing professionals.

"High heels and makeup," Phoebe said. At twelve, she was at the age where she was too old to trick-or-treat but still wanted the free candy. She had pierced her ears and overnight seemed to acquire a complete collection of tiny butterflies, daisies, and hearts. Her lobes were dotted with two startled black cats, their tails upright.

"Dad always wears the same costume," Benjamin said.

I turned to Randy. "You dress up?"

"Sure," he said. "It's Halloween."

"As a what?"

"A pirate!" both kids said.

Randy stopped coloring long enough to smile at them.

"Sounds like fun," I said, winking at their father.

"He's got a hook," Benjamin said.

"And an eye patch," Phoebe said.

"And a cape," Randy said.

That called for a second wink. Capes were hot.

"What are you going to be?" Benjamin asked, poking one blade of his scissors through his pumpkin to cut an eye.

"Will you come trick-or-treating here?" I asked, changing the topic. Halloween fell on a Wednesday night, their mom's night. "Will we be on your route?"

"This building?" Phoebe said. For a kid, she had a real tal-ent for conveying adult-like disdain.

"No way," Benjamin said.

"Too small," Phoebe said. "Our building's much better."

Randy explained how the goal was to gain entry into the highest high-rises in the city, start at the top, and work your way down.

"Wow, no coats," I said.

I can't remember one Halloween as a child when, despite spending weeks assembling my costume, I didn't get screwed by the weather. Like clockwork, even if the city had been blessed by warm skies and a burst of Indian summer only days before, on October 31 the temperature plunged.

"You can't go trick-or-treating without wearing a coat," my mother would say.

"All right," Brenda, the future religious zealot, would say. She was always dressed as a Jewish martyr or a refugee from a czarist pogrom, so a coat was never a hindrance to her overall ensemble.

But for me? "Jackie Kennedy does not wear earmuffs," I protested. "And the only coat I can wear is one designed by Oleg Cassini and it's certainly too late to arrange for that."

"Here's the deal," my mother would say. "You want the candy, you wear the coat. I'm not spending the next two weeks nursing a houseful of sick kids. So make your choice, First Lady—button up or broom the free Baby Ruths."

Every year my mother won. Every year we looked like all the other Chicago trick-or-treaters with our costumes hidden beneath wool hats and scarves and heavy overcoats. Even UNICEF suffered. Burdened with mittens, we could barely manage our brown paper candy bags let alone stuff pennies into a milk carton. I could see the appeal of indoor soliciting.

"Some people don't give out anything," Benjamin said, holding up his pumpkin and angling it right, then left, as he cut a nose triangle. "They're candy Nazis."

"Do you soap their front doors?" I asked.

Both kids looked at me like I'd just suggested they vacuum the neighbors' carpets. "Never mind," I said. "It's an old Chicago custom."

"Some apartments leave candy bowls in front of their doors; you're supposed to use the honor system and only take two pieces," Phoebe said.

"Yeah," Benjamin laughed. "Losers."

Suddenly inspired, I had a brilliant idea. Good or bad, Halloween memories were an important part of childhood. What a perfect opportunity for me to spend some quality time with the kids, connect, even in a small way—be a bigger part of their lives. I said, "Need an escort?"

"What?" Phoebe said.

"We're not babies," Benjamin said.

"Even our mom doesn't go with us and she's our *mom*," Phoebe said.

"Sorry. I just thought it might be fun."

"For who?" Phoebe said.

"Well, maybe I can help with your costumes."

Phoebe stopped drawing. "You can't do that. That's Mom's job."

"She's been making mine all week," Benjamin said.

"She sews," Phoebe said.

Of course she did. I said, "I bet it'll be a really cool costume."

"The coolest," Benjamin said.

Pirate Boy finally joined the conversation. "We'll have fun handing out candy at home," he said to me, his expression wistful. "Hey—who wants to tape pumpkins on the front door?"

*   *   *

Usually I sleep with my head on Randy's shoulder, our legs intertwined like a challah, but that night I stayed on my half of the mattress, looking up at the ceiling, neutral territory. Even with the lights off, the room's never really dark. Three hundred thousand New York City streetlights take care of that.

"Thanks a million for all your help today," I said. "It sure would've been nice if *somebody* had steered me in the right direction. The kids felt patronized by my going-with-them offer, insulted by my costume offer."

Randy reached over to me. I scowled at him. He sat up. Now he was scowling.

"There's no right or wrong direction," he said. "Just be yourself. The kids aren't judging you."

"Really? Then why did that conversation feel like the emotional equivalent of a sucker punch?"

I wanted to get it right, join the club, didn't want to be the poster child for idiot stepparenting, but I was constantly second-guessing myself. What did it take to be privy to the inner sanctum of child-rearing—besides a child?

Randy said, "Don't you think you might be reading into things too much, that you're *looking* for trouble? You act like you're scared of the kids. Whenever Phoebe calls here she feels bad that you don't talk to her; you immediately say, *I'll get your dad.*"

"She told you that?"

He nodded, a brusque, curt nod, like *of course my daughter tells me things.*

"But I know she's calling to talk to you, not me, so why should I make her talk to me?"

"Why do you assume she doesn't want to talk to you?"

"Because when—*Really*? She wants to talk to me? She always sounds so impatient. Like she's disappointed that I'm the one who picked up the phone and then I feel, well, you know."

"How? What? Do we have to do this now?"

"Do what?"

"Analyze every little thing my kids say or do and how it makes you feel!"

"I'm not doing that." I was doing that. And I felt like shit that he'd said *my* kids meaning *his* kids and not sort-of-my-kids, too.

"Every time you feel hurt or unhappy I feel like you're blaming *me* for taking you away from your home and putting you in this terrible position of living in New York and dealing with my kids. Kids are kids. They grow up; they change; they don't always say the things you want or do the things you want, but that doesn't mean they don't care about you. Your relationship is evolving. Let it go and let them be."

"Let them be?"

Randy plopped down and punched his pillow; he rolled over with his back toward me. "Yes, and let me get some sleep!"

I was too stunned to respond. *Where'd that come from? What was that all about?* Within moments I could hear his steady breathing.

I was mad at myself. Mad at Randy. But not half as mad as I was that he could fall asleep while I was still mad.

*   *   *

On Halloween I snuck out of work early. The good news is, I still had a job to sneak out of. I exited the subway at Seventy-Ninth and Broadway and realized the entire city had snuck out of work early. The weather was warmer than any Halloween in the history of Chicago; the Upper West Side in full holiday mode with marauding sugar-crazed fairy princesses and glow-in-the-dark Pokémons.

I arrived home and was greeted by Captain Hook. "Where'd you hide the candy?" he asked. "I can't find it." He was annoyed.

"Gee, you'll have to make me walk the plank," I said. "I hid it in the kitchen behind the cups and saucers on the top shelf over the stove, where it's not easy for me to reach." Otherwise it would have been eaten already.

Randy hurried to the kitchen and I followed. He opened the cabinet door and retrieved our booty—Charleston Chews and Life Savers—and dumped everything into a stainless mixing bowl on the counter. He frowned at my choices.

"You better get moving," he said. "What are you dressing up as?"

"Who, me?"

"Yes. Sure. Of course, you."

"How about a Chicagoan? I'll put on a coat."

"There are observers in life," he said, "and participants."

This was turning out to be some Halloween. I'd screwed up on the stepmom front. I was screwing up on the costume front. Randy didn't like my Charleston Chews. Maybe I'd feel more like a participant if I were a real mom. Having your own kids is like a ticket to the party; but women like me can't even hang out in a public playground without getting arrested.

Randy rearranged the candy in his bowl using an intricate system I couldn't follow. He checked the time. "I'm surprised nobody's shown up yet," he said.

"Small building," I said.

"Well, the kids who live here will show up. At least the little ones. They're too young to handle a big building."

We waited. We sat in the living room and watched the six o'clock local news. We watched the six-thirty national news. It was easier for one of us to watch than it was for the other because one of us was wearing an eye patch.

"Slow night," I said. I could see the disappointment in Randy's eye.

Finally, halfway through *Wheel of Fortune*, the doorbell rang. Randy jumped out of his chair and grabbed the candy bowl. "Fee-fi-fo-fum!" he called out. "I smell the blood of a trick-or-treater!"

He opened the front door at the same time as our next-door neighbor Mackie. She was wearing a long white cotton nightgown with a wide gold belt and two fake braids coiled around each ear. Randy looked down at his mixing bowl of carefully organized loot. Then he looked at Mackie's crystal punch bowl overflowing with small gold boxes of Godiva chocolate, each box tied with a brown ribbon.

Our super, Ed, was standing between the two doorways, dressed like a super. "Put away your candy," he said. "Nobody's coming."

I hovered behind the princess and the pirate. "What happened?" I asked.

"6A happened," Ed told us. "Mr. Kartun dressed up like a mummy, completely wrapped himself in toilet paper, and scared the children half to death. They all went home peeing in their pants."

"But we bought so much candy," Mackie said, acknowledging her magnificent gold boxes and our pathetic offerings.

"Yeah, that's what I figured," Ed said. He stood there waiting. He twirled his thumbs, whistled the opening bars of "The Halls of Montezuma." So 4B looked at 4A, 4A looked at 4B, and simultaneously got the message.

"Want some candy, Ed?"

"Fan of Godiva, Ed?"

Like a miracle from Halloween heaven on high, our super produced a large plastic garbage bag, holding it wide open with two hands as Randy and Mackie flipped over their bowls to fill Ed's bag.

"Have a good night," my pirate said.

"Happy Halloween," Lady Godiva said.

"I like your eye patch," Ed the Super said.

Randy removed our paper pumpkins from the front door; he looked like a disappointed child as he crumpled the drawings. It's then that the candy corn in my head cleared away.

His kids were growing up, changing; they didn't always do the things he wanted or say the things he wanted—like asking *How 'bout joining us, Dad?* or *How 'bout we trick-or-treat in your building, Dad?* Their relationship was evolving. He had to let them go and let them be.

Phoebe Takes Up with a Horse

~~~~~

Phoebe fell in love with a horse. Horses were a subject I knew little about other than they have four legs and a tail and attract flies. Phoebe had been riding for five years, since she was seven; she'd show up on Saturdays wearing smelly boots and carrying a crop. The last horse I ever rode was a pony at Kiddieland.

Much to my surprise, and probably the profound displeasure of the surrounding neighbors, there was an actual barn on the Upper West Side. I say *was* because after protests both pro and con, eventually a condo developer sent its residents off to a "farm" (glue factory), ending their careers of trotting around while little girls with crops rode them stir-crazy. My stepdaughter among them.

But before the evil developers showed up, Phoebe spoke of Jazmine with the ardor of a romantic lover. Jazmine's gait.

Jazmine's coat. Jazmine's bowel movements. Despite my efforts—and efforts were made—I never seemed to say the right horse-type thing to Phoebe, resulting in her dismissal of me as an idiot.

"Hi, Phoebe, nice hat."

"It's a helmet."

"I like your slacks. They're so roomy in the thighs. Does Jazmine get dizzy from walking in circles all day?"

"No, she does not get dizzy. She's a horse."

Randy's Jazmine conversations with Phoebe were shorter but more successful.

"Dad, I have a class. Can I have forty dollars?"

"Get my wallet."

I realized then that I should start giving Phoebe money. I was not above buying a child's love.

"Hi, honey. Do you need money for your horse?"

"Sure," she said. "We could probably buy him for about three thousand dollars."

Two Friday nights later I came home from the video store with three tapes. *The Black Stallion. The Black Stallion Returns.* And *The New Adventures of the Black Stallion.* There were a few more movies at the store with *Black Stallion* in the title, but they were in the Adults Only section.

"How soon will the kids be over?" I asked Randy. He was standing at the kitchen counter, stabbing a pack of frozen hot dogs with a knife, trying to separate them.

"Did you buy buns?" he asked.

"No. Was I supposed to? I rented movies. I thought we could have a family movie night, watch horse movies."

I showed Randy my selections. He paused in his whacking of hot dogs and said, "This black stallion returns. He comes back. He has adventures. He has a busier social life than we do."

My beloved pointed toward the cupboard that holds the dinner plates, his not so subtle hint that I should set the table. The kids did not have chores in our household. Randy was still trying to compensate for the divorce. "I'm really not too keen on horse movies," he said. "And I can guarantee you, Benjamin is definitely not keen on horse movies."

"Perfect. You two can do something father-and-son-ish, and Phoebe and I can have our own time together. Girl time."

"Bun time," Randy said. "We need buns."

After a dinner of hot dogs wrapped in slices of white bread, Randy and Benjamin set up a gin rummy game in the kitchen and I sprang my surprise on Phoebe.

"I've seen them," she said, reading the movie titles.

"All of them?"

"A million times."

"Well, they sound like they're real favorites. Want to see one again?"

"I've already seen them."

"Oh. Okay."

I would have volunteered to escort Phoebe to class, maybe sit on a haystack and call out encouragement yippee-ki-yay style, but even on Daddy weekends, Susan met Phoebe to watch her ride. I hesitated to step on Susan's turf, along with other things in the barn I didn't care to step in.

Some days I'd wear myself out trying to be a good stepmom. I monitored my moves like I was wearing an electronic ankle bracelet. I didn't admit I felt hurt when the kids only asked for Randy's opinion, not mine. I always made a point to ask, *How's your mom? Please say hi.* I knew not to discipline the kids—that was Randy's job; that was Susan's job; and yes, at times I screwed up.

Can somebody please explain why a dirty dish can't make it all the way from the sink to the dishwasher?

Why is there only one grape left in this bowl?

All right—who forgot to flush?

I tried to find some way to connect with Phoebe that was ours, unique to us, some interest or activity that we could share. I ran through options in my head.

Cleaning her room together sounded appealing. To me.

Make jewelry? Polish our nails? Call up boys after midnight and hang up?

My knowledge of adolescent girls hadn't progressed much since my last sixth-grade slumber party.

Benjamin was easy. We were pals. As long as you didn't make him cut off a video game in the middle of some major move, he never complained. He'd launch into long, intricate explanations of his Mario Donkey Kong world while I grinned and nodded and tried my best to follow, my brain waves flipping into an immediate test pattern as he went on and on about how Mario jumped through green tunnels to the dungeons of Bowser's castle climbing through nets across lava while giant fire balls sprang up from the ground.

Phoebe would often sit and patiently watch her brother play while she seemed endlessly fascinated. She demonstrated an innate grace and ability to understand another person's passion, a talent I admired and still hoped to emulate.

I called my mother.

"Mom, how did you relate to me when I was a girl?"

"I've always been related to you."

In my family, everyone's a comedian.

"I need advice. I want to get closer with Phoebe, do stuff together. But I don't know what to do."

"Why are you asking me? Ask her."

"Ask her what?"

"What *she'd* like to do."

"Oh." Insightful. Astute. "Good advice. Thanks, Mom. You always come through."

"That's why we're close," she said.

"How's Dad?"

"Ask him yourself. He's standing right here."

I heard mumbling in the background. More mumbling as the telephone was passed from parent to parent and my mother filled my dad in on my half of the conversation.

"Honey?"

"Hi, Dad."

"Sounds like you're scared of a kid," he said. "Just remember—she's a kid."

I heard my mother saying, *Give me the phone, Bernie.* "You don't need her approval," she said. "Thank goodness I never asked for yours."

"Mom, did you ever question yourself as a mother?"

"Any woman who doesn't is an arrogant fool."

"Ditto," I heard in the background.

The phone shifted.

"Ditto, Dad?"

"Ditto for dads. All parents screw up."

I could hear my mother saying, *Who screwed up?* as my father told me, "Good luck, pumpkin."

The name caught at my heart. To him, I was still a kid.

My next piece of advice came a few hours later. Randy was asleep in the bedroom. I was in the kitchen eating Cap'n Crunch and talking to Claudia between political revolutions.

I told her, "I need a good activity to share with a twelve-year-old that doesn't require my climbing on a horse."

Claudia coughed into the receiver, her cigarette cough. "Twelve-year-old girls don't want to spend time with grown-ups. God knows I don't want to spend time with any twelve-year-old girls. They're moody. Opinionated. Boy crazy. They sleep late and stay up all night."

Claudia had just described herself.

"Remind me again why I called *you* for parental advice?"

"Because I'm the only other person you know awake at this hour. Make her share your interests. Show her what you like to do. Or just wait until she turns twenty. Bond with her then."

Benjamin's class was putting on Gilbert and Sullivan's *Gondoliers*. I considered this high-class material, several notches above Rodgers and Hammerstein or Lerner and Loewe, who weren't exactly slouches themselves.

"What part are you playing?" I asked Benjamin, over Saturday afternoon bowls of macaroni and cheese.

He smiled with pride, half his lunch in his teeth. "A gondolier."

"The title role. Great."

Down went the smile. "We're all gondoliers."

He seemed to like showbiz, though. He kept bursting into song at the oddest times singing about roses red and roses white and laws of maidens' making. I'd ask, "Benjamin, did you change your socks?" and off he'd go, practicing for the show at ear-shattering decibels.

By the night of the performance, even the neighbors must have learned the entire libretto. Only two tickets were available per student; private school auditoriums being like private schools, small and exclusive. Randy and Susan would attend. I was sending my husband and his ex-wife off on a date.

Phoebe and I stayed home and ordered in pizza. While we waited for our half sausage, half green pepper with extra cheese, I pulled out my eighth-grade vinyl-covered scrapbook, the one I never showed anybody, that I kept stored under my shoe boxes. I asked Phoebe if she'd like to see it.

When I was Phoebe's age, I wanted to be famous; I wanted to mingle with stars. I wanted some of their magic to rub off on me and make me magical, too. Being famous would mean I was memorable. But in a good way, not in a Lee Harvey Oswald way. I wrote letters to famous people. I requested autographs, offered to be pen pals. I must have been pretty good at it, because the responses started rolling in.

Dear Linda,
Unfortunately Vice President Lyndon Johnson cannot attend your birthday party in Chicago on Sunday, May 22. But he does thank you for the invitation and wishes you a happy birthday.

Dear Linda,
I am writing on behalf of Mr. Cecil B. DeMille, who cannot send you his autograph. It is with regret that I inform you he died five years ago.

My television crush, Kookie Byrnes, mailed me an autographed photo of himself leaning against a red Ford Thunderbird, one hand holding a comb while the other hand poufed his famous hair.

The letters were stuck in plastic sleeves with lines of sticky glue that had turned even browner than the letters.

"I never heard of any of these people," Phoebe said, after she'd thumbed through the pages, holding each one at the corner with two fingers, like the tail of a dead mouse.

"They're people I know. You can write to people you know."

"Why would I want to do that?" She focused on Kookie. "You knew this guy with the weird hair?"

"Well, not personally. I'd watch him on TV."

"So this is a *fake* letter? He didn't really answer you back?"

"I suppose. Maybe. Now that you mention it. But aren't there any famous cowboys you'd like to write?"

"*Cowboys?*"

"Yes, other horseback riders."

I was then given a lecture on English-style riding versus Western and posting the trot versus sitting the trot, none of which I understand to this day other than that the hats are different. Obviously an autograph collection was not about to compete with a horse. I felt grateful when the doorbell rang, so grateful I overtipped the pizza guy.

During dinner I asked, "Phoebe, can you suggest something we can do together? Just you and me?"

She seemed to contemplate the possibility, then said, "No," and refocused on her pizza.

While we ate she talked about Jazmine; how responsive Jazmine was, how sensitive, with the sweetest temperament ever. I wondered if Jazmine would've appreciated my autograph book. As Phoebe chatted, I found myself watching more than listening, she so pretty with her fresh complexion and shiny curls; me aware of my own aging.

Would I have felt differently if Phoebe were my own daughter? Would I have felt pride in her beauty, instead of envious of her youth?

I offered her more of the sausage half, her half. "Phoebe, besides riding Jazmine, what do you like to do most?"

"Be with my girlfriends."

"Besides that."

"Hang out in my room."

"What if after dinner we hang out in your room together?"

I used to like hanging out in my room. Not with my mother, of course. But I wasn't Phoebe's mother. I was her friend.

She made a face. "I have homework."

"What are you working on?" I didn't want her to leave. I wanted to keep talking. But I felt intimidated by the fine line between getting involved and being invasive.

"I'm rereading *The Count of Monte Cristo*. For English class. It's my favorite book ever."

"So what's the story about?"

"A sailor goes to prison because his enemies falsely accuse him and when he comes out he pretends he's a count and goes after them for revenge." She pushed her chair back and stood up. "I'm done eating," she said. "I've got homework."

"Revenge? Your favorite book's about revenge?"

She left her plate on the table and retreated to her room.

After the playgoers and the gondolier returned and I heard Benjamin's full report (he didn't forget any lyrics except for one line that didn't count because everyone else was drowning him out anyway), and Susan took the kids home, their other home,

I asked Randy if he thought I'd ever connect with Phoebe. We were walking around the living room, turning off lights.

"You're already connected," he said. "The kids are fine with you. Everyone gets along. Nobody fights."

"I'm aiming a little higher than *nobody fights*. I feel like Phoebe's mad at me all the time and I can't figure out why."

"If she sounds snotty it's because she feels close enough to act out."

"You're saying it's a compliment?" Randy turned off the kitchen light. I turned off the hallway light.

"Yes."

Why not *you've got a nice smile*? Or—*that dress makes you look slim*? I was never good at accepting compliments, and certainly didn't know what to do with *I'm snarling because I like you*.

"Weren't you difficult at twelve?" Randy asked, turning on the bedroom light.

I said, "Not that I remember."

On Saturday, a kids' weekend Saturday, I scoured our neighborhood bookstore loading up on horse books. *Black Beauty*. *Horse Whisperer*. *Seabiscuit*. *The Red Pony*. I spent a considerable amount of time making my selections, homing in on the classics, which I defined as anything I'd personally heard of.

And then—what luck!

Black Stallion, the star of my rejected movie tapes, had apparently scored a book deal. The shelves were groaning with tales of him and his offspring. Black Stallion had turned out to be quite the stud. *Son of the Black Stallion; Black Stallion's Filly; The Black Stallion's Sulky Colt.* I was just sorry there was no *Black Stallion of Monte Cristo.*

I headed home feeling fired up and proud of myself until I opened our door and was assaulted by the sorta reggae sorta pop music of a gentleman I later learned was named Shaggy.

Randy was standing in the entry to the living room watching his young colt.

"Why is Benjamin in the middle of the floor spinning on his head?" I asked.

"He's learning break dancing."

"Can't he practice at his mother's?"

"It's for school. They're learning it in phys ed."

"So you're telling me this is *homework?*"

Perhaps bonding with Benjamin would also prove challenging.

"Yes," Randy said. "Phoebe's in her bedroom doing her homework."

Hopefully she wasn't in her room riding Jazmine. I left the menfolk to their dance activities, walked down the hall, and knocked on Phoebe's door.

"I'm busy!" she called back. "And lower that awful music!"

I opened the door a crack, stuck my head in, and waved my hand like a white flag. She was stretched out on her bedspread—*with her shoes on*—not that I commented, reading her Count book. Gingerly, very gingerly, I entered and presented my offerings. She shuffled through the books.

"If you already read one or your mom bought it for you, we can return it," I said. "But I thought maybe you'd like some of these."

She never told me whether she already owned them or had read them or hated them.

"Maybe I should try one," I said. "Which one do you think I'd like?"

It was a lovely afternoon. Quiet. Once we lowered Shaggy. Companionable. Once I stretched out on the other twin bed. With my shoes on.

We didn't talk much. But we shared time together. Me reading about Black Stallion. Phoebe reading about revenge.

How Now Brown Brow

~~~~

Pia Mollback wore hats perched at jaunty angles, ankle boots with patterned hose, layers layered over layers, each peeking out to make its own provocative statement. She was one of those women who enter a room armed with confidence; she copped an attitude. To me, Pia was New York. She dressed like she was invited to a cocktail party. I still dressed like I'd been asked to run over for a beer.

Pia and I first met on a Jell-O Pudding Pops assignment; Pia was a food stylist, somebody who gets paid to make Pudding Pops look beautiful. Seated on adjacent stools, sipping tea in the window of an East Side coffee shop, I told her how much I admired her appearance. She took the compliment as an invitation to critique mine.

"About all these *colors* you wear, Linda. They're too—how do I say this?" Pia fluttered a few fingers against her lips as she studied my outfit. "Colorful." She said, "Think Holly Golightly, Coco Chanel, think subway soot not showing on your hems. There's dirt in this town and black's the only way to hide it."

I looked down at my blouse. My skirt. "But I have so much red in my wardrobe."

Pia rolled her perfectly mascaraed eyes. "The only person who should wear red in New York rides a sleigh in the Macy's parade."

I glanced out at a Park Avenue matron walking past, tiny flashes of red blinking off the soles of her high heels with each step. "*That* lady's wearing red."

"New York women buy those shoes just so they can scrape red on dirty sidewalks."

"How about green?"

"Not even on St. Patrick's Day."

"Orange?"

"Only if you're an Hermès shopping bag." Pia picked up a lemon wedge and aimed a squirt into her teacup. "You want to be unique without sticking out. Ever see a guy walking down Fifth Avenue in a cowboy hat and lizard boots? You immediately know *he's not from here.* Perhaps it's time to look like *you* live here. Doesn't your husband care? Doesn't he want you to look more, you know—local?"

What could I say? There are women who dress for men and women who dress for other women and then there are those of us who are just grateful we manage to get dressed in the morning.

Standing on the sidewalk before Pia headed downtown and I headed crosstown, we were passed by dozens of New Yorkers all in black wool coats, black knit hats, black leather boots. "Develop your own style," Pia said, giving me the once-over. "Just not this style." She air-kissed me good-bye on each cheek. "It will change your life."

From day zero I was off to a bad start. According to photos, even my layette set was tacky: bibs and onesies splayed with flamingos, a gift from an aunt in Boca. Even as a young girl I never rushed into any fad. I'd wait to make sure a look was really acceptable, so by the time I purchased my suspender skirts or turtleneck dickeys or white Hullabaloo boots, I was tragically passé. If you had to pick me out of a police lineup of fifth graders you wouldn't think twice. "That's her, Officer. The one wearing a *Ben Casey* shirt two years after the show was canceled."

The summer between seventh and eighth grades I shot up four inches. Suddenly I was the *tall girl* banging into walls and tripping over her own feet, trying to regain a modicum of coordination; the one who towered over the boys and wasn't chosen in dance class. The last thing I wanted was clothing that drew attention to the high-rise sitting alone on the sidelines, forcing herself to smile, pretending she didn't care.

After Pia's unsolicited pep talk, I observed women on the street, women in restaurants, women dashing into cabs—determined to learn what looks they chose for their black pants and skirts, how they accessorized their black sweaters and blazers. What if Pia was right? What if all this time Randy loved me *despite* the way I dressed; that on some subconscious, besotted level he felt embarrassed by my lack of style?

Even Phoebe let it be known that I could use some sprucing up. Almost thirteen, she was turning into a self-proclaimed expert on any topic. She'd be watching television or flipping through a magazine appraising outfits. *That sucks. That's embarrassing. She should be shot.* She'd compliment her own clothing choices. "Isn't the proportion of this jacket *perfect?*"

When I was a kid, proportion meant my mother saying, "Buy it a size bigger so you grow into it."

One Saturday Phoebe said to me, "Hey, Linda—maybe we can go shopping together. There's a cool store on Broadway called New York Look."

I was thrilled that she wanted to spend the time with me, pick out her clothes, and get my viewpoint. "Sure," I said. "I'd love to help you find things."

She looked at me and said, "I meant for you."

Maybe if I dressed more like a New Yorker, I'd feel more like a New Yorker, have a stronger sense of belonging. A week later, loaded down with anything jet black, midnight black, or ink black, ducking past the three-or-less sign, I headed into a Bloomingdale's fitting room and worked my way through the pile. Nothing knocked my red socks off. A little black dress hung like a big black mess. I looked at my arms and knew my sleeveless days were over. One pair of pants must have been cut for basketball players; the hems pooled around my feet.

Out of desperation I slipped on a pair of communal heels stashed in a corner of the fitting room, and to my surprise, the pants improved. I grabbed a black cashmere sweater with black trim, pulled it over my head, and stood back to gape at the total effect in the mirror, all three views. I looked, somewhat, well . . . *sophisticated*. I shimmied a few dance steps, twisted around to appraise my butt. Checked out the price tag on the sweater. Marked down 40 percent.

I heard gentle tapping on the outside of the door.

"This room's taken," I called out.

"Do you need assistance?" the tapper's voice asked.

The door opened and a saleslady glided in, her reflection smiling behind mine in the mirror. She looked sleek and knowledgeable with her silver hair pulled into a chignon.

"Sarah Jessica Parker bought this same sweater yesterday," she said.

I spun around to look directly at her. *"Sarah Jessica Parker shops on sale?"*

The saleslady shrugged.

"And she bought this same black sweater?"

"I sold it to her myself."

"I'll take it."

The saleslady smiled. "It will change your life."

I waited for Randy to admire my big score.

"Honey, how do you like my new sweater?"

I held it up by each shoulder, turned it frontward and backward so Randy could admire it.

He was stretched out on the living room sofa, trying to admire the business section of the *New York Times*.

"Nice," he said.

"Really?"

"Yeah. Really nice."

"It was a steal," I said.

"How much?"

"I saved forty percent."

"No. How much did it cost?"

"Practically nothing."

"How much is practically nothing?"

I told him.

"For a *sweater*?"

I let him go back to reading his newspaper.

Later that night I called my mother to complain how Randy didn't seem to understand the value of a great bargain. My mother never calculated her purchases in terms of dollars outlaid but only in terms of dollars saved. That way nothing cost her anything.

"Why'd you tell him it was new?" she asked.

"Because it *is* new."

"For the first few years after I married your father, I never told him anything was new. He'd comment on something he hadn't seen before and I'd say, *This old thing? It was stuck in the back of my closet.*"

"And that worked?" I'd always considered my dad to be really smart, a read-between-the-lines kind of guy.

"Eventually he started encouraging me to go shopping, told me to go out and have a little fun."

This was my mother's idea of motherly advice.

"I'm sitting here trying to convince myself that Dad fell for all that."

"Oh, you know men," my mother said. "They see whatever they want to see." Then added, "Thank God."

Roxy Buskin and I were discussing which dessert to split at Cafe Lalo, a Parisian-style coffeehouse predominated by a sweeping glass patisserie case.

"Amaretto cheesecake's always good," Roxy said.

"Lemon meringue pie's healthier," I said.

"Sacher torte?"

"Tiramisu?"

"Split both?"

Roxy and I had met a month earlier in adjoining rinse stations at a hair salon. Most of the Lalo customers were women with strollers parked alongside their tables. Roxy and I were strollerless with no toddlers to attend to, just cake. I felt good in a black knit top and black pants. Roxy looked nice, too, in a black knit top and black pants.

Halfway through our desserts, Roxy suddenly dropped her fork and held up her hands, palms toward me, thumbs out, forming a square to frame my face, tilting her head from left to right, moving the frame closer then farther until she asked, "Who does your brows?"

"Who does what to them?"

"Shapes them. You know—professionally?"

I paused en route to mascarpone. "Tweezing eyebrows is a profession? Like butcher? Baker? Candlestick maker? There's somebody out there who's a *tweezer*?"

"That's what I thought," Roxy said. "You do them yourself. Would you be insulted if I make a suggestion?"

"Can I withhold my answer until after I hear the suggestion?"

"You should make an immediate appointment with Eliza Petrescu. She's the eyebrow guru of New York."

I stopped eating, no longer able to concentrate on sugar. Roxy did have fabulous brows. But I'd always thought they were a genetic gift like flawless skin or straight toes or being able to add numbers in your head. She was rifling through her handbag, pulling out pen and paper. "Eliza will arch them. Shape them. Clean out the fuzz. You'll look a million times better."

"Okay. Now I'm officially insulted."

"Trust me," Roxy said, scribbling down a phone number. "Eliza changed my life."

Roxy was out of work, always borrowing money, and didn't have a boyfriend. I wondered what her life was like before Eliza.

"Oh—and don't touch them until your appointment," she said. "Eliza likes to work with a full crop."

The woman on the telephone spoke in the clipped, self-assured voice of someone who had never known the ignominy of misshapen brows. "Eliza's next opening is in two months," she said.

"Two months to have someone pluck hairs out of my face?"

A long pause ensued. "You're lucky I had a cancellation."

After scheduling my appointment I started getting psyched about my new opportunity for self-improvement. I found myself walking down Park Avenue checking out all the perfect brows. Meanwhile mine were growing in like a brush fire. I called Roxy, desperate for guidance.

"Are you sure I can't tweeze until I see this woman?"

"That would be a terrible mistake," Roxy said.

"A terrible mistake is the Archduke of Austria starting World War I or eating uncooked shellfish."

"Eliza will scold you," Roxy said. "And you never want Eliza to scold you."

"I can't go three more weeks without tweezing. I already look like Bert's backup on *Sesame Street*."

"Wear low hats with floppy brims," Roxy told me.

"I can *braid* my brows into a brim."

"Be patient," Roxy said, "and don't show up late. Eliza abhors tardiness."

I arrived twenty minutes early, not wanting to incur Eliza's wrath. Eliza had her own floor on the mezzanine of a Fifth Avenue salon where I waited in a small sitting area, its walls covered with framed magazine articles extolling Eliza and framed autographed photos of Eliza's celebrity clients.

How could I have gone my entire life without knowing about this brow thing?

The first time I shaped my brows was in eighth grade, when my mother handed me tweezers and said, "It's time." She instructed me how to hold them at a proper angle and to clean the strays under my natural arch, but to *never* tweeze above the brow—the implication being something along the order of a dire fate befalling my firstborn. Of course that was before we knew I'd never have a firstborn. With practice, I learned to shape a decent brow, but rarely a matching set.

Two other women were sitting in the waiting area. Across

from me was a leggy redhead whose brows looked exquisite. Beautifully arched. Well balanced. And this was *before* her appointment. The receptionist smiled at her and said, "Abby, you can go in now."

The other woman, wearing a leopard print hair band and a mink vest, was flipping through a *W* magazine, giving me the opportunity to examine her brows. Also lovely.

I smiled and said, "So, how long have you been coming here?"

The woman looked up from her magazine, glanced around, and when she saw she was the only other person in the waiting area, she answered in a moneyed voice. "Twelve years. I followed Eliza here from Bergdorf's." I assumed she meant Eliza used to work at Bergdorf's, versus she trailed her during a shopping spree. "It's your first time, isn't it?"

I nodded yes.

She said, "It will change your life."

I entered the inner sanctum. Eliza sat perched on a stool next to a long table covered with fresh white paper. I was no longer certain if she was going to pluck my brows or check my cervix. She patted the table. I got on and stretched out.

"You're new," Eliza said, her Romanian accent sounding elegant and mysterious.

"Yes," I said.

Eliza studied me for all of two seconds and before I could say another word she whipped! whipped! whipped! waxy paper *above my brows*. A couple of finishing plucks with a tweezers here and there and we were done.

"Nice to meet you," she said, handing me a mirror.

And there I was—or at least, there was *the movie star version of me*. My eyes looked wider. My forehead looked smoother. I wanted to track down every man who ever broke my heart and mail him a photo; call my high school and find out how long until the next reunion. I wanted to kiss myself.

"You're a genius," I said to Eliza.

"I know," she said, totally bored.

I waltzed out of the bedroom wearing black pants, my Sarah Jessica Parker sweater, and black boots; my brows a perfectly arched matched set.

Newspapers covered the living room coffee table. Randy was sitting on the edge of the sofa leaning forward and examining an electric can opener. Socket wrenches, claw hammers, needle-nose pliers, and a Phillips screwdriver were spread out around him on the floor.

Okay, a little overkill in the tool department, but there's something sexy about a man who can mend an appliance.

I asked, "Honey, do I look different?"

"Uh-huh," he said, concentrating on the can opener, not paying attention.

Did I really want an answer?

I twirled and modeled my outfit, twirling myself sick until Randy noticed.

"You look great," he said.

"Regular great or different great?"

"Always great."

My mother was right. Men see what they want to see.

Randy refocused on his project. My life hadn't changed because of reshaped brows, and other than lower dry cleaning bills, it hadn't changed thanks to new clothes. My life changed when I married a man who looked at me, *really* looked at me, and still considered me beautiful.

He was squinting at the back of the can opener, twisting a screwdriver. "Do you mind stepping out of the way?" he said. "You're standing in my light."

A Card-Carrying New Yorker

At first I'd fly back to Chicago for any excuse—eighth-grade reunions, Tupperware parties, somebody needed me to pick up their dry cleaning. By Year Two the trips became more discretionary:

Cousin Robin's wedding.

Nephew Ethan's bar mitzvah.

Aunt Sophy's ninetieth birthday.

Aunt Sophy's funeral.

And with each visit I began to feel more like a spectator and less like somebody returning home.

In February, I flew back for Claudia's Very Special Birthday. Waiting outside in the O'Hare taxi line, freezing through my coat while rubbing my gloved hands together, I decided to see if I could trick my driver into thinking I was a native New Yorker. When it was finally my turn, I hurried into a taxi. Most of the driver's face was hidden by a blue knit cap pulled low on his forehead above aviator sunglasses. I could see my breath in the cold air as I gave him an address. After we pulled onto the highway, I smiled into the mirror and said, "I hear Chicago's a nice place to visit."

The sunglasses looked back at me. "Not in February it's not. Who's your travel agent?"

"I live in New York."

"New York? You sound like you're from here."

"No. New York. I pick up accents fast."

"Between the airport and cab?"

"Very fast."

The city looked cleaner, shinier, but no longer mine. Seeing the skyline was like running into an old boyfriend after we'd each moved on. Driving down Michigan Avenue felt like browsing through an old high school yearbook. Was I a Chicagoan living in New York? Or a New Yorker from Chicago?

Claudia swore she'd kill anyone who mentioned, acknowledged, or even *thought* to celebrate her birthday, but she did permit me to take her to dinner at one of those Japanese restaurants where everyone takes off their shoes and sits around a low lacquer table drinking sake while a chef juggles knives.

"Can I at least *toast* you?" I whispered, holding up my white porcelain shot glass.

"No!" she said. "And what did you do to your eyebrows?"

Over sliced steak I told her how I was having an identity crisis, and not the easy kind that men have, the kind that can be resolved with a new sports car, but the where-do-I-fit-in kind. Claudia refilled our sake glasses. "I haven't even bothered switching my Illinois driver's license for a New York one," I said. "Not that I drive anywhere."

Knives were clinked, carrot slices appeared on our plates. The chef, laughing and smiling, bowed in several directions, then flipped a santoku knife over Claudia's head, catching it right in front of her face. The other diners applauded.

"Jesus," Claudia said. "You can get killed in a place like this."

We both tossed back more sake. It's a good thing we weren't flipping any knives.

Claudia glared at the chef. "Were you aware that Japanese ultranationalists tried to murder their prime minister after World War II?"

I silently congratulated myself for not arranging to have the waiters sing "Happy Birthday."

Claudia turned to me. "Y'know, that driver's license is a symbol. You aren't committed to New York. You're keeping your back door open." Claudia lifted her sake glass but kept her eyes focused on me. "This isn't your Teddy marriage; this is your Randy marriage. The happy one."

At work, back in New York, Jennifer, a tall, robust know-it-all who actually knew things, told me about Driver's X-Press, where citizens of Manhattan can zip in and out and obtain a new license within half an hour. I figured, a lousy thirty minutes? Okay, I'll commit.

I ducked away from the office and my Tickle Me Elmo copy and dashed over to Thirty-Fourth. Driver's X-Press even looked speedy with its short counters and short lines. With one last sentimental sigh, I surrendered my Illinois license remembering the day I had waited in three different lines for over two hours to acquire it, only to be horrified at the end result. "Who's bright idea was *this*?" I asked the pubescent-looking young man who had just handed me my license. My face was cut into the shape of Illinois, a natural fit since my face happens to be the shape of Illinois.

My public servant shrugged. "Not happy? Move to another state."

So here I was in another state getting my picture snapped after combing and arranging my hair, administering the type of attention more commonly warranted for a wedding portrait. I whipped through the vision test, checked off the organ donor box, signed two forms, and paid the requisite fee.

I praised the woman behind the counter as she handed me my license, told her how impressed I was with the system, the efficiency, the foresight, the sheer thoughtfulness of it all, until the man behind me in line x-pressed his opinion.

"Hey, Chatty Cathy—can we move it along here?"

I frowned at him over my shoulder. "I was just saying thank you," I told him.

He motioned me onward with his thumb. "Send her a card."

Three months later I received a jury duty summons.

"Can you believe this?" I said, staring at my notice. "I barely just got here. Shouldn't there be about eight million people ahead of me?"

Randy was busy pulling a *New Yorker,* a *New York,* and a *Time Out New York* from our mailbox, my latest subscriptions. He looked so imposing and mature in his business suit, more like somebody's parent instead of my husband. "Everybody gets jury duty," he said. "Even the mayor."

"That's not jury duty. That's a photo op."

"What have you got against jury duty?" he asked, shuffling through bills.

I jammed the notice inside my handbag, hoping it would disappear. "I don't want to be responsible for somebody going to jail. Unless they're a terrible person in which case I hope they do go to jail. But what if they go and get beat up by mean guards when they don't deserve to because they weren't *that* terrible in which case I'd feel terrible."

Randy looked at me. "Interesting logic. Why do the words *hung jury* come to mind?"

As a freelancer, two other words came to mind: *no paycheck,* my other big excuse for shirking my inalienable rights.

Mrs. McElnea from 4C, emitting her usual torrential wafts of Shalimar, hurried past us into the mailroom.

"I don't even know how they got my name," I said.

Randy peeked in the mailbox one last time before locking it. "From your driver's license."

"*Really?* I thought they got the jury names from the voting pool."

Civics was never my strong point. I stood a better chance of naming the seven dwarfs than the nine Supreme Court justices.

"Let me guess," Randy said. "You're not registered to vote in New York."

"Not exactly," I said.

*   *   *

I delayed jury duty by checking the *not available on this date* box and mailed back the card, but by then figured I might as well register to vote.

Jennifer the know-it-all knew where to go and which subway to take. "Go on your lunch hour," she said. "You'll be back in ninety minutes."

The Board of Elections was in one of those buildings that scream government as only a government building can: ornate lobby, bland offices, lots of flags. I rode the elevator to the right floor, found the right door, and stood in the wrong line. One state worker and one new line later, it was my turn. The clerk looked up and greeted me with a nod as she used the sleeve of her cardigan to wipe her eyeglass frames. She was sitting behind a steel desk beneath a picture of the New York state bird. Mr. Bluebird was on her shoulder. I loved her haircut: angled on the sides, gently layered in the front. I thought, *only in New York would the government workers have fabulous cuts.*

"So what's it going to be? Republican, Democrat, or Independent?" she asked.

"Excuse me?"

"Declare your party." She slipped her glasses back onto the bridge of her nose, making her look more bureaucratic. And mean.

"Well, that's not exactly your business now, is it?"

She answered me with exaggerated patience, enunciating each word like she should have been working down the hall at INS. "It is if you want to vote."

For a government worker she sure had a lot of attitude. It must have been the haircut.

I tried to convey an equal amount of attitude. "And I don't suppose you've ever heard about a *secret* ballot? I believe that's why there are *curtains* hanging on all the voting booths."

"Listen—" She looked down at my application, then back up at me. "Listen, Miss Yellin—you wanna vote? You gotta declare."

On election day, Randy voted before work. I voted after work because I snagged my panty hose getting dressed in the morning, an emergency requiring a trip to the drugstore instead of the road to democracy. When I arrived at my polling site, a halfway house on Broadway adjoining a pizza parlor, I was surprised to see a long line; the media had predicted a low turnout. The line crawled so slowly I could have run next door and ordered a pizza.

I get impatient in long lines. Grocery lines are the worst. I always end up behind the shoppers sneaking twelve items into the eight-items-or-less line. But I don't have the nerve to confront these people, mainly because I don't want to own up to having become so intimate with their carts that I was counting the items.

But the poky voting line didn't bother me. There was something electrifying about being a part of the process that I hadn't expected. It's not like I'd been all that involved in Chicago politics. I'd grown up in a *keep your nose out of trouble* family; we never declared affiliations. Our motto was *Lie low*—the motto my grandparents brought over on the boat from Russia, the one they hopped on two steps ahead of the czar. Benjamin was studying state government in school and along the way I did pick up a few tidbits, like how to spell Schenectady and how Peter Stuyvesant was called Old Peg Leg and how the state's garbage is shipped to Virginia. I could have asked Benjamin to teach me more, but it's embarrassing to learn history from a fifth grader.

It was my turn to approach the election table. Two women sat behind it, both plump with curly hair. They looked like relatives.

"Name?" one asked. When I answered she pointed to the other woman, who checked my address, made me sign on a dotted line, and pointed to her right. I handed my voter card to a ruddy-faced young man slumped low in a folding chair, legs straight out, arms folded, who I assumed was the poll watcher. The man pointed me toward my booth. There sure was an awful lot of finger-pointing in this election.

I examined the inner workings of the booth. In Chicago all I had to do was stick a pin through cardboard holes. Here the instructions read: *Pull the large red handle to the right to begin.*

I gave the matter some serious thought, studied possible options. Red handle . . . red handle . . . red handle. I poked my head out of the booth. "Pardon me," I said to the poll watcher, calling for his attention. "I can't seem to locate the red handle."

"Look *down*," he said.

I turned and noticed a large red handle sticking up out of the floor like a captain's steering wheel on a yacht. I said, "Oh. *That* red lever." With both hands I swung the lever from left to right; the curtain closed.

More relaxed now that I was hidden, I scrutinized the voting board with its flippy little doodad flags. Flip the flag one way, an X appeared. Flip it back, it went blank. A political arcade game. Fascinated, I flipped the flag for the Democratic senator to an X, then back to white. X . . . white . . . X. Until I heard somebody outside the curtain say: "Everything okay in there?" like I was tying up a stall in a public bathroom.

"I'll be out in a minute!" I called back.

I was surprised to see so many names on the ballot for political contests I'd been completely unaware of. Candidates were running to be state senators and judges and assemblymen. The last time I was in any type of assembly it began with the Pledge of Allegiance. I made choices based on gut instinct. *A guy named Constantiner was in my high school photography class and he was a good guy, so I'll vote for Constantiner. Who will make a better attorney general? The man or the woman? The woman, of course.*

After I'd done enough voting for one election, I pulled the large red handle back from right to left, and all my votes disappeared to the sound of a satisfying thunk.

By the time I walked the three blocks home to my living room, the polls had closed and Randy was watching CBS project the winners. Either my votes were counted really fast or they didn't count at all.

"Citizen Yellin here," I announced.

I slipped off my coat, dropped it over the armchair and sat down beside him. I was a registered voter with a New York driver's license and a husband kissing my neck.

Committing to New York was getting easier.

THE WIVES OF RANDY ARTHUR

~~~~~

I never thought of Benjamin as much of an athlete. The only muscles he ever seemed to use were in his thumbs and attached to a remote control. So it came as quite a surprise to me when Randy mentioned we'd be spending Saturday afternoons at Little League games.

"*Baseball?*" I said. "Please pass the duck sauce."

Phoebe and Randy and I were sharing egg foo yong while Benjamin navigated a pizza. The kitchen table was covered with spilled chow mein noodles, the crispy kind nobody ever eats. And tomato sauce from Benjamin's fingers. The repertoire of food items Benjamin was willing to ingest was limited to hot dogs, pizza, and macaroni and cheese. That was it. Benjamin wouldn't even sample unfamiliar foods. Offer him a taste of something new and he'd look at you like you were trying to poison him. Randy indulged him. Cooked separately for him, let him eat what he wanted.

My mother indulged me, too. She'd slap the food on the table and say: "Here's the drill, young lady. I cooked it and you'll eat it."

"Does your team have a name yet?" Randy asked, scooping white rice from a cardboard carton.

Benjamin burped in response, then Randy burped, resulting in a burping contest. You'd think I was eating with *two* ten-year-olds. After no agreement could be reached as to whose burp was more impressive, Phoebe and I being the arbiters, we returned to the subject of team names.

"We're the Steaks," Benjamin said as he plucked a pepperoni slice off his pizza.

"Excuse me?" I said.

"Steaks," he said. "As in—steaks."

"That's the lamest name ever," Phoebe said. Having recently turned thirteen, her personality had become a moving target. Within five minutes she'd change from Daddy's Little Girl into Lolita followed by two acts of Camille.

"You won't even eat steak," I said.

"How'd you end up with a name like that?" Randy asked. He was mushing his chow mein into his rice. His table manners regressed around the children.

"If you think I'm giving up riding to stand on the sidelines screaming 'Go Steaks!' you're crazy," Phoebe said.

Benjamin held the pepperoni slice up to his nose and studied it, like he was searching for strychnine. "We voted on a different name. But some of the guys' parents got mad and made us change it."

"What was it?" I asked.

"Raw Meat."

"Good thinking," Randy said.

"Lame names," Phoebe said.

Saturday morning Benjamin was upset that Randy *made* us walk to 102nd Street. "I'll be getting enough exercise today. I don't need any more," he said.

His father said, "Keep moving, pal."

The one other detail Randy forgot to mention—not that I shouldn't have foreseen it—was that Susan-the-Ex would also be attending the game. When we arrived at the playing field she was sitting on a bench chatting with another mom, surrounded by a wheeled cooler and plastic grocery bags overflowing with boxes of doughnuts and granola bars and juice boxes. Susan had volunteered to be Snack Mother that week. I didn't know it was possible to be something called a Snack Mother. I wondered if I should volunteer one Saturday. Maybe be a Snack Stepmother.

Benjamin looked all embarrassed and uncomfortable while his mom hugged him hello and pulled a loose hair off his shirt and straightened his red baseball cap. He picked up his leather glove and headed out to the field to warm up with the other Steaks. He looked adorable with his red number 18 T-shirt tucked into his goofy striped baseball pants. But even I knew not to tell a guy going out to slay an enemy sports team that he looked adorable.

Phoebe squeezed in between Susan and the other mom and somehow Randy ended up between Susan and me.

Susan fussed over Phoebe, asked if her blue hoodie was warm enough, finger-combed her hair. The other mom was wearing a T-shirt the same color as the opposing team so I didn't have to be nice to her. I'd never see her again.

"This is my daughter, Phoebe," Susan said to the woman, then turned toward Randy and me. "This is Catherine."

I leaned over and waved to Catherine, said, "It's lovely to meet you." If Susan was warm and gracious, I wanted to be warm and gracious. I wanted to offer Catherine a doughnut.

Susan turned back to Catherine and continued her introductions. "This is Benjamin's dad, Randy, and this is Linda."

Randy nodded at Catherine, who was now busy looking from Randy to Susan to me, probably trying to figure out the game plan. The fact that Susan and I looked like sisters only complicated matters.

Other parents were crowding onto the bench or setting up canvas folding chairs behind the chain-link fence surrounding the field. Susan said several hellos. She knew everyone's name. I envied her being the real mother, the involved mother, the Snack Mother.

After the coin flip, the Steaks batted first. Up, down, three players in a row. Randy smiled and squeezed my shoulder. Phoebe sat with her chin on her hands, elbows on her knees, looking bored out of her mind. Clearly, future Phoebe appearances would be limited.

Benjamin covered the left outfield in the bottom of the inning, slapping his fist into his glove, crouching low, then spending most of the time studying his shoelaces. The pitcher for the Steaks was the coach's son. Apparently, coach's sons are always the pitchers. The teams were well matched—both of them pathetic. But it was fun to be surrounded by all the eager parents encouraging their sons, half of them cheering "Go Tigers!" and the other half cheering "Go Steaks!"

During the game, I'd sneak looks over at Susan and try to imagine her as Randy's wife. How could my predecessor not fascinate me? She had been the young wife, the nubile, dewy-faced let's register for crockpots and fondue sets, life is full of potential isn't love grand wife.

I was the older, been-around-the-block, no-false-illusions wife. Randy could never look at *me* and say, "I still picture you at twenty-four."

Randy seemed oblivious to any awkwardness from sitting between the two women he'd married. If there was someone on that bench who felt like a third wheel, it sure wasn't him. I twisted my plain gold wedding band around on my finger, reminding myself that it was right where it belonged.

A few innings later—I lost count—the Gods of Nepotism were no longer shining; the pitcher walked seven players and the coach benched his son. Watching a grown man pick on his kid was somewhat surprising, but what was really surprising, practically shocking, was when he sent Benjamin in to pitch. *Benjamin? Our* Benjamin? Mr. Why-Walk-When-You-Can-Hail-a-Cab?

Benjamin moved toward the pitcher's mound, nodded at

the catcher with a professional curt bob of the head, then nodded at the first baseman, whom I recognized as his friend Josh.
Turning his body toward the plate and leaning back into the
pitch, Benjamin narrowed his eyes and glared at the batter
with a look so evil, so menacing, I hadn't seen anything like it
since the one time I suggested he sample sushi. He threw the
pitch; the Tiger swung and missed; the umpire called a strike.
One after another. Three Tigers up. Three Tigers down. Benjamin struck them out.

Susan hooted and shouted. I whistled through my pinkies.
Randy cheered his heart out. Even Phoebe was impressed. I
heard her mumble, "Not bad." Randy leaned over and hugged
me, but as he did so I saw Susan, proud Susan, looking forward, watching her son, and for the slightest moment I felt
like I'd stolen her hug.

Two more innings and six more strikeouts later, *Benjamin
was pitching a no-hitter*. All those hours sitting in front of his
Nintendo were paying off. The kid had perfect hand-eye coordination.

Okay, so he choked in the last inning, allowed two guys to
score. The coach used the two runs as an excuse to restore his
son to the pitcher's mound the following week. But that day
Benjamin was a star. A hero. Life was good. And I was part of
it. All because I married Randy. I wanted everyone in the world
to be happy and in love. Everyone.

Introducing Susan to a man she liked became my new goal.
And not because a new husband would save Randy money.

Married or not, Susan collected alimony until Benjamin turned twenty-one. My motives were pure.

The day after the baseball game was quiet at home. Phoebe was stationed at the kitchen table writing a paper on the U.S. involvement in Laos. Tom Seaver was on the sofa reading about Aztecs. I would have volunteered to help the kids with their homework except I knew nothing about either subject. And one of the events I'd actually *lived* through.

Randy was also quiet. And cranky. He'd spent the afternoon walking around the dining room table filling out legal forms and sorting through receipts in preparation for our annual tax return, giving me plenty of time to consider romantic candidates for his ex-wife.

Vincent the traffic coordinator at work was between marriages but he was too short.

My sister Toby had a work buddy who moved to New York. I once met him for coffee. Like a surrogate Welcome Wagon. He was tall enough. Smart enough. Sweet enough. But Mohammed wasn't Jewish.

Then I thought of Jack-America's-Most-Eligible-Bachelor. Jack was my friend who used to live in Chicago when I lived in Chicago and moved to New York two years after I moved to New York. I liked to tell him he moved because he missed me, but the truth had a lot more to do with the big fancy-shmancy corporate job he was offered with all sorts of perks like free Knicks tickets and a personal driver. And for anyone who's now wondering why I never dated Jack-America's-Most-Eligible-Bachelor, let me explain it this way: men who tell you that you're the kind of girl they can really talk to, just want to talk to you.

First I called Claudia. "Why are you home on a Sunday afternoon?" I asked when she answered the phone. I was calling from the bedroom, stretched out on the bedspread with pillows behind my back. I didn't want to disturb the kids from doing their homework or Mr. H&R Block from doing his taxes.

"Mike's not around today," she said. "Hang on while I get my cigarettes." For the past six months Claudia had been hot and heavy with a man she described as "currently not all that available," which meant—married. I heard her set down the receiver and go mumbling around in the background. *Where are those damn matches? What's my diaphragm doing here?* By the time she got back to the telephone, lit up, and settled in, I could barely remember why I called.

"Is everybody comfy?" I asked.

"Sure," she said. "What's new in Gotham City?"

"Remember Jack? Bachelor Jack?"

Claudia groaned in the affirmative. She thought Jack was narcissistic, but that's because Jack once told her that she was the kind of girl he could talk to.

"I'm thinking of introducing him to Randy's wife."

"Aren't you his wife?"

"I mean Susan. The first wife."

After what was either a sigh or an exhalation of cigarette smoke, Claudia said, "Okay, I'm going on record here. That's a little odd."

I twisted around and rearranged pillows with one hand while holding the phone with the other. "I like Susan. I think of her as a friend. And it's not like I don't know her taste in men. She needs someone smart. With a certain amount of stature. Someone I wouldn't mind having around at family dinners for the next twenty years."

"Fixing up your husband's ex-wife is like selling a used car to a neighbor. It'll come back to haunt you," Claudia said. "She's in real estate now, right? Why don't you just send her a real estate client?"

"I don't know any real estate clients."

"Have you discussed this plan with Jack?"

"No."

"Or Susan?"

"No."

"Or Randy?"

"Not yet."

"Well on behalf of all of them: it's a terrible idea."

"I'm going to call Jack and ask him what he thinks."

Before we hung up Claudia griped about Hugo Chávez and how pissed she was at him and how she'd like to fly right down to Venezuela and set him straight. I left her to deal with Hugo and I called Jack even though I didn't expect him to be home.

He was home.

Jack Salzer had been dating women in their twenties and early thirties ever since he was in his twenties and early thirties. Other than a short break in the festivities for a seven-month ill-advised and expensive marriage, he claimed all the finer bachelor requisites right down to the second home on the shore and the silver BMW. Susan would like him. He'd be

good for the kids, too. Jack liked kids and Phoebe would like
his beach house; Benjamin would like the BMW. Everyone
would get along beautifully. Jack was always asking me if I
knew anyone exciting. Were there any pretty girls at my office? What he didn't seem to notice was that young pretty girls
didn't necessarily want to date guys in their fifties. A mature
woman like Susan would be much better for him.

I went straight for the pitch. "Great news. I know someone
you should go out with."

I had moved from the bed to the carpeted floor. I was
stretched out on my side doing leg lifts while talking to Jack.

"What's she like?"

"Classy. Poised. Intelligent."

"I mean how old?"

"A little older than you're used to."

"Thirty?"

"Not quite."

"Twenty-eight? Twenty-nine?"

"More like over forty." Left leg up. Left leg down. "A lot over."

"You're kidding. Don't you know anyone good who's
younger?"

I flipped onto my other side, switching the phone from one
hand to the other. Right leg up. Right leg down. "Jack, why
would any twenty-year-old want to go out with *you*?"

"I'm rich and I'm handsome."

"Besides that."

"Isn't that enough?"

"Okay. So let me get this straight. You're looking for a gold
digger?"

"Yes. A gold digger with a good body. What about that Italian friend of yours? The one I met at the chili party."

"She said you're too old for her."

"Really? She said that? I thought European women don't mind an age difference."

"They do when it's three continents wide." Leg up. Leg down. "Forget this entire conversation. I withdraw my offer. My friend's too good for you."

"Well, thanks for thinking of me, but call me when you know someone who'd be a better fit."

"Fine. As soon as Phoebe's out of puberty, I'll give you a buzz."

That's the kind of friendship Jack and I have. Like a brother and sister who adore each other but fight all the time. I hung up the phone, leg midair, just as Randy walked into the room with a handful of tax forms. He smiled at me. Leg up. Leg down. Smiled even harder and set his papers aside. Randy can appreciate an old leg.

Stuart Moeller worked in the finance department at the ad agency. Stuart was recently divorced.

We became friendly when I stopped receiving my paychecks after somebody in accounting transposed two digits of my Social Security number and I showed up on the company computers as deceased. Stuart brought me back to life. He was even-tempered, a little shy, but played Mendelssohn and Verdi in his office all day, so I figured he had some couth. Susan liked couth. He was the kind of man who's comfortable wearing neckties with little Christmas trees in honor of the holiday season or colored kerchiefs that match his socks.

Monday afternoon I dropped by his office, plopped down on his cordovan leather sofa. The agency finance guys get much better furniture than the creative people. Of course, they're in charge of the furniture budgets.

Stuart liked when I dropped by to say hello. The only visitors he usually got were people with problems. Like the first time I visited. But this time I was there with a solution.

"Stuart, have you started dating since your divorce? Because if you are and you want, I have someone for you to meet."

"Okay."

"Okay?" His desk was tidy. Susan liked tidy.

"Okay, I'll meet her," Stuart said.

"That's it? You don't want to ask any questions?"

"It's hard to meet women. Whatever you've got, I'll take."

"Great. Fine. Let me check with her and I'll get you her number."

Stuart nodded okay.

I was about to fix Susan up with the Anti-Jack.

Susan sounded more than a little surprised when I called to tell her about Stuart and ask if she was game for a coffee date or maybe a movie with him. I tossed in a few *Why nots?* and *What the hells?* for good measure.

"Don't you think this is a little unusual?" she said.

"It's what I'd do for any friend," I told her.

We chatted like girlfriends. She admitted that she hadn't

dated for a while; it wasn't easy finding decent men. She sighed. "Most of the ones my age want to date twenty-year-olds. Can you believe it?"

"Unbelievable," I said. While we talked I doodled with a ballpoint pen on an ad for a Lil' Laugh & Learn Swing, scribbling a mustache and eyeglasses on a baby's face. "They're so immature."

Susan told me that if I really thought Stuart was special, a good guy and somebody she'd like, I could give him her number.

After I hung up I felt excited. Hopeful. Like a true do-gooder. I wanted Susan to be as happy with someone as I was with . . . well . . . whatever.

Stuart called my office from his office the next day to thank me; said he spoke with Susan and they'd be meeting for drinks Thursday night; said she sounded nice.

Thursday was perfect. That was Randy's night with the kids. Susan could go out and have a great time, even stay out late if Stuart and she really hit it off.

"What did you talk about on the phone?" I asked, feeling quite pleased with myself.

He said, "Directions to the bar."

Friday morning I was watching Randy walk around in his underwear. There's something about hairy legs that makes me happy. Unless they're my hairy legs.

He padded around our bedroom, barefoot, walking from

the closet to the dresser and back again to reconsider which Polo shirt to wear with which khaki pants. Randy hates Fridays ever since they became casual Fridays. He finds them stressful, thinks throwing on a suit is much easier. He rummaged through his sock drawer, studied his loafers. Randy has flat feet. Funny, endearing feet. If they didn't have toes on them, they'd qualify as pancakes.

I was in front of the dresser mirror watching his reflection over my shoulder and studying a scratch on my cheek. I often wake up with mysterious marks on my face. I never know how they got there, whether I'm clawing at myself during dreams, ripping my fingernails down my face like an Edvard Munch painting.

Randy had seemed somewhat taken aback when I told him I'd arranged a date for Susan. He looked puzzled, said things like, "You what?" "How come?" "That's peculiar."

I asked, "So what kind of mood was Susan in when she got home last night?"

He was holding up a leather belt in each hand. "The brown or the black?" I turned and pointed to the black.

"Did she seem happy? Excited? Dreamy-eyed?"

He frowned like *How would I know?* He said, "Linda, I have no interest in poking into my ex-wife's moods."

I was sitting at my desk eating an egg salad sandwich and writing headlines for a Little Superstar Sing-Along Stage when Susan called to report in about the date, give me the after-date update. That's what girlfriends do. But I could tell she was choosing her words carefully. And she didn't sound as friendly as the last time we spoke.

"Stuart's a little . . . let's see, what's the word I'm looking for . . . oh, yes . . . *dull*."

Dull's not good. But I jumped to Stuart's defense. "Maybe he was nervous."

Susan laughed. One of those sour laughs that mean the person's not really laughing. "Maybe he was asleep."

Asleep's not good.

My vision of happy extended-family outings with Randy and both of his kids and both of his wives and Susan's new boyfriend was off to a rocky start. I asked, "Should I try again?"

Susan's answer was cool, measured, and not too genial. "Thanks, but I'll pass for now," she said. "There is something you can do, though."

"What? Tell me. Anything. Snacks for the next Little League game?"

"Benjamin wants a sleepover party for his birthday. About five of his friends and him." Benjamin's eleventh birthday was two weeks away. "I was wondering if Randy and you would mind having the party at your place. I've just repainted and everything's still in boxes all over my apartment."

Five eleven-year-old boys. How much trouble could that be? I loved the idea. I'd be the hostess.

"I'll help, of course," Susan said. "I'll bring the cake."

I said, "Yes. Yes, we'd love to do it. Sounds like a blast."

"Excellent," Susan said. "I knew I could count on you."

Before I went back to writing headlines I started a list of things to remember for Benjamin's birthday party. Invitations.

Birthday streamers. Were eleven-year-olds too old for hats? I also avoided Stuart for the rest of the day, in case he wanted to tell me he had a wonderful time on his date.

In case anyone else besides me also didn't know: eleven-year-old-boys are too old for party hats. Benjamin quickly confirmed this fact when he said to me: "You're kidding, right? That was a joke?"

The night of his sleepover party I was excited. Probably more excited than Benjamin. I'd never been in charge of a kids' party, having never really being in charge of any kids. Benjamin invited the guests (after my offer to design party invitations was summarily dismissed); Randy rearranged Benjamin's bedroom so there'd be enough space for the sleeping bags; Susan, as promised, showed up with the cake (chocolate, home-baked, three layers); and Phoebe volunteered to spend the night at one of her Ashleys so she could avoid the entire event. Which didn't leave much for me to do other than be excited.

Benjamin chose the dinner menu in advance. Hot dogs. Pizza. Macaroni and cheese. Individual juice box cartons were passed around. The boys ate in the kitchen while Randy and Susan and I hovered in the living room trying our best to be attentive without being intrusive, like three English butlers. I asked Susan what movies she'd seen lately, who cut her hair, was she planning any cool vacations? Girlfriend-type talk. Randy didn't join in the conversation but every five minutes or so he'd call out to the kitchen, "Anybody need anything? Ketchup? Mustard? *Napkins?*"

The boys talked quietly, more like businessmen at a board meeting than what I expected: a bunch of wild crazy Indians. They were a tight group, friends since kindergarten, with assigned roles. Eric was the brain. Jasper the best runner. Malcolm was the one girls liked best. Sam was poised around adults and Josh owned the most Pokémon cards.

After the pizzas were devoured and the hot dogs scarfed down, Susan carried in the cake lit with eleven candles and one for good luck. I was sorry I didn't buy the cake so I could carry it in. Instead I snapped pictures on the Instamatic, which meant I didn't end up in the pictures.

The boys disappeared into Benjamin's room to watch *Austin Powers* on tape. Susan offered to help fold empty pizza boxes and load the dishwasher. Randy and I said no, no, we can manage. Susan retrieved her handbag from the hallway table, her coat from the front closet.

"Got any fun plans for tonight?" I asked. More girlfriend talk.

"See you tomorrow," she said, leaving without answering.

Austin Powers was followed by a boisterous Nintendo tournament followed by Randy announcing it was almost midnight and time to get some sleep. An *it's-not-late!* protest erupted into grabbing for the primo spots on the floor, unrolling sleeping bags, shirts and jeans flying across the room, bodies sliding into place, zipping sleeping bags, and discussions of whose unfortunate faces ended up next to whose stinky gross feet and who just let loose that disgusting fart.

The farting accusations generated the most laughter until Randy stood in the middle of the room, lit a match, defumigated the air, and told the boys to settle down or they'd be tired the next day.

Yeah. As if they minded.

But Randy was tired and I was tired so with one more pseudo-parental admonishment we shut off the light and escaped to our own room.

In retrospect, maybe it wasn't such a swell idea to schedule a family dinner the following night, on Benjamin's actual birthday. He did stay awake long enough to choose the restaurant, based on its serving gigantic slices of the gooiest fudge cake in all of Manhattan. Most of the dinner conversation was of the making-conversation variety. *How's your burger? Where's the waiter? Benjamin, open your eyes.*

Somehow, I ended up sitting on the side of the table with Phoebe and Benjamin, across from Susan and catty-corner from Randy. I felt like Randy and Susan were the parents and I was one of the kids. Especially at the end of the meal—when Randy and Susan split the check.

We were waiting for the waiter to bring back the change. Rap music was playing on the overhead speakers. A huge communal hunk of cake sat still unfinished in the middle of the table. Susan leaned across and spoke to me in a low voice, like she was about to confide in me, girlfriend to girlfriend. "I heard what happened at the party last night," she said. "Lorra called."

"Something happened? What happened?"

Lorra was one of the moms and friends with Susan. All the moms were friends with Susan. I hardly saw the moms. I could never remember whose mom was who. And even after three years, I'm sure they still thought of me as *Randy's new wife*.

I focused on Randy's former wife. Randy and Phoebe were busy playing thumb hockey. Benjamin took the opportunity to wake up and pull the entire cake plate toward him.

"Well, I guess some sons confide in their mothers more than others." Susan held three fingers up against her mouth, shrugged her shoulders, and smiled. Whatever news she had to report, she sure was amused by it. "Lorra told me about the contest the boys had."

"Nintendo?"

"Not quite." Susan was back to all business but still enjoying herself. Randy was sorting out the tip and change with the waiter. Phoebe was talking to Benjamin. "It seems a second contest took place. After you went to sleep." Susan looked at the kids to make sure our tete-à-tete was just girl-to-girl. She lowered one hand to the side and below the table where only the two of us could see, then held her thumb to the tip of her index finger and made an up-and-down jiggling motion, one I recognized but that wasn't quite registering. She whispered to me: "They call it a whack-off party."

It registered.

"On *my* carpets!"

"Happens all the time." Susan laughed, sat back, and held out the same hand for Randy to tender her half of the change. "It's the age they're at."

Did Susan know about these games? Did Randy? Whatever happened to Pin the Tail on the Donkey? Or Telephone? I didn't dare ask how the boys determined a winner.

"Anyone want to share my last bite of cake?" Benjamin asked.

I immediately answered *No!*

After dinner we all walked home together down Broadway, except the kids were going home with Susan and I was going home with Randy. One extended family. Five in total. Maybe someday we'd extend to six if Susan remarried. Something she was fully capable of doing with no help from me.

Sign Here and Here and Here

After three years as renters we were ready to buy. When Chicagoans go in search of housing they start with a dream list and cross items off as reality sets in.

"Okay, we can live without a fireplace."

"Forget the powder room. Guests can use the kids' bathroom."

"A patio really isn't a priority."

Turns out New Yorkers go through a similar process.

"Okay, we can live without closets."

"Forget the kitchen. We'll just call out."

"Indoor plumbing really isn't a priority."

We were working with the locally famous Frederick Peters. Whenever there's a real estate article in the *New York Times*, there's always a quote from Frederick. He wears bow ties and suspenders and looks like a college professor, instilling trust.

At each apartment we visited, the seller's Realtor would give us a sales spiel and then Frederick would tell us the real story.

Realtor in pashmina shawl: "Custom-made cabinetry."

Frederick: "Lowe's."

Realtor with comb-over: "The sweetest lady lived here for sixty years and now she's moved to Florida."

Frederick: "Aneurysm on the bathroom floor."

Realtor in leopard-print eyeglass frames: "Eighteen hundred square feet."

Frederick: "Sixteen hundred."

Me: "Where are the other two hundred?"

Frederick straightened his bow tie. "In New York it's legal to measure a room from inside the walls."

Me: (Speechless.)

Randy called. "Can you leave work immediately? Something just came back on the market." I was in the middle of trying to write snappy lyrics for tampons, searching for words to rhyme with "plastic applicator."

I said, "I'll grab my coat."

Thirty minutes later we were standing in front of a twelve-story building on Riverside Drive. Many New Yorkers would never consider living on Riverside Drive. It's too cold, too windy; they don't want a view of New Jersey; but I hailed from an entire city known for cold and windy and I've got nothing against looking at New Jersey. Along with Frederick and two lady Realtors, we scrutinized iron scrollwork, bas-relief columns, and a copper cornice.

"Note the limestone façade," the first woman said.

"Yes, limestone," the second woman said.

"Prewar," they said in unison.

The women introduced themselves as Nancy and Ronnie. Nancy said something and Ronnie would repeat it. Ronnie said something and Nancy would repeat it. They were conjoined Realtors. They even looked alike in their gray pantsuits, shoulder-length blond hairdos, and solitaire diamond pendants around their necks; marquis for Nancy; emerald cut for Ronnie. Fric and Frac whipped us through the lobby to the elevators. On the ride up, Ronnie told us the building had a gym and a playroom.

"We'll have to show you the gym and playroom," Nancy said as the elevator doors opened onto a dark, stucco hallway.

Ronnie fumbled with the front door key and then Nancy fumbled with the front door key and finally led us inside.

The apartment did not "show well." It showed nightmare.

Every surface—walls, doors, radiators, moldings, trim, all the wainscoting and paneling—had been sponge painted. Gold and brown splotches offset forest green blobs. A mural in the hallway, painted by somebody with no integrity and even less talent, depicted the interior of a Greek temple with mauve and white marble pillars and no relationship whatsoever to the rest of the apartment.

The carpeted rooms seemed to be carrying out some sort of African safari theme. Leopard in the second bedroom. Zebra in the third. Green snakeskin on the floor of a walk-in closet. Whatever the intent, I just knew it was wrong, wrong, wrong. But what made the apartment truly unique were the mosaics. The microwave, gas meter, door frames, bathroom mirror frames, a freestanding watercooler—all looked like ashtrays made at summer camp.

Nancy told us that the owner was a true artist and the apartment was worth even more because of her contributions. Then Ronnie told us that the owner was a true artist and the apartment was worth even more because of her contributions.

Frederick told us the owner's husband left her for the live-in nanny. "She smashed all the china and mirrors and went crazy with a glue gun."

The body of a mosaic snake wove along the side of the bathtub up onto the wall, splitting into a two-headed mosaic snake. A fuse box door was covered with the decapitated heads of Barbie dolls.

Standing in the living room beneath overhead track lights as large as family-sized cans of Hawaiian Punch, I stared down at the wood floor. "Something's off about this shade of brown," I said.

"It's eggplant," Nancy said.

I looked closer. "Ohmygod, you're right. It's purple."

"Eggplant," Ronnie said.

I immediately dubbed the place the over-my-dead-body apartment, but Randy pulled me into the kitchen for a private conversation, leaving Frederick to chat with the Doublemint twins.

"This is a good apartment for us," Randy said. "Decent room sizes, river views, a logical layout. We should make an offer."

"Make an offer? Just like that? I've spent more time contemplating a pair of slacks at Macy's."

"If we don't move on it, we'll lose it."

I considered that good news. Randy waited for my response. I said, "Can we at least start with an insulting offer?"

Five days and three counteroffers later, Randy broke out a bottle of champagne, uncorking it over our kitchen sink. "To our contract," he said, clinking his glass against mine.

"To sponge painting," I said.

"Now we keep our fingers crossed that we pass the board interview."

"Why wouldn't we? It's not like we're Bonnie and Clyde."

"Co-op boards are peculiar." Randy tossed back his champagne like he was swallowing a couple of aspirins. "You never know what they're looking for."

I refilled our glasses with the last champagne we might ever be able to afford. "Well, it all sounds illegal to me, making people fill out personal information, picking and choosing who can or can't live in your building. If they vote us down, do we at least learn why?"

"The law says they aren't obligated to provide a reason."

"So you spend the rest of your life wondering why they didn't like you?"

"No. You spend the rest of your life hunting for another apartment."

We were surrounded. The kitchen counters were covered. The kitchen table was covered. Stacks appeared on the floor. Randy and I were compiling a financial dossier for the co-op board:

W-2 forms, bank statements, credit check reports, charge card bills, tax returns. Which explains why Susan-the-Ex wasn't our Realtor.

"I can't believe millions of New Yorkers are willing to put up with this rigmarole," I said, pausing to massage the cramp in my fingers. "I feel like I'm transcribing *War and Peace*." Randy moved the pile of charge card bills next to the pile of credit check reports. He was in charge of piles. "It's not fair," I said. "The neighbors will know my salary, but I don't get to know theirs."

"Who said anything about fair?" Randy checked an item on his yellow legal pad. The room was stuffy but I was afraid if I opened a window or turned on a fan all the papers would blow out and we'd have to kill ourselves. Reading off the pad Randy said, "We still need the letter stating we're up to date on our current rent payments." He was in heavy concentration mode, studying his list.

"Is there anything else? What about urine samples?"

"And we need twelve letters of recommendation."

"Excuse me?"

He looked up like he was surprised to see me. "Three professional ones for each of us and three personal ones for each of us."

"Saying *what*?"

Randy shrugged. "It's standard procedure. All the buildings ask for them. It helps them judge your character, tells them what kind of person you are."

"It's stuffy in here," I said. "Let's turn on a fan."

*   *   *

I called Claudia to ask for a letter of recommendation. I could hear her strike a match, inhale and exhale before she asked, "Recommending you for what?"

"To live in the apartment we want to buy. The building requires references."

"You need permission to be a *neighbor?*"

"Well, actually—yes. That's how it works."

"I'd run my neighbors out of town if I had a deal like that. What's this letter supposed to say?"

"That I'm not noisy, not messy, not rude."

"Not *human?*"

"And at the end you say if they have any questions they should call."

"They damn well better not call. I don't want to talk to these people."

"Please, Claudia. It won't take long. And who knows my character better than you?"

"How's this?" she said. *"Linda's restraining order should be lifted any day now and I think everyone is eager to move past the incident with the underpants on the bus."*

That night in bed while Randy and I were making love, my mind wandered, and not to naughty dentists or being the sultan's number one harem girl. I kept thinking of reasons why the board might turn us down. *They hate mid-westerners. Somebody squealed that I snore through walls. They found out I copied my fourth-grade report on George Washington Carver from the* World Book Encyclopedia. I seemed to be spending an awful lot of energy cultivating the approval of people I didn't care about. Wasn't that what high school was for?

Above me, Randy shuddered and gripped me tighter.

"Incredible," he said.

"Incredible," I said.

I had plenty of time to come up with other rejection possibilities because it took six weeks before we were scheduled to meet the board. Apparently they weren't as eager to meet us as we were to meet them.

In the meantime, Frederick arranged for us to bring the kids to see the apartment. Walking around bug-eyed, surveying with her hands planted on her hips, Phoebe said, "You're kidding about this, right?"

"No," Randy said.

"Do I have any say in this?"

"No," Randy said.

"Not unless you want to help pitch in for the mortgage," I said.

"Well, I hope you don't expect me to bring any of my *friends* over here?"

No teenage visitors. I wasn't about to protest.

Benjamin was more interested in playing with the mosaic watercooler, making it splash. His only question was, "Do I get a television in my room?"

*   *   *

The evening of our interview we arrived twenty minutes early for our 7 P.M. appointment. We'd been instructed to wait in the lobby while the board met in apartment 1A to ransack our credentials.

Randy introduced us to the blue-uniformed doorman. "Hello, we're here for the—"

"Interview," the doorman said. "I'm Emilio. Have a seat across from 1A." Emilio winked. "So nice to meet you. Mr. and Mrs. Arthur, right?"

"Right," Randy said. I could tell he was pleased to be recognized, like that was a good indication.

I wondered if it was an indication that Emilio had also read our board package and knew that twice a month I charged visits for electrolysis on my Visa.

We sat on chairs covered in worn black velveteen, department store King Louis–like reproductions, and I studied the lobby's prewar details. The prewar cracked windows. The prewar tarnished wall sconces. The prewar peeling paint job. I leaned toward Randy and whispered, "Is it too soon to volunteer for the decorating committee?"

Randy's posture was so upright that he might've been applying for sentry duty at Buckingham Palace. He kept staring at the door with the brass 1A. He was wearing a dark gray suit, white shirt, and red tie—a look that said: finance. I'd settled on a black knit dress, black hose, and black heels—a look that said: funeral.

I watched Emilio wave through every tattooed twenty-year-old guy in a torn T-shirt carrying anything that vaguely resembled a pizza box or semiautomatic.

I whispered to Randy again. "Security's not too tight in this building."

A man with tortoiseshell glasses poked his head out of 1A. Randy jutted up, his posture now even straighter, if that were possible.

"We're running a little late," the man said. "We haven't completed our review."

We responded with big accommodating smiles.

"No problem!"

"Take your time!"

"Don't rush on our accounts!"

As soon as the man disappeared and the door closed I said to Randy, "I'm scared to death and I barely like the place. I just don't want to start all over again with twelve more recommendation letters."

Randy reached over and squeezed my hand, which would have been reassuring if his hand weren't dripping with sweat.

"I bet they don't even read those letters," I said. "We should have written them all ourselves and signed them from Charles Manson, John Wilkes Booth, and Clarabell the Clown just to see if anyone noticed."

We waited in silence, watching as a series of dogs on leashes was paraded through the lobby; dogs heading out for walks, dogs heading back from walks, even more dogs than pizzas, led by frizzy-haired women in Birkenstocks; men in crew neck sweaters who looked like they taught economics at Columbia University; and couples in well-cut wool coats, probably subscription members of Lincoln Center.

Finally, the door to 1A opened again. The tortoiseshell glasses were back. "You can join us now," he said.

"Good luck," Emilio called after us.

"Too bad the doorman's not on the board," I whispered to
Randy as we entered 1A. "He'd let anyone in."

Apartment 1A's layout looked like our future layout, square
entry hall, rectangular living room, only without the wacko
paint job and the scorned woman mosaics. Randy and I were
motioned to a blue brocade sofa facing seven board members
sitting on a variety of chairs: stuffed, wooden and folding,
the same seating arrangement I'd expect if we were having a
friendly get-together with the Spanish Inquisition. The board
members were spread out like they were posing for a Christmas
manger scene except instead of a cradle with Baby Jesus in the
center there was a substantial woman with short gray-blond
hair holding a clipboard. She introduced herself, saying she'd
been the board president for ten years. I tried to look properly
impressed.

The other members also gave their names, some along with
titles: Vice President, Treasurer, Head of Christmas Committee.

The president smiled, ruffled her notes. "I see here you pay
alimony," she said to Randy. Nice opening.

While Randy talked finances, I worried that my panty hose
were twisted. I hadn't noticed when we were waiting out in the
lobby, but now I was positive that something was wrong with
the crotch and maybe I'd put one of the legs on backward. I
crossed my legs one way, then the other, but stopped, afraid
that now I looked like I needed to pee.

A stone-faced woman taking notes questioned us next.
"Will you be planning any renovations?" she asked.

I wanted to answer, "Are you kidding? Have you seen the place?" but I wasn't sure if that was the correct answer. If we said yes, extensive ones—would they think, *Wonderful, they're improving the property,* or *Uh-oh, noise and dust.* Before I could finish my lively conversation with myself, Randy said, "The kitchen needs updating."

"I'll say!" Madame Secretary laughed.

"And we'd like to restain the floors," Randy added.

A man with the biggest ears I'd ever seen said, "Oh really? Purple's not your color?" The board members all shared a good chuckle.

"Tell us about your children," tortoiseshell said, peering down at a stack of papers. "I see the daughter is fourteen."

"Yes," I said, making eye contact with the two women who looked young enough to be raising kids. "And she babysits."

Paydirt. The women smiled like I'd just handed over a cash bribe.

"Good to hear," the first one said.

"I'll get her number," the second one said.

"And what about your eleven-year-old son?" El Presidente asked. "Is he loud and active?" El Presidente lived in the apartment below the one we'd be buying.

"No," Randy said. "Not at all."

"He sits on his butt and plays Super Mario all day," I said. "The kid hasn't moved since birth."

After another half hour of the board wanting to know everything short of our preferred coital positions, we were ushered out.

Frederick called the next morning. "Congratulations," he said.

We'd been approved to buy a New York co-op with purple floors and nosy neighbors.

NINA THE
STONEHENGE CONTRACTOR

~~~~~~~~~

I don't know why I listened to the account guy at the ad agency.
He's the one who recommended Nina. She was the third contractor we invited over for a video screening. She showed up
with her partner, Franco, and we all sat around the living room
like guests at a tea. Randy commandeered the remote control
on the VCR.

Nina complimented Randy's camera angles, stuck her finger in her mouth, and feigned barfing over the sponged walls.
Clearly, we shared the same sensibilities.

"So why can't you get into this place?" she asked, after our
video ended with the scene of me pointing out the cracked
glass transom over the bedroom door.

"The owner's cleaning lady was packing things up and
misplaced the silver," I explained. "The owner decided *we*
must have stolen it and even though she discovered we

didn't steal it, she doesn't want us around in case we decide to steal something else."

"A real loony tune, huh? And how 'bout those mosaics!" Nina laughed heartily with her head tossed back, like one of those fake laughs in beer commercials. She was squat with close-cropped red hair, dark eyebrows, and no makeup. The first time we met Nina she was wearing army pants and a gray T-shirt. The second, third, twelfth, forty-ninth, sixtieth, and every time after that, she was wearing army pants and a gray T-shirt. On some level Nina must have equated contracting with combat, a nuance we failed to notice.

Nina informed us that she'd sung backup with the E Street Band before Bruce Springsteen was a star. Making what later turned out to be the miscalculation of her life, she decided Bruce would never hit it big and quit, figuring the real money was in renovations. She could change a drill bit, hammer straight, and loved to spackle. During the interview Franco didn't say much but he had the burly build and gnarled hands of a man who knew his way around a construction zone.

"Franco manages the crew. I manage Franco," Nina said, making a joke that she seemed to find far more amusing than Franco did.

"Well, I think we'll all get along beautifully," I said.

"There's just one more thing you need to know," Nina said.

"What's that?" Randy said.

"I'm a lesbian."

Randy and I looked at each other, then back at Nina. It was several moments before anyone spoke.

"Okay," Randy finally said. "Why is that relevant?"

"I just don't want there to be any surprises later on," Nina said.

"What kind of surprises?" I asked.

Nina shrugged. "I've had clients in the past who couldn't deal with it."

"Well, we weren't planning on dealing with your sexual preferences," Randy said. "We just want a new kitchen."

Three days later Nina submitted a bid and we agreed to start demolition the day after our real estate closing.

The phone machine was blinking when we returned from the closing. There were two messages. One from my mother screaming with excitement: *How are my New York apartment owners!* Another from Nina. I called Nina back while Randy opened a bottle of wine.

"It's a go," I said. "Tomorrow the walls come tumbling down."

"Well, that's why I called," Nina said. "We need to delay the start for two days."

I covered the receiver with my hand and whispered to Randy, "You might want to listen in on this. Pick up the extension."

Nina explained to us the importance of starting the renovation on the New Moon. "The job will go twice as fast if we start on the New Moon," she said.

"But we'll already be two days late," Randy said.

"We'll make up for it. I promise," Nina said. "And you'll thank your lucky stars."

*   *   *

Nina showed up two days later with a suntan and four guys in overalls.

"Where's Franco?" we asked.

"Oh, I meant to tell you that," she said. "Franco quit. But don't be concerned—I have an amazing crew."

Nina's amazing crew was assembled every morning when she drove her truck to a paint store where illegal immigrants gathered outside on the sidewalk in hopes of day work.

"Let's hit it!" she said, turning to the crew member standing to her right. "Vámonos, Luis!"

"Me llamo Miguel," he said.

Randy and I left for our jobs, and by the time we returned to the apartment that evening the old kitchen cabinets had been carted out, the carpets ripped up, closet doors removed.

"This is so much fun!" I said, the last time I was to say those words for the next six months.

The following morning we walked over to the apartment and Nina greeted us at the door. "Exciting news!" she said.

It's never good when a contractor announces exciting news. And it's never cheap.

"What, Nina?" we both said. Her eyes lit up. I checked her pupils to see if they were dilated.

She said, "I hired Sal to do the electrical and plumbing!"

Sal was our new super. Nina was going to mark up the work done by our super.

"Fine," Randy said. "Excellent idea."

On the way to the subway he said, "I get the feeling that if our pipes explode or electricity wipes out someday, it'll be a whole lot easier to track down Sal than Nina."

I was making decisions on things I never realized required decisions.

"What color grout do you want?" Nina would ask.

"Grout comes in colors?" I'd say.

"Talk to me about hardware finishes," Nina would ask. "Chrome? Brass? Nickel?"

"The one that costs a nickel."

I was in charge of decorating. Randy was in charge of budget and confrontations. I looked at the kitchen design the way I'd look at a movie set. I didn't care if the appliances actually worked; just so they looked good.

"We need to choose the kitchen fixtures," Nina said. "We have to go to Home Depot."

"Fine," I said. "When?"

"Any time after eleven is best."

"I can't go in the middle of the day."

"I meant P.M."

"As in *almost midnight*?"

"Less crowded then," Nina said. "How 'bout I pick you up in front of your place at eleven-thirty? But my truck only holds two. And it's a pigpen. Dress casual."

"Thanks for warning me. I'd hate to be overdressed for Home Depot."

*   *   *

Nina was waiting for me out front when I headed downstairs exactly at eleven-thirty. I told Randy, don't wait up. Nina was smoking a cigarette, the radio in her truck cranked up high, blasting an old ZZ Top song.

"Did I ever tell you I sang with Bruce Springsteen?" she said.

"Yes," I said, as she tossed the remainder of her cigarette out her window, rolled the window back up.

The truck really was a pigpen with discarded soda cans, crumpled sandwich bags, tool boxes, newspapers, an acoustic guitar, empty Marlboro cartons, sneakers, and a baseball mitt cramming the back and covering the floor. The grip on my door handle was filled with little paper-covered wads of old chewing gum. And everything smelled from stale cigarette smoke.

"So, Nina," I said, as we drove up the Westside Highway toward Yonkers, "you ever think of getting out of the contracting business?"

"Every day of my life," she sighed.

"Of course I don't mean in the middle of *our* job, but I was just wondering and all because—with all due respect—you don't seem to have any particular skill set for contracting. You aren't a plumber or a carpenter. You don't have an electrical license."

"I'm in management," she said, gripping the steering wheel with both hands, leaning forward and staring intently on the road. "That's my talent. Management."

Nina told me how her most recent relationship didn't work out, not that she was surprised. "Virgos and Sagittarians are never a decent combo," she said. "I don't know what I was thinking." She glanced over at me. "Randy and you seem to be a good couple."

I nodded.

"Second·wife, right?"

"Right."

Nina lit another cigarette, lowered the window on her side of the car, and for the rest of the ride blew smoke out the window while singing, *Love can still be found the second time around* . . .

We pulled into the Home Depot parking lot. The place was packed. Nina circled three times before she found a spot for her truck.

"What is this—the contractors' version of Skull and Bones?" I asked.

Inside, Nina greeted stock boys by name, chatted with other shoppers in overalls and baseball caps, while I observed the secret rituals of Home Depot after midnight: contractors selecting ceiling fans, examining door frames, debating be-tween faucets, all against a backdrop of beeping forklifts playing bumper car in the aisles.

"You've got quite a nightlife going on here," I said to Nina while we waited in the checkout line, our shopping cart piled high with fixture boxes.

"Yeah. It's a great place to meet guys," she said, then threw back her head and laughed. "Like I give a damn."

Standing in our kitchen-under-siege, Nina informed Randy and me that our granite countertops would not be delivered in time for our move-in date. "But at least you'll have plumbing." She kneeled down to address a pair of legs sticking out from the cabinet beneath the sink. "Right, Sal?"

"Right, if you stop bothering me," Sal said, between the clinking sounds of his wrench. That was their routine. Sal installed new copper pipes, ran new electrical wires, and rerouted old plumbing while Nina hovered over him telling him to hurry.

"We've got five days until we move in," Randy said. Every day he reminded Nina how many days we had left.

Moving day was bright and sunny. So much for good omens. I don't know what other plans that moving crew had that evening, but they sure didn't want to be spending it with us. Tables and sofas went flying down the hallways, bumping up against walls and doors, careening around corners. Artwork and planters were jammed against packing cartons piled high in haphazard formations; boxes of china and glassware teetered on edge. I spun around in circles, trying to keep track of the airborne pillows and swaying lamps. In the background, Nina's crew was still pounding nails.

I said to Randy, "I can't wait until all these people just go away."

And once again a familiar adage proved to be painfully true. *Be careful what you wish for.*

Unable to unpack in my unfinished kitchen, standing next to Randy next to an unusable sink, Nina mentioned a slight upcoming delay in our schedule.

"I don't know if I ever told you this . . . ," she began.

"That you used to sing backup for Bruce Springsteen?" we said.

"Yes. But one other thing." She smiled big. Too big. Nervous big. "I'm a Druid."

"A what-id?" I asked.

Nina spoke all in one big rush of words. "A Druid. And next week starts the celebrations for the last summer solstice of the millennium at Stonehenge and we're hoping for more open access to the stones to see the shadows and of course I have to be there with the other Druids for the celebrations and the ceremonies which basically amounts to—I'm sure you'll understand—a three-week pause as of Monday."

"A pause?" Randy said.

"A Druid?" I said.

"Shadows?" we said.

Nina clasped her hands in front of her chest, bopping her head from side to side as she grinned. "Think of me as a Celtic priest."

"I'm finding that difficult to do on all sorts of levels," Randy said.

"Three weeks?" I said. "Nothing's going to get done here for three weeks?"

"Trust me. The time will fly," Priestess Nina said.

Lying next to Randy in our bedroom with the missing closet doors, I stared up at the exposed electrical wires sprouting from a ceiling box and said, "Okay. So she feels obligated to tell us up front that she's a lesbian but forgets to mention she's a Druid."

"Maybe she was afraid we had Druid issues."

"I *do* have Druid issues. They leave in the middle of contracting jobs."

"She'll be back," Randy said. "We still owe her money."

"This is the worst renovation job in the history of renovation
jobs," Phoebe said when we informed her about the holdup.
Now she was an expert on construction. "Is the contract based
on a time and materials basis? Is Nina liable or deemed in
default for any delays?"

We shook our heads no.

"Well, then, serves you right," Phoebe said.

She was beginning to scare me.

By the time Nina did return, Randy and I were looking for *our*
shadows. "She called me at work. She'll be here on Tuesday,"
Randy reported.

"Did she check the moon first?" I asked. "I don't want to get
my hopes up only to discover it's waxing in the wrong direction."

On Tuesday an ebullient Nina appeared, springing right
into action with her two-man crew.

"How was the solstice?" I asked.

"Cloudy," she said, pissed.

Over the next two weeks Nina grouted her last grout, spackled
her last spackle, installed kitchen counters, and hung closet

doors. Randy handed Nina her final check. She held it up in two hands and kissed it. "By the way"—I hated when Nina began sentences with *by the way;* it was never good news— "I've signed my name in a secret place in each of your rooms. I'm proud of this job."

"You did a wonderful job," Randy said.

"And we'll enjoy spending the rest of our lives hunting for your signatures," I said.

After she left Randy and I stood arm in arm looking out the window at the barges on the Hudson River. "I'm just glad we finished before the warranties ran out on all the new appliances," he said.

"It's the luck of the Druids," I said.

We never spoke with Nina again, but later heard from the account guy at my office who originally recommended her, that she had moved upstate to be a painter. Walls or canvases, we don't know.

On our first Thanksgiving in the apartment I was standing at the kitchen sink, trying to decipher a cookbook, and dropped a cranberry on the floor. It rolled off and I squatted down to retrieve it. There, in florid script, on the baseboard beneath the cabinet, I saw *Nina.*

Out of My Ivy League

~~~~~

The invitation read, *black tie optional*.

"Who are these people who think their dining rooms warrant tuxedos?" I asked Randy. It was the week before Christmas and the taxi had just dropped us off on Park Avenue. I looked what I considered presentable in, well, all black. Randy looked like a maître d'.

While waiting for the doorman in the brass-buttoned uniform to call and request permission for our entry, I whispered to Randy, "You must be a pretty good broker if your clients live here."

"Thank you," he said. "I am."

Somehow my hostess gift of roasted nuts no longer seemed quite right. On the elevator ride, I said, "If you're such a good broker, how come *we* don't live in a penthouse?"

* * *

I dreaded New York dinner parties. The sizing up and looking down. The dropped names and lifted faces. The inevitable
alma maters. Somehow they always came up in the natural
progression of conversation.

"Excellent tartare."

"Please pass the goat cheese."

"I went to Yale."

My Chicago friend Bruce once confessed that he graduated dead bottom in his class at Dartmouth. Bruce was smart
enough to realize that it's better to be last in an Ivy League
school than first anywhere else. I never even considered an
Ivy League school, not that any Ivy League school would have
considered me. I had one option and only one. The University
of Illinois in Champaign-Urbana, which let's face it, wasn't
exactly a mecca of champagne or urbanity. But matriculating
there was nonnegotiable.

"There's nothing wrong with your own state school," my
mother said. "I went there and look how well I turned out."

That was what I called a no-win argument.

It wasn't difficult to get into Illinois back then, not much
harder than getting accepted into the Ray-Vogue School of
Design, which advertised on late-night television. On the day
of my departure my parents packed a trunk, handed me a train
ticket, and said: "We hope you learn something." Four years
later they picked me up at graduation and said: "What's new?"

There was no talk of graduate school or higher education.
In my family, higher education meant you spent four years of
college stoned.

Our hostess, Cynthia, Radcliffe '78, rang a tiny bell to announce dinner. Tinkle. Tinkle. *Get your butts to the table before the food gets cold.*

The dining table was the length of two Lincoln Continentals studded with silver candelabras and porcelain place card holders. I was seated next to a woman who introduced herself as "Bobbie, patron of the arts." I think that meant she went to museums all morning followed by lunch at the Whitney. Randy was sitting on my left, talking to the woman sitting on his left.

"I was an art history graduate at Cornell," Bobbie informed me. "Cum laude."

"Cum laude. Very laudatory," I said.

"Summa for me," a woman in a jeweled hairclip jumped in.

"You majored in wrestling?" I said. Only I was amused.

"Where did you matriculate?" Bobbie asked.

I delicately patted both sides of my mouth with a napkin and mumbled my answer. "U of I."

"I? I-what?" Bobbie apparently had sonar eardrums.

"I have to go to the bathroom. Excuse me," I said, hoping Bobbie would be left thinking I attended the U of Italy.

While lingering longer than necessary in the powder room with its Sherle Wagner fixtures and *heated* Toto toilet seat, I wondered how these New Yorkers always managed to make me feel apologetic for my midwestern education. It's not like the Midwest doesn't boast a few prestigious institutions of higher learning. The University of Michigan has managed to garner a great deal of cachet over the past thirty years, probably by not mentioning what their winters are like. Northwestern University, which should really be named Midwestern University unless it relocates two thousand miles north and west, is even more impossible to get into now than when it was impossible for me to get into before. And the University of Chicago continues to spit out graduates capable of building A-bombs.

When I returned to the dinner table, Randy was engaged in conversation with the man sitting across from him, something about hedge fund returns. I would have joined right in, but knew Randy would be annoyed when I immediately dozed off. Bobbie was now chatting with Krinkie, the woman sitting opposite her, still talking alma maters. Everyone had moved on to the salad course. I was the only woman who didn't request her dressing on the side.

"So where were we?" Bobbie said, turning back to me. "You were about to tell me what that mysterious *I* means."

The woman was like a dog with a rag in its mouth.

"Illinois," I said. "I went to the University of Illinois."

"Illinois? Oh. How sweet," Krinkie said from across the table. Krinkie wore vintage eyeglass frames, which meant she was current. "What are they known for there?"

It would have been nice to answer something along the lines of fifteenth-century Spanish liturgy, but I decided to just tell the truth.

"Cornfields and cows."

Bobbie responded with a bemused chuckle until I said, "No. Really. It's the number one agriculture school in the country."

"So you're saying you went to school with farmers?"

"Well, yes, I suppose I am."

Bobbie sliced a cherry tomato in two. I refrained from pointing out that it was a *farm-fresh* tomato.

"Illinois is part of the Big Ten," I said with pride.

"The Big Ten what?" Bobbie asked.

"That's a football conference."

"Oh."

"Did you ever hear of the Rose Bowl?" I asked.

"Is that any relation to Monaco's annual Rose Ball?" Krinkie said.

"I don't believe so." I helped myself to a refill of wine, something with a fancy French name that I'd pronounce *red*.

"Columbia was so disappointed when I rejected them for Brown," Judy, the woman two seats down from Bobbie, said, talking across her husband, Brad, who was busy dissecting his arugula. It's not enough to mention where you attended college, but also which other prestigious schools accepted you.

"They kept throwing scholarship dollars at me. But Amy Carter was attending Brown at the time and I felt safe knowing there were Secret Service agents on campus."

"That makes good sense," I said, "what with Rhode Island being such a hotbed of crime."

"Renee Schottenfels called me up the other day, *heartbroken*," Bobbie said, ignoring me. "It seems her youngest has absolutely no interest in going to grad school."

Krinkie and Judy tsk-tsked in sympathy.

I started praying that nobody would ask me what grad school I attended. Aside from the subject never even coming up in my family, what was the point? Sears Roebuck signed me up as one of their catalog copywriters without my needing a master's degree. I was totally capable of writing *Save $5 on*

Harvest Gold Toasters without requiring additional education. But at the moment I regretted that all I had was a B.S. Who wants letters like that after their name?

Bobbie sighed as she daintily pushed her salad greens around on her plate, not actually eating them. "I hope Renee can talk some sense into him."

I contemplated quietly shoving my elbow into Randy's ribs, signaling him: *I'll give you all the sex you want in exchange for pretending you have stomach flu so we can leave.*

But instead I reminded myself that thanks to Randy, I did have *some* academic credibility. Thanks to Randy I had a Harvard-degree-through-marriage.

Randy's academic history was typical of its time: College. College dropout. Two years spent wearing unwashed jeans, hitch-hiking around the country, and living on Mexican communes. Followed by resuming college and, in his case, wangling his way into Harvard.

I'm still not quite certain how he made the transition from flower child to Harvard grad, but after insisting on seeing the diploma, I know it's true. Plus he's a member of the Harvard Club, which is impossible to join without first attending Harvard.

The club is on Forty-Fourth Street between Fifth and Sixth Avenues, one block over from the Princeton Club, which nobody from the Harvard Club likes to acknowledge. A giant flag hangs over the front door sporting a big white *H* against the official crimson red backdrop. It helps the Harvard grads locate their club. The front room looks like a corny stage set for a Harvard Club movie: stone fireplace, leather club chairs, wood-paneled walls, and a portrait of FDR.

The week following the dinner party, Randy wanted to hear a lecture on "Frederick Law Olmsted's Central Park: The Lungs of the City." Randy's a big fan of bushes and dirt, probably because as a New Yorker he'll never own any.

We arranged to meet at the club after work. I arrived first and sat in the front room waiting for Randy, scared silly somebody would pull me over to frisk me and check my identification. *Imposter! Wannabe!* they'd accuse.

I couldn't wait in the bar and order a drink because I didn't have signing privileges. Signing privileges start with forty thousand dollars a year in tuition. Instead I swiped some free pretzels and checked out Harvard memorabilia, T-shirts, pennants, key chains, all with the white Harvard *H* and all under lock and key in a big glass case. As soon as Randy walked in, his overcoat draped over one arm, a briefcase in the opposite hand, he leaned over and kissed me with proper Harvard decorum. No tongue. I pointed to the glass case and asked, "Hey, how come you guys don't have a mascot? All you've got are these giant *H*'s plastered all over everything."

"We're the Harvard Crimson."

"Crimson's not a mascot. It's a color. And not even a normal color."

"So what are you suggesting? We should hire an Indian like Illinois? That's not even politically correct."

"Okay, maybe a football game with a Native American dancing like a madman all over the forty-yard line isn't in the best of taste, but it sure beats just having a color."

Randy must have been upset. His ears turned crimson. "Can we discuss this later?" he said. "I don't want to miss the talk."

The lecture was held in the club's great hall, a two-story-high room with thick tapestries, saggy leather sofas, oil paintings of past Harvard grads, and a stuffed elephant head the size of, well, an elephant, probably shot by Teddy Roosevelt, whose portrait also happens to be hanging in the great hall. Rows of folding chairs had been set up facing a wood podium and a projection screen extended from the ceiling. Randy and I sat on one of the sofas lining the mahogany walls, offering me an ideal opportunity to study Harvard grads. They looked like they went out of their way to dress like intellectuals with their clip-on ties, comb-overs, and ill-fitting sports coats.

"Check out this bunch," I whispered to Randy. "Welcome to the Wonk Parade."

"Excuse me, but I happen to be one of these wonks," he whispered back.

"Present company excluded."

The lecture lasted about an hour; a man from the park conservatory showed slides and talked about Olmsted's visionary genius. Then the question-and-answer part of the evening began. The questions always seem to be posed by people whose true subtext is: *I'm smart! I'm smart!* The more complicated and incomprehensible the question is, the smarter the person must be. *"I recently read Olmsted's 1850 monograph on public gardens in England and was struck by his keen observations regarding social class. How do his interpretations juxtapose against yet still embody the purity and designs of Calvert Vaux's architectural ideals?"*

Of course, it would have been bad form to roll my eyes because I was the one person in the room who did not attend Harvard, which may explain why I'm capable of composing a simple one-sentence question like: *"What the hell are you talking about?"*

Two nights later, Randy was standing at the kitchen counter shuffling through the mail, sorting it into the usual piles: bills; magazines; catalogs; and the-mailman-stuck-this-in-the-wrong-box. Randy always retrieves the mail, that's his job, and in return he retains the privilege of being first to look through it.

"Something for you," he said, handing me a white envelope with my name and address stamped in black ink. I read the return address and ripped the letter open.

"It's from the University of Illinois asking for a donation," I said. "Apparently those money-grubbers don't think the three hundred and sixty-five dollars I coughed up for tuition every semester was enough. I don't even know how they tracked me down across state lines."

I was feeling in a sentimental mood, though, and promptly wrote a check. I attached a note that read: *Kindly use these funds for PR.*

Then I signed it—Linda Yellin, B.S.

LOVE IN THE TIME OF CHOLESTEROL

~~~~~~

The first few weeks of the new century everyone walked around on high alert waiting to see if Nostradamus was right and the entire planet would be smashed to smithereens by a comet, or what Benjamin considered *a good excuse not to do homework*. By February, after everyone had calmed down and written off Nostradamus as a quack, and it had been made clear to Benjamin that, no, he was absolutely not getting out of his seventh-grade book report, my seventy-three-year-old in-laws started planning for the future.

Larry said it was Ruth's idea to sell their house and Ruth said it was Larry's idea but they both agreed it was time to move. The market was hot. They could cash in on their split-level with the backyard that now felt more cumbersome than enjoyable, and the stairs that hurt Larry's knees.

For the past several months Randy's sister had been on a

campaign to get Ruth and Larry into senior housing, orches-
trating their lives from her command headquarters in Oregon.
She'd call them with subtle hints. She'd call us with dire pre-
dictions. "They could both keel over and end up in wheelchairs and then what?" Or "they could both have strokes and
need full-time nursing care and then what?" Just that week
Andrea called and said, "If Dad dies before Mom, she'll be
stuck packing the whole house by herself and then what?"

We called them the *then what* calls. The words became part
of our daily vernacular.

"We better stop at the grocery because we might run out of
eggs and then what?" I said.

"We better buy dog food because someday we might own a
dog and then what?" Randy said.

"We could change our phone to an unlisted number and
hire thugs to strangle your sister and then what?" I said.

Randy took out a map and drew a radius around his parents' house, knowing they'd want to live no farther than twenty
minutes from their doctors, their friends, Ruth's hairdresser.
Ruth spoke with friends who'd already made a transition; she
researched and wrote out lists. Randy made the phone calls
and arranged the appointments with the independent living
centers.

Andrea made us promise to call her with a full report after
every outing, reminding us, like a couple of ninnies, of the
three-hour time difference.

Even on weekends that were officially kids' weekends we'd
drive around New Jersey. Our schedules were open. It took us
a while to notice the shift in the kids' priorities; how they blew

us off for concerts, movies, slumber parties, school dances, sporting activities, and in Phoebe's particular case, a horse. We kept our calendars clear hoping the kids might squeeze us into their plans, bless us with their sought-after companionship. Half the time they no longer slept at our apartment. Staying at their mom's was just *easier*, they said.

Instead we checked out the lifestyles depicted on the shiny brochures that showed up in Ruth and Larry's mailbox on a regular basis. Most of them mailed by Andrea.

The train out to Ruth and Larry's left from Penn Station. Gray, cavernous Penn Station with its creepy fluorescent lighting. If I were Pennsylvania, I would insist New York take my name off the door. The station's big focal point is a colossal sign suspended overhead. I don't know who's running the show up there, but clearly they're having scads of fun. The sign is for listing departure gates, but somehow the gates never get posted until three minutes before departure time, a scenario designed to result in a New York buffalo stampede.

As Randy and I stood among our fellow travelers, the foot tappers, the hand wringers, the hair tuggers, all of us staring upward, afraid to blink and miss a gate, I could just picture those sign managers, sitting at their controls behind a window in some secret upper booth, looking down on the crowd and laughing their asses off.

"C'mon, Lloyd, put it up there."

"Naw, let's make 'em sweat a little more."

"Check out that lady down there in the brown pantsuit juggling the full set of American Tourister. No way she's catching this train!"

"Ha ha ha."

"Ha ha ha."

Ruth and Larry lived in Clark, on the Northeast Corridor line and ten minutes from the Rahway station. The day before at work, I mentioned to Wendy—a copywriter known for her overbleached teeth and free M&M's jar—that I was taking the train to Rahway over the weekend to visit my husband's parents.

"I'm so sorry," she said. "What are they in for?"

Rahway is home to one of New Jersey's state prisons. I explained to Wendy that my in-laws were not felons and that I've never actually visited Rahway prison, but for the rest of the day she looked at me cross-eyed.

Two minutes and forty-one seconds before departure time our gate was posted. Randy and I elbowed and jammed and charged forward, ran a few expert NFL plays, and hurried down the stairs to our platform, rushing onto the train. Finding seats was our next major challenge because even though most of the seats are designed to hold three passengers across, they inevitably end up occupied by one person, a backpack, and some loose Food Town flyers, all spread out in a fashion intended to assert: *I hate sharing*.

We lucked into a totally empty three-across seat. We took the two outer seats and plopped Randy's backpack in the seat between us. We hate sharing, too.

*   *   *

As we stepped off the train onto the open platform, the February air felt brisk but not miserable. After Chicago, nothing was miserable. We walked downstairs rather than wait for the elevator. The red Chevy van was parked across the street from the station. As soon as they spotted us, Ruth and Larry nodded and waved like two little bobbleheads; they opened their doors and climbed out. Ruth was wearing a bright blue down coat with a hood and ankle-high, fur-trimmed galoshes, even though there was no snow on the ground. Larry wore his usual uniform: cuffed pants, plaid shirt, an unbuttoned fleece-lined jacket.

After exchanging kisses and keys, Larry slid open the van's side door; Ruth and he moved to the backseat, first Ruth, then Larry, following behind her and squeezing her puffy down behind.

Randy drove. He always drives when we're with his parents. Larry and Ruth sit in back so they can backseat drive, telling their son who grew up in New Jersey where to turn left and where to turn right and when to slow down and when to speed up and be sure to watch out for that eighteen-wheeler.

New Jersey's just one big maze to me. I never have an opinion on which way to turn. In between direction giving, Ruth read from her brochures. "This one says they have five acres with walking trails. Randy, honey, signal left."

"Left, unless you want to take the shortcut," Larry said.

"Larry, there's no shortcut."

"I know where we are. I don't need help," Randy said.

"Take the shortcut," Larry said.

"Larry, there's no shortcut."

"Tell me about the walking trails," I said, twisting toward my mother-in-law as the seat belt cut across my neck.

"That's all they mention. Just that they have them. Andrea recommended this place."

"Andrea lives three thousand miles away," Randy said, turning left. "What does she know?" I detected some younger brother–older buttinsky sister resentment.

"I don't want any place where all you do is sit around and wait to die all day," Larry said.

So far every place we'd visited was either too small, too dark, too dull, or too expensive.

"Nobody's dying, Larry," Ruth said, patting his hand.

Randy turned off the parkway as he read aloud the name of the exit: "Pleasant Valley Way."

"Sounds like a good name for a cemetery," Larry said.

I was beginning to suspect that Larry was not as enthused about changing residences as we thought.

We drove another ten minutes and after passing every square, flat, boring franchise store in America, Randy turned into a driveway lined with evergreens. The driveway continued around a parking area until he stopped in front of a long white clapboard building with red awnings, a broad staircase, and a covered veranda. The *Gone with the Wind* version of independent living facilities.

"Hoity-toity," Larry said, peering out the car window. I wasn't sure if he meant that as a good thing or a bad thing.

"I'll park," Randy said. "You three wait for me inside."

I loved how he respected his parents, listened to them, but as they got older and more vulnerable, he guided them with a, well—*parental*—hand.

Larry helped Ruth out of the car, patted her chest, and closed the van door.

"I hate the cold," Ruth said.

"We could move to Florida," he said.

"I hate Florida," she said. Larry held her elbow as they started up the stairs. I followed. "All those old men walking around shirtless exposing their hairy chests and surgery scars."

"Too bad the women aren't topless," Larry said.

"If you want to spend your days boiling in the sun looking at eighty-year-old breasts, suit yourself."

"I love *your* breasts," he said.

"Larry," she said.

"Ewww," I said.

Randy bounded up the steps, past the three of us and onto the landing, throwing open the double oak entrance doors. "Show-off," I whispered to him as we walked into a large lobby area with dark green carpeting, flowered curtains, wing chairs, and a grand piano. Randy headed over to a reception desk where a young man with a shaved head was watching a hockey game on a small portable television. Ruth and Larry and I studied the surroundings. The two of them held hands. According to the photos in the brochure, the residents could not be any busier, healthier, or happier, or more unlike all the people we saw snoozing in wheelchairs. The place smelled like detergent.

Randy returned with a woman who introduced herself as Chrissy, a tall, wide-shouldered blonde wearing a beige wrap dress and gym shoes. It was difficult to tell how old Chrissy was; my mother would say she was a woman of *indeterminate age,* somewhere between forty and a really good plastic surgeon.

Chrissy pumped all our hands enthusiastically, asked all our names, and then proceeded to call Ruth and Larry Mom and Dad, which seemed to please them and made me cringe. "Let's go!" she said, calling out hellos along the way to various aides and residents, even the sleeping ones. Chrissy was the sort of person I'd politely describe as a bundle of energy, or impolitely as *somebody's been dipping into the uppers at the meds station.*

Her questions were all rhetorical. Isn't this library cozy? Aren't these silk ferns precious? Don't you just adore the hand-rail moldings?

The dining room was painted bright pink ("Didn't we just love it?"), the round tables covered with canary-yellow table-cloths and rose-colored napkins. Cheery gone crazy. We all leaned in to read the day's menu posted on a gilt-framed bulle-tin board. Chrissy clasped her hands to her heart. "Homemade croutons," she said.

"Yesterday's stale bread," Larry said.

Chrissy led us through the arts and crafts room and pointed out watercolors and clay ashtrays and paper gum-wrapper chains. A row of cigar boxes filled with soil and little sprouts constituted the garden club. Chrissy told us about the weekly laundry and housekeeping service and showed us the on-site beauty salon and the empty exercise room. She spoke in eu-phemisms: *Memory challenges. Reminiscence care.*

She said, "You'll be pleased to know there are quite a few couples here, Mom and Dad."

"Any single men?" I asked.

"Why?" Randy asked.

"I'm curious whether the women fight over them."

In the sample "couple's suite"—a living area barely large enough for two walkers, a bedroom barely big enough for a double bed, kitchenette with half-size refrigerator, microwave, and minibar-sized sink—I saw the color drain out of my in-laws' faces.

"We can go to my office now and I'll show you the price sheet," Chrissy said.

"Perhaps another time," Ruth said.

"Mail it to us," Larry said.

"Not even a stove. Not even a full refrigerator," Ruth said after we'd all piled back into the Chevy. "I hated it."

"We have two more appointments," Randy said.

"No more looking. No more places."

"Let's go eat," Larry said.

Over burgers at the Livingston Diner, they discussed waiting at least another year to move.

"That might not be possible," Randy said, watching Ruth wipe some ketchup off Larry's shirt.

Ruth said they could hire a gardener.

Larry said he'd take extra aspirin if his knees hurt.

"Maybe we'll get one of those chairs that ride up and down the banister," Ruth said.

Larry elbowed her and winked with a lascivious grin. "That'd be a new one."

"Oh, Larry, shut up," she said. Then giggled.

When we drove back to the Rahway train station and once again exchanged kisses and keys, they stood outside the van in the frigid air, holding hands, a united front, until we waved one last good-bye and headed up the stairs to the platform.

Randy was in the kitchen talking on the telephone. I was sitting in bed, pillows scrunched against the headboard, flipping through a *CosmoGirl* I'd found in Phoebe's room, but not paying attention, not focusing, too busy thinking about growing old, being forced into changes, feeling guilty that I was away from my parents, spending time with Randy's parents while *my* parents were aging, my parents might need me, my parents would one day die.

Ruth and Larry had been together since they were teenagers, meeting right before Larry was shipped off to France during World War II. Ruth saved the letters they'd exchanged; she kept them tucked away in her lingerie drawer tied with a silk ribbon.

"Do you ever reread them?" I once asked.

"Of course," she said. "All the time."

Randy worried how either would survive the loss of the other. You hear about couples who don't; how they're too intertwined, too codependent. Within six months of one death, the other dies, too.

Do coroners have a box they check for cause of death: HEARTBREAK?

When Teddy died I hated being the one left behind. I wasn't good at grief and anguish.

My cousin J.E., a woman who travels through life with two initials instead of one name, advised me to view his death as a growth experience.

I wanted to physically harm her.

"You'll move on," she said.

"What if I don't want to move on?" What I meant was: what if I *can't?*

"Linda," she said, "you have no choice."

This time I want to go first. I'm scared of dying, *terrified* of eternal nothingness, relatives in tunnels, coming back as somebody else. All of it sounds hideous. But any option feels more bearable than imagining myself alone, without Randy. He's stronger. He'll manage. He'll do fine. Women will be crawling all over him at my funeral offering him tuna noodle casseroles and theater tickets.

And of course, he'll have his children.

Phoebe and Benjamin. Calls and visits. Care and concern.

But me?

If I'd stayed in Chicago, cultivated *my* blood relations, been more of a presence than a voice on a telephone or a birthday gift that shows up in the mail, maybe I wouldn't feel haunted by the prospect of dying alone.

If I hadn't put childbearing on hold, waiting for the right marriage, the right circumstances, the right time, waiting myself right out of my reproductive years, maybe I'd have given birth to my own children, whom I could've raised to love me enough or at least feel obligated enough to oversee my last years with a modicum of tenderness.

But no, I opted for throwing myself at the mercy of practical *strangers.*

I'd end up rocking away with my untweezed brows and fuzzy upper lip, ungroomed, unloved, with no visitors at all.

Who's going to care about me? Worry about me? Who's going to wipe *my* butt? By the time I hit seventy, my nieces and nephews in Chicago won't even remember me. They probably barely remembered me now.

Did Phoebe and Benjamin like me well enough that they'd look me up for old times' sake? Maybe send me a postcard on my birthday that I could read through my cataracts? Or would they just count the minutes until I died so they could lop off the top of the QTIP trust, money that should've been *theirs theirs theirs* that the old driveling stepmother was using *up up up,* damn her. They could wreak their revenge for all the times I said get your shoes off the sofa or don't leave dishes in the sink.

Okay. I was feeling sorry for myself. They weren't heartless kids. They were just busy kids whom I'm sure would be even busier adults. If they couldn't make time to visit us on weekends now, how would they possibly make time to visit a nursing home later?

I could picture myself lying in a semiconscious haze, unable to speak, incapable of lifting my head in protest as I overheard the bedside chatter.

Benjamin: Doctor, is it too soon to pull the plug?

Doctor: There is no plug.

Phoebe: We're double-parked.

I vowed to phone my parents first thing in the morning. I also vowed to be nicer to Phoebe and Benjamin.

"I called the kids," Randy said when he walked into the bedroom. He looked all hairy-muscular-adorable in a white undershirt and red briefs. "They'll grace us with their company at dinner tomorrow night." I could tell he was pleased. "Phoebe wants Italian."

Randy climbed into bed, leaned over, and kissed me.

I asked, "How'd it go with your sister?"

"I told her they want to wait another year."

"What did she say?"

"She said: *then what?* I said we'd figure it out then."

I rearranged my pillows, set the magazine aside, and said, "Honey, wouldn't it be romantic if we die together?"

"Like in a fiery plane crash?"

"No. Like Romeo and Juliet."

He looked perplexed. "*Poison* ourselves?"

"Not quite like that. Something gentler. Like we both die in our sleep on the same night."

"That sounds like an excellent plan," he said. "Does it have to be tonight?"

"No. Of course, not."

"Great." He reached up and turned off the light. "See you in the morning."

THE BIG OH-FOUR

~~~~~~

In spring, unable to look at one more plastic toy without the urge to smash it, I changed jobs. The new agency specialized in financial clients: banks, insurance companies, brokerage houses. I might as well have been writing copy in hieroglyphics. I kept making secret calls to Randy's office, whispering questions into the phone. *What's a corporate spread duration? What's an accrued market discount?* I had no business accepting the job, but the day rate was good and the workday was short; the agency kept *bankers' hours*, the one financial term I understood.

Standing outside the agency's glass and steel office building, breathing in the scent of candied nuts roasting on a sidewalk cart, I thanked the gods above that I'd survived another day of speaking in tongues. The air was too light and the sky too sunny to descend into a dark subway for my commute home. I decided to live in the moment and walk.

The walk turned into a wander up Sixth Avenue and through Central Park with its Rollerbladers, soccer players, . Frisbee tossers, benchwarmers, and stroller-pushing nannies, everyone emitting a combustive joy. I emerged from the park at Seventy-Second Street and Central Park West, passed the spot where John Lennon was assassinated and the barbecue restaurant where three months earlier I'd stained my shirt. The day was gorgeous. The world was happy. I was heading home to my man.

I wandered into a Gap store on Broadway and ended up chatting with the woman sharing my three-way mirror, both of us examining our butts in the jeans we were trying. She said I looked great in mine and I said she looked great in hers but neither of us ended up buying the jeans because we both looked fat. Then I stopped at the drugstore to purchase fade cream for a brown spot on my hand and poked around trying on reading glasses, an activity I abandoned when I realized I needed stronger ones than my last pair. By the time I got home I felt fat, old, and blind.

Randy was standing over the kitchen sink shining wingtips, rubbing black polish on them until they gleamed. "Hi, beautiful," he said. "You're late. Everything okay?" I kisssed him hello. "Have you been thinking about where you want to celebrate our anniversary tomorrow?"

"Tomorrow?" I said.

"Yes. I'm excited. Four years and counting."

He was excited. He slipped a shoe on one hand and held it out for inspection. I pointed to a spot he'd missed.

"I set up a reservation at Aureole but we can go anywhere you want," he said.

"Aureole tomorrow? Don't you think it's a little, you know, *soon* to go back there?"

"Not if you like it," he said.

We had dined at Aureole to celebrate our third anniversary. One does not eat at Aureole; one *dines*. The Zagat restaurant guide described Aureole as an American "treasure." I think they meant to say: *Stop at the U.S. Treasury Department before you arrive if you plan on paying your bill.*

I picked up the other wingtip and a cloth and helped rub.

For our second anniversary Randy took me to the Gotham Bar and Grill, where all the food comes out tall. No matter what you order, it's served in a pile.

"What is this?" I asked, staring down at my plate.

"A tower of Swiss chard, crisp potatoes, wild onions, and sliced filet," Randy said.

He was right. That's what I'd ordered. I studied my stack of filet. "What's the point of this?"

Growing up in Chicago, my family didn't frequent fancy restaurants. We'd go out for dinner and two minutes after we placed our order my father would bark, "Why's it taking them so long?"

"Be patient, Bernie," my mother would say. "We just ordered. They need time to cook the food."

"How long's it take to fry some chop suey?" He'd wait another fifteen seconds, then push back his chair, dropping his napkin on the table as he stood up. My dad was an imposing man, formidable in his height. He'd announce, "I'll get to the bottom of this."

"There's no bottom, Bernie. They're cooking. Sit down. You're not at the office." My mother would shoot a helpless look across the room toward our waiter as my dad headed off to the kitchen, the double swinging doors banging behind him. He'd return from the kitchen, a big satisfied smile on his face.

"The food'll be right out." He'd sit down, tucking his napkin back into his shirt collar, while my mother mumbled, "Well, here's one more place in town I can never show my face again."

Most nights Randy and I ordered in. The fastest telephone conversations on earth take place when ordering from Ollie's on Broadway. I wish they'd open a franchise in Florida for my father. The Ollie's lady answers the telephone in her I've-only-been-in-this-country-two-days English and immediately snaps: "Phone number!"

You rattle it back and before you can finish spitting it out she's blurting your address out of her computer. Then demands: "Order!"

You tell her the items, then she rapid-fires them back at you and says: "Cash or charge?"

"Charge."

"Last four digits!" (She doesn't even take time for *all* the digits.) "Bring your card to the door," she instructs as she slams down the phone, at which point your bell immediately rings and the delivery guy is waiting downstairs.

"Choose whatever restaurant you like," Randy said. "If not, I'll pick something special." I could see he was already contemplating options. He had that same intense look on his face that he gets when he's standing in a drugstore aisle going back and forth between Crest Regular and Crest Extra Whitening.

We each set our wingtip down to dry, side by side.

Randy began to clean his shoe brushes with the rag he used to clean his shoes. "Oh! I forgot!" he said. "Claudia called. She's got a business meeting and a dinner in New York on Thursday and wants to have lunch with you. I told her you'd call back."

"When'd she call?"

"Before you got home."

Men are terrible at giving messages.

"Did you have a nice chat?"

The relationship between Randy and Claudia still hovered somewhere between cordial and lukewarm. Claudia had never quite forgiven Randy for being *the man who took me away* and Randy had never quite forgiven Claudia for not forgiving him. I'd feel caught between my loyalty to him and my history with her.

"It wasn't a long conversation. More on the order of *Hi, how are ya? Is she home? She's not? Okay. Have her call me.*"

Of course, I'm the only one who realized they weren't close friends. They each thought they got along great.

Claudia answered the telephone after two rings.

"Where've you been?" she asked. "I called an hour ago."

"I've been shining shoes." I walked around the living room with the telephone in one hand and a dust rag in the other, wiping around the lamps and books on the end tables; more of an attempt at dusting than actual dusting. "I hear you'll be gracing our fine city."

"Thursday. I have to convince the national sales manager

that I'm a genius, take a muckety-muck to dinner, and see your shiny face." I could hear Claudia striking a match and her long inhale. She rattled off questions and news. *How's your weather? I cut my hair. They raised my rent. Where's someplace good to take the muckety-muck? Will I need a heavy coat?*

She can switch subjects within a nanosecond but I always manage to track her. I think that's why she loves me. "It's warm. Light coat. I'll get my Zagat's." I dropped the dust rag on the sofa and carried the phone back to the kitchen.

The Zagat was in the drawer next to the kitchen sink, the same drawer where we stored takeout menus. Randy had finished cleaning his brushes and was now lining them in orderly fashion inside his official shoe equipment box. He pointed to the menus when I opened the drawer, indicating that he wanted to order dinner. I held up my hand to indicate I'd be off the phone in five minutes, which we both knew was a lie. I blew him a kiss and headed back to the living room sofa.

"What neighborhood? What kind of food?" I asked Claudia.

"Something impressive."

I turned to the index. "How about a restaurant listed under *Cool Loos?*"

"Why would anyone pick a restaurant based on the bathroom?"

"Beats me. I'm just happy if the lady ahead of me remembers to wipe the seat."

"Well, toilets aren't going to impress my client. Are there any listings under *Expensive?*"

By the time Claudia and I finally hung up, Randy was sitting in the chair across from me. Pouting.

I hurried over to kiss him and apologize. "I'm sorry, honey. We'll call Ollie's right away."

Five minutes later the doorbell rang.

Claudia's meetings were taking place at the New York headquarters of the radio network she worked for as a Midwest sales rep. Her job was to convince advertisers to spend money running radio spots on her stations instead of buying print ads in newspapers, commercials on television, or handing out balloons on street corners.

I was recording a radio commercial at a studio a few blocks away. Something I wrote about something called fixed annuities.

We planned to meet halfway to share a cab to the East Side except that somehow my halfway was four blocks and Claudia's halfway was two blocks so I was late. I was also late because my voice-over talent kept tripping over the phrase "accelerated death benefits."

Claudia was waiting on our prearranged street corner, smoking a cigarette, when I arrived. She looked wonderful in a shiny gray trench coat, her blond hair shorter than I'd seen it before, kind of a sexy Joan of Arc cut. She was wearing her usual four-inch high heels—this time black patent pumps with gold pilgrim buckles. She always wore high heels to compensate for basically being shorter than a fire hydrant.

After we hugged and air-kissed and Claudia swore that I never looked better and I swore that she never looked taller, we hailed a cab. Claudia wanted sushi at Hatsuhana. Chicago also has a Hatsuhana but Claudia prefers the New York Hatsuhana. She's on expense account.

The cab got as far as two blocks east and stalled in traffic. Our driver sat face forward bobbing his head to some private concert of the mind. A green cardboard pine tree dangled from the rearview mirror. The taxi smelled of pine-scented french fries. All around us horns were bleating and drivers rolled down windows to curse.

"I can't believe I've lived here four years," I said.

Claudia made dagger-eyes at the back of a FedEx truck blocking our lane. A bicycle messenger zipped by her side of the cab, almost clipping the door. "Ever consider moving to New Jersey?"

"There's traffic in New Jersey. They've got traffic. Their tomatoes are good and they've got a Six Flags Great Adventure park, but New York's better."

"That was a rhetorical question," Claudia said.

"Oh."

The taxi moved forward. Two feet. Our driver emerged from his personal revelry long enough to slam the horn with the heel of his hand. Other drivers joined the fun. Peer pressure. Claudia rummaged through her handbag and produced a cigarette pack. I pointed to the NO SMOKING sign mounted five inches in front of us. The cigarettes went back into her bag.

"Looks like I'm living here for the long haul," I said. "I goeth where my man goeth."

Claudia groaned, as if to say don't bore me with your romantic crap. This from a woman who's described her boyfriends' penises to me in all their purple hairy detail.

Even though we talked on the phone all the time, in-person reunions often started out feeling awkward. We needed a warm-up period to get back in stride. I used to share every detail of my life with Claudia and now most of my confidences were shared with Randy. You can't be married to a man and reporting the intimate details of your life to a girlfriend, so as much as we adored each other, the distance between Claudia and me had grown wider than a plane ride.

"How is he?" she asked.

I don't think she was aware how rarely she referred to Randy by name. Usually he was He or Him.

"Great," I said.

Claudia wanted me to be happy. She just wanted me to be happy in Chicago.

Our cab inched ahead. I don't know why drivers do that—*inch*.

Claudia started eyeing her purse again. Ten minutes without a cigarette and she goes into withdrawal.

"How about we walk?" I said. "We can window-shop on my favorite street."

Claudia looked down at her four-inch heels and up at the dangling pine tree and out at the angry traffic, then looked at me and nodded. I paid the driver along with enough of a tip to hopefully make up for the fact that *he* was still stuck in the cab, and we escaped into fresh spring air. If you didn't count the car exhaust.

Chicago has a building dedicated to selling diamonds. New York has a *district* with a gateway of two soaring helixes capped by gigantic fake diamonds. Someday I want to meet the committee that came up with such a stellar tribute to tacky. But giant fake diamonds aside, I like to walk down Forty-Seventh Street and look in the windows. I play a game where I can select one free item out of each display. By the time I walk from one end of the street to the other I've lost any desire for diamonds. This game has saved Randy a great deal of money. Every human in New York—except, for some reason, Randy—is best friends with a diamond dealer who sells the finest-quality wholesale stones. And everyone claims that their dealer is the one dealer who supplies diamonds to Tiffany's.

"Check out these engagement rings," Claudia said, her face against a window. She won't ride a subway but she'll lean her personal flesh against a public piece of glass. "Is all this junk real?" Rows of sparkling stones in blue velvet-lined trays rested on billowing folds of white satin.

"Yeah. That's why the street's lined with trucks. They look like normal delivery trucks but they're really security trucks. Guards with guns hide inside to ward off heists." It pleased me to be the New York expert.

"Bullshit," Claudia said. She moved on to the next window, digging into her handbag to pull out a fresh cigarette. In the past year she'd switched to smoking menthols, not because she liked menthols, but because it cut down on the number of moochers bumming free cigarettes. "Well, I sure won't be needing any engagement rings soon." She lit a match and updated me on her latest boyfriend. They'd met at the Chicago Council on Foreign Relations after a lecture on the international trade legacy of Richard Nixon, a man Claudia still referred to as President Scum of the Earth. Dave shared her anti-Nixon sentiments and within days was sharing her bed.

"So you don't see Dave as long-term material?"

"Not at all."

Claudia moved to the next window. I followed.

"Dave can be kind of critical," she said, avoiding eye contact with me. "*Comb your hair. Your feet are cold. Your cooking sucks.* We fight a lot."

Commenting on other women's relationships has always felt dicey for me —even with Claudia. I never know when to scream *Red flag!* and when to keep my trap shut. I figure if you tell a friend she's dating a jerk, don't expect to be a bridesmaid if she marries the jerk. Then again, couldn't at least one of Eva Braun's girlfriends have sat her down and said, "Eva, sweetheart—trust me. You can do better."

Claudia sucked on her cigarette. "What can I say? I picked a nitpicker."

"Why would you tolerate criticism? Who needs critical?"

"Aw—I don't pay attention to half the things he says and after we argue we make up." Claudia favored me with a meaningful wink.

"So let me get this straight," I said. "You're one of those fight-and-make-up-with-hot-sex couples?"

She said, "Who needs diamonds?"

At Hatsuhana, we deliberated between sitting at the sushi bar or a table and opted for a table. Claudia said it'd be better for talking *privately*—which meant I was probably going to hear a description of Dave's penis.

I studied the menu, mentally comparing the photographs

to things I remembered from my high school science dissection class. Just as we were about to order, a man sitting two tables over with either an overdressed wife or his dolled-up mistress called for the waiter's attention. Suddenly the waiter was taking *their* order.

"Excellent sense of entitlement," Claudia said. "How do you develop one of those?"

When it was our turn again, we each ordered a Box of Dreams because the menu promised *"a culinary and visual marvel that is sure to please the senses."* It turned out to be nine miniature bowls filled with rice and mysterious fish products. I swapped my ugly Spanish mackerel and creepy-looking sea eel for Claudia's egg omelet and cooked shrimp. She's always been more adventurous when it comes to men and fish.

"This is a very nice culinary and visual marvel," I said.

"It's certainly pleasing my senses," Claudia said, plucking a bite of ginger with her chopsticks. "We should order sake to toast your four years here."

"Sake? Don't you have an important meeting after this?"

Claudia poured us each a cup of green tea from the little iron teapot on our table. The only weaker toast possible would have been water.

"To Linda," she said as she lifted her teacup. "My girl's no quitter."

I was touched. Surprisingly touched. Claudia knew the pre-Randy me; the inept, bad-judgment, often disastrous me. She knew about the good relationships I screwed up, the bad relationships I stayed in too long, the depression and self-recrimination after Teddy died.

It was Claudia who insisted I break up with a guy after I told her that he asked me to keep silent in bed—so I wouldn't interrupt his sexual fantasies. And it was Claudia who made me cocoa and wrapped her arm around my shoulder the night I suffered a low self-esteem meltdown, after failing to convince an aloof but alluring man that I was worth loving. Claudia remembered things about me that I wanted to forget, like how I wasn't brave, that love scared me, how I actually did consider myself the cut-and-run type. If it weren't for Randy being Randy, I'd have probably hopped on the first Greyhound bus out of Manhattan two weeks after I arrived. Quitting was in my nature. Few people knew that. Maybe not even Randy. But Claudia did. She was my touchstone and would probably be there up until the time I needed a tombstone.

We sipped our tea and shared a plate of orange slices. Claudia signaled for the check. She didn't want to be late for her meeting and I needed to make an appearance at the ad agency.

"Do you think I've changed since I've moved here?" I asked.

"Yes. You pluck your eyebrows and dress like Edith Piaf." Claudia set down her corporate credit card. "And you're happier." Claudia grinned. "You did good, New Yorker. It's good that you married him."

I was touched. I'd underestimated Claudia. She understood more than I'd realized. Randy and she would be fine. Even though she still called him Him.

That night in bed Randy asked if I'd had a nice visit with Claudia. He said he was surprised she didn't stay for the weekend.

My head was resting on his shoulder, affording me a bird's-eye view of his chest hair.

"She had to go home and fight with her new boyfriend," I said. "It's foreplay." I propped myself up on one elbow for a bird's-eye view of Randy's face. "You don't mind when I'm on the phone with her so much, do you?"

He trailed his fingertip around my breasts. "Sometimes. Just a little. Because I want to be with you. But she's important to you, too. I know that."

I ran my fingers along his arm.

"If Aureole's out, tell me where you want dinner tomorrow night," he said.

I rolled on top of my husband. "Surprise me."

Friday morning I woke to discover a blue velvet box next to my toothbrush; inside was a pair of delicate diamond earrings purchased at a dealer on my favorite street. Randy said he went there because he heard the dealer supplied Tiffany's diamonds.

That afternoon Randy called me at work and gave me the address of where we'd celebrate our first four years of marriage. His choice was perfect. The weather was warm enough to sit at a sidewalk table right in front of the deli. We were surrounded by noise, dirt, and car fumes. I didn't tell him it wasn't our anniversary, that it was the anniversary of his marriage to Susan. Our anniversary was three weeks later. I'd mention his mistake then, and maybe score another corned beef sandwich.

STEP STEP SLIDE TOGETHER

Benjamin's feet exploded. Every week the kid needed new sneakers, which was what Randy and he were doing—out shopping for shoes again—when I walked into our kitchen on a Tuesday night and found Phoebe slumped over the table. Weeping and howling, shaking and sobbing.

I scared the bejeezus out of both of us when I screamed, *"Ohmygod Phoebe, what's wrong!"*

She stopped crying long enough to sit up and frown at me with the scornful disapproval only a teenager can bestow: What's wrong with *you*?

Apparently the grown-up isn't supposed to sound like she's shifted into immediate panic mode.

"Are you okay?" I asked.

She spoke through her tears, saying three of the most painful words in any woman's life: "He dumped me."

Three months earlier Phoebe had replaced her love of Jazmine the horse with Brian the stud. For the past three months Phoebe—and hence all other human beings within her orbit—had lived, breathed, and experienced the magic of Brian. Three months of her ignoring her family and grades because she was too busy hanging out with Brian or talking on the phone with Brian or off with her girlfriends discussing Brian. Your basic high school nightmare.

He was a confident boy. He shook hands like a businessman. Walked with a lanky stride. He reduced everyone's name to a diminutive. Phoebe was Phee. Randy was Ran. I was Lin. I don't know when kids started calling grown-ups by their first names but this kid didn't bother with more than first syllables.

His full name was Brian Robinson the *Third*. Evidently there were two more of him running around. Phoebe had transferred to a coed school for high school (that all-girl thing having worn extremely thin) and she met Brian in algebra. He was Student Council president, captain of the football team, number one in the National Honor Society, had won the Pulitzer, a Peabody, the Nobel Peace Prize, spoke eleven languages, could multiply up to eight digits in his head, and was so handsome women chased him down the street and begged for his sperm.

Okay, I might not have some of the details correct, but I am positive that they met in algebra and Phoebe was crazy about him. Crazy miserable with her face buried in her hands, her shoulders shuddering with each convulsive sob.

I pulled out a chair and sat next to her. I wished there was a Heimlich maneuver that removed pain. I debated how to help without feeling I was overstepping boundaries, or worse, patronizing her. I handed her a napkin to wipe her face.

"He told me I was too good for him, that I deserved better, that he really cared about me and would miss me every day of his life, but someone as special as me made him feel inadequate and we should break up."

I'd always wondered at what age guys started serving up that crap.

"Phoebe, honey," I said, "do you want to talk about it?"

She scowled at me. "I *am* talking about it."

"Well, he sounds like a jerk."

"No he's not!" she howled, back in full force with the tears.

I wasn't too hot at this teenage broken heart business. My first boyfriend sat in front of me in high school study hall. His name was Alan Wynkoop. (We sat in alphabetical order.) Alan had a head shaped like a lightbulb, longish brown curly hair, and silver wire-rim glasses that wrapped around the back of his sweet little ears. That was the view of Alan I saw the most. We passed notes back and forth below our desktops. Alan gave me his school ring to wear. I went home and showed it to my parents. My father made me give it back the next day.

"Do you think he'll change his mind?" Phoebe suddenly asked, peeking out between her splayed fingers.

I'm sure Claudia would have said, *Of course not!* But I was talking to a fifteen-year-old about her first-ever real boyfriend. Was I supposed to tell the truth? Randy's biggest priority with raising his children was: Never crush their spirits.

Way before any theories about how television could rot your brains and lower your IQ, my parents placed no restrictions on the number of hours I planted myself in front of our TV. My favorite show of all my favorites was *Sky King*. The star was Sky King. I don't remember if that was his name because he was the king of the sky or if his first name was Sky and his last name was Mr. King, but I do remember that his niece Penny never got to do squat. Some sky crisis would occur and the sky king would hurry off to his airplane and *every single time* Penny would perkily ask, "Can I come, too, Uncle Sky?" and *every single time* Uncle Sky answered: "No, Penny, you wait by the radio."

That poor girl never went anywhere. I often wonder what happened to Penny when she grew up, but I bet she ran off with the first airline pilot she met to escape from Uncle Sky crushing her spirit. The last thing I wanted was to discourage Phoebe and be a spirit crusher. What would Randy say? What would Susan say? What would Dr. Phil say? Why'd Brian the Third have to break up on a Tuesday night while Randy was out shopping for sneakers?

The kids had taken to hanging out at our place on Tuesday and Thursday nights instead of Randy going to their mom's, so I saw them more often. Sometimes they stuck around to do their homework; often they'd go home to study, but we'd eat dinner together discussing pop quizzes and unsympathetic teachers and lousy cafeteria food. The last time I ate meals like that I was the one going to school and taking pop quizzes. I tried to remember what it felt like to be a teenager, which wasn't as difficult as one might think. I feel decades younger in my head; the truth can hit me like a jolt, the sudden realization that I'm *how old?*—followed by *when did that happen!*

Leslie in Chicago always said that until your parents die a part of you always feels like a kid; and after that, a smaller part still feels like a kid, only one who's been orphaned. Talking with Phoebe made me feel grown-up in a way all the other grown-up parts of my life—corporate jobs, personal charge accounts, an address book filled with the names of my lawyer, my accountant, my podiatrist—did not. The parent role, even the once-removed stepparent role, humbled me.

Phoebe's tears had downgraded to sniffles, a blessing because at the rate she was going she'd need an IV to ward off dehydration. While she sniffled, I whipped through platitudes in my head. *It's not the end of the world. It hurts less with time. When a door closes a window opens;* things I'd learned the hard way.

I'd heard them all after Teddy's death and like any grief-crazy woman I dismissed them as so much rubbish. But they had indeed proven true. A window did open. It hurt less with time.

I handed Phoebe another napkin.

"I realize these words might sound hollow today," I said, "but hearts do mend. Time heals all wounds." I laughed. Tried to make her laugh. "And wounds all heels."

She wailed in response.

When my sister Toby was ten years old she had a boyfriend, Howie Netsky. Howie wasn't a real boyfriend, a *boyfriend* boyfriend, because they weren't allowed to date, or talk on the phone past eight-thirty at night, but he was enough of a boyfriend to break up with her for another ten-year-old. Howie wrote Toby a mean letter on crumpled lined paper and stuck it in our mailbox. Devastated, she showed us the letter.

My mother, who'd spent a year teaching fourth grade before giving up her career for marriage and motherhood, read the letter muttering, "Uh-huh. Uh-huh. Hmm." She took out a red pencil from the junk drawer in our kitchen, circled all of Howie's spelling mistakes, handed the letter to Toby, and said: "Now mail it back."

"Did Brian write a note?" I asked Phoebe.

She seemed so distraught. Where was her Phoebe fury? Her sense of revenge? Her inner Count of Monte Cristo?

"I once egged this guy Richie Yochum's Volkswagen after he dumped me," I said. "Of course I waited until it was dark out but then I took a dozen eggs and smashed them all over his windshield and the hood of his car."

Phoebe was paying attention now, which I found gratifying, like I was really getting through to her and helping her feel better, until I realized she was looking at me like I was some weird specimen in a petri dish. "You broke eggs all over some guy's car?" she said.

Perhaps that wasn't the best example I might have chosen while in the parental role but I said, "Yes. Not that I recommend it. I heard later that he thought it was done by street hoodlums, which was lucky because we got back together."

Phoebe brightened. "You got back together?"

"For a week. Long enough for me to buy him a silver key chain for his birthday. Then we broke up again. Getting back together never works because at first you forget why you broke up and then you remember why you broke up so you break up all over again."

The tears kicked in for another round. My fault. I was an idiot at love advice. Claudia never asked me for love advice.

Leslie had never asked me. JoAnn never asked me now. No-body asked me. I was famous for lousy love advice.

"Oh, honey," I said. "I want you to be happy."

If only I could protect her from future heartaches and mis-calculations and making the wrong choices that feel so right at the time; shield her from false starts and false hopes, wish-ful thinking and unfulfilled expectations; men who'd woo her and pursue her and then let her down. Of course along the way she'd break some hearts of her own, followed by lonely nights when she doubted herself and wondered why love came quickly for others but not for her. Until there was finally a matching up of souls and it seemed that every event in her life had led up to this one man, and she realized that if love were any easier, any less fateful—it wouldn't feel like magic.

No, I couldn't spare her the journey. For once, I stopped trying to say the right thing, come up with the perfect step-mom words. I leaned over and wrapped my arms around her. She cried on my shoulder. Enough with stepping on eggshells. They belonged on Richie Yochum's car.

I squeezed her tighter.

When she hugged me back, I thought, maybe, hopefully, after all this time, I'm finally getting this right.

THE WINDING
DOWN PART

~~~~~~~~~~

The Ambassador of New York

～～～

Every other week a bus pulled into town from Pennsylvania or another plane arrived from Chicago and out popped a niece or nephew with a duffel bag.

In Chicago I had a million cousins. For three generations Chicago was the layover point between Russia and the family's eventual landing spot. All the relatives must have used the same travel agent and itinerary:

Today, after an exciting heart-stopping pogrom, we'll pack our bags (quickly) and board a big cruise ship to America. (Steerage class!) After a delightful three-day wait at Ellis Island (influenza shots will be served), enjoy a scenic un-air-conditioned train ride to Union Station in Chicago. There you'll spend several captivating

decades breaking your backs to earn a living and raise
your children—until we all head south to the beaches
of Miami!

Russia. Chicago. Miami. That was it. Except for my sisters
and me. Brenda and her equally religious husband raised their
children in New Wilmington, Pennsylvania, a town that could
make anyone crave the excitement of a pogrom. Toby settled
in Naperville, Illinois, a cornfield disguised as a suburb.

For years I encouraged visits from my sisters' children. Come
vacation with Aunt Linda in New York City. View sites! Talk to
natives! Eat food off sidewalk carts! I was secretly hoping to
imprint their minds, plant seeds of future New Yorkhood.

Brenda's son Neal was first to show up. He attended Yeshiva
University, passing through various stages of religious fervor
until he discovered spareribs and cheeseburgers. First he attended as a biology student. Then he attended as a premed student. After that particular foray lost its charm, he attended as
a prelaw student. The following semester, when he discovered
that Yeshiva U did not offer a pre-stand-up comic major, he
just attended as an I-can't-wait-to-get-out-of-here major, finally
graduating and moving on to a telemarketing job in New Jersey.

His sister Rebecca, who was hired for a job designing
graphics for things that needed graphic designs, followed Neal
to New York.

I felt personally responsible for helping the recent arrivals find
their way. I'd be their beacon of light, their voice of experience.

I asked Rebecca if she'd learned the subway system yet.
She said, "Yes."

"Have you learned the bus system?"

"Yes."

"Do you understand the street grids?"

"Yes."

"Even that tricky part where Broadway and Seventh Avenue cross and everything gets screwed up?"

"Yes."

"How'd you do that? You've lived here—what?—twenty minutes, and you've already got everything figured out? It took me years."

"I read maps."

"Maps?"

"Yes, maps. They're posted all over the city."

"Oh. I see." I chucked her on the upper arm to let her know she was doing an impressive job of assimilating.

Toby's nineteen-year-old son Ethan moved to New York to become a famous musician, and thank goodness for that because New York doesn't have nearly enough musicians. He bid farewell to his Chicago suburban life, enrolled in a New York city college, and met half the population of Brooklyn while interviewing for a roommate, all of whom he looked upon as potential fans. Strangers gave him credit applications. He gave them flyers in return.

Ethan introduced me to the New York club scene, about twenty years too late for me to actually qualify. With a home-produced CD in hand, and his rock-star-in-the-making scrawny build and requisite sneer, he managed to book shows at several downtown clubs. Randy and I, feeling like the chaperones at a high school prom, attended Ethan's performance at CBGB, the famous underground club famously about to go out of business.

CBGB was dark, the walls painted black, and plastered with posters four inches deep going back thirty years. My shoes stuck to the floor. The room smelled like stale beer.

"The Ramones played here!" Ethan said, twisting the pegs on his guitar, all excited as he tuned up for his set.

"Yeah," I said, "I think that's the last time anyone's cleaned this place."

"Be cool," Randy whispered to me.

Another gig took place in the sub-sub-sub-subterranean level of a club called—for no apparent reason—the Knitting Factory.

"What's he going to be playing?" I asked, as Randy and I worked our way down a twisting narrow staircase, plunging deeper into the bowels of the earth, stair by stair, floor by floor. "'Sympathy for the Devil'? We're about to hit oil."

Each level opened onto another cavelike room with a band, presumably a more desirable band than the ones submerged below it. Randy stopped on a landing, pausing to catch his breath. "Have we hit bottom?" he asked a young man sitting at a folding table, collecting money and stamping hands.

"Keep going," the guy said.

"We should have brought oxygen masks," I said.

My favorite sci-fi movie ever as a kid was *Journey to the Center of the Earth*. James Mason, the main star, led an expedition into the earth along with the semi-star, Arlene Dahl—who was dressed in a big skirt and hat, an unfortunate choice considering she was climbing rocks all the time. The expedition also included Pat Boone, a popular singer from Sunday night TV variety shows; and a Swedish guy with a pet duck. There was a bad guy, too, but all I remember about him is that halfway through the journey he got hungry and ate the Swedish guy's duck. Finally James Mason found the center of the earth, where everyone spun around in a makeshift boat and then went home to London to be famous. Trudging down to Ethan's performance, I'm sure Randy and I were only one or two floors above that boat. But much to our amazement—when we finally unburied Ethan—there were actually other people listening to him play. Maybe they were POWs or institutionalized mental patients who'd been locked up below-ground for years, but it was a respectable showing.

Ethan called the next day. Randy and I each picked up a phone extension allowing us both the opportunity to hear Ethan say: "Wasn't that amazing last night! I'm thinking of dropping out of college to tour!"

"Let's hold on here, Mr. Mick Jagger," Randy said. "How much money did you clear last night?"

"Twenty-three dollars! Usually the first time somebody plays there they don't make *anything*."

"Great," Randy said. "I want you to take that twenty-three dollars, pay your landlord, pay your phone bill, gas, food, and electric bills, and then with whatever's left over, hire a manager to book your tour."

Ethan's sister Zoe moved to New York to take fashion courses. She was majoring in How to Pick Out Clothes. I think she was

pissed that she was the only kid left at home to walk the dog
and take out the garbage. Either that or all those *I Love New
York* T-shirts I'd been sending every Christmas finally paid off.
She moved in with Ethan, sleeping on a futon in his cramped
living room. He'd been away from home long enough for them
to both forget that they drove each other nuts.

Zoe's first week as a New York newcomer, I took her to
lunch on Madison Avenue, then window-shopping from Barneys on Sixtieth uptown to Ralph Lauren on Seventy-Second.
That's all she could afford, views of the windows. Zoe would
check out a few mannequins, then scope out the street, study
a clothing display, then study the street.

"Is it really safe around here?" she finally asked, twisting
a strand of her long brown hair. "Mom keeps calling worried
about crime."

"Hey—look around," I said. Zoe turned right, then left. "Do
you see anyone getting mugged?"

"No."

"No murders or kidnappings taking place over my shoulder?"

"No."

"What do you see?"

"Lots of stylish women."

"Right. And they may criticize your shoes, but they'll never
harm you."

Free food for relatives has become a big draw at our home.
Ethan has proven to be more than willing to commute over
an hour from Brooklyn to appear for any meal at any time.

We order in special for Rebecca from one of the Upper West Side's numerous kosher restaurants, all featuring chicken and falafel, and all priced as if the food includes airfare from Israel. Zoe picks at whatever she eats, no matter what it is or where it comes from. Neal angles to take home leftovers.

I love seeing my ever-growing, squeezed-together New York family crowded around our dining room table. I try to pass along my knowledge, my New York savvy, my hard-won comfort zone. Phoebe and Benjamin are now surrounded by cousins they never knew they had, nor wanted, and all of them my potential organ donors.

CLAUDIA CAVES

~~~~~~~~

Claudia met a man online and much to her embarrassment fell in love with him. She flew to New York to shop for a wedding dress.

"What am I going to tell our grandchildren?" she said. We were heading down Seventy-Seventh Street past town houses with imposing staircases and wide doorways, on our way to Madison Avenue. "People are supposed to meet by looking across a crowded room or bumping on sidewalks in the rain. Not over the same computer they use for eBay."

I said, "First off, you're too old to even have children, and if ome miracle—the kind that hasn't taken place since Jesus orn—you *do* have children, you'll be dead long before ow up and have children."

ld happen, you know. A fifty-eight-year-old woman in e birth to twins."

"Great. When you're fifty-eight, move to Russia and sign on with her fertility doctor."

Claudia shifted her tote from one shoulder to the next. She was lugging bridal magazines all over the city. For the last two months I'd get calls at all hours asking my opinion on raspberry sauce versus chocolate, lilies versus stephanotis. She'd unleashed her inner bride. The one element that had apparently been missing from her secret wedding all these years—a groom—turned out to be seven years younger, also a first-timer, and owned a wine store in Lincoln Park. Charlie was in charge of the wine.

Claudia stopped at a sidewalk cart filled with sunglasses and wallets. She modeled a pair of Chanel knockoffs so big they wiped out half her face. I shook my head no. She bought a pink headband instead. Claudia had entered her strawberry period. Her blond hair was now reddish-blond hair. She wore a pink trench coat and bright pink flats. Even her skin tone was pinker; she had stopped smoking since falling in love. She said she had better things to suck on now.

We walked past a doorman standing in front of a ritzy apartment building; the gold-colored epaulets on his uniform matched the gold braiding on his hat. A dog walker exited a brownstone. Three dachshunds. A poodle. A beagle and a boxer.

"Are you going to change your name?" I asked Claudia.

"Too late," she said. "I'm too used to my name. And it's too much paperwork."

I'd been scared to change my name. I kept obsessing over women who'd changed their names, then divorced and changed them back. Farrah Fawcett-Majors back to Farrah Fawcett. Roseanne Barr Arnold back to Roseanne Barr. Me after my first marriage; Teddy's last name back to my maiden name. But I'd found myself regretting that I hadn't taken Randy's name, that I hadn't had enough faith in us, that a part of me expected things to fall apart, to fail. My fear eclipsed the reality of who Randy and I were as a couple; I kept protecting myself long after necessary. Now it felt too late, we'd been married too long, it was too much paperwork. But I turned to Claudia and said, "Maybe you should reconsider."

We waited for the elegant beige-and-gold woman behind the Vera Wang reception desk to hang up the phone. The reception area was small, beige and gold and elegant. Other than a dress in the window, two chairs, and two glass display cases and the desk in front of a spiral staircase—leading to the *exciting* stuff—that was it.

Claudia studied the items in the cases, examining the back-lit satin pumps, the silk gloves buttoned at the wrist, the pearl and rhinestone headpieces. "Check out this sweet little number," she said. "Can you imagine me walking down the aisle with a tiara on my head?"

The receptionist gently replaced the telephone receiver in its cradle, smiled at us, and apologized for not being immediately attentive. She asked our names. "How lovely to meet you," she said, checking a leather-bound appointment book. "And when will the bride be arriving?"

Claudia said, "I'm here."

"Pardon me," the woman said, patting the chest area of her peach silk blouse. "I thought you were the mothers."

"I'm the mother," I said, pointing at me and then at Claudia. "She's the bride."

We were invited to climb the stairs to the inner sanctum, where we were greeted at the top by another beige-and-gold woman, clipboard and silver pen in hand, who introduced herself as Dara-I'll-be-helping-you. After ascertaining once again that Claudia was the bride, Dara asked a few key questions. Sleek? Simple? Sophisticated? She seemed to be making assumptions based on Claudia's age and for the slightest moment blanched when Claudia announced she was looking for something big and poufy.

Dara led us into a mauve-colored room, its four walls lined with white confections. Claudia sucked in the air as if savoring every drop of Vera Wang oxygen. At first Dara presented each gown, relaying details about its exceptional materials and exquisite construction, but somehow Claudia managed to take over, whipping through the racks like she was in the back room at Loehmann's until she hesitated at a gown with petal embroidery, ruffled straps, and a draped tulle skirt. "Oh my," she said. "How much?"

Dara checked a tag. "Eight thousand." She read the number like she was reading *eight dollars.*

"I love it," Claudia said. "I must try it."

Dara showed us to a dressing area with a three-way mirror in front of a low pedestal and a separate dressing room with another mirror and a narrow upholstered bench holding a strapless corset. Beneath the bench two pairs of satin pumps in different sizes also awaited Claudia. Dara excused herself to retrieve and prepare the gown.

"Wow—the Vera Wang equivalent of scuzzy bowling shoes," I said, grimacing at the pumps as soon as Dara left. Claudia gave me a look. I was marring her Vera Wang experience. I volunteered to wait outside on one of the *mother* chairs while she changed. I left as Dara, carrying an armload of a gown, returned and disappeared with Claudia behind a closed door.

Minutes later the dressing room door opened. Somebody resembling Claudia emerged, self-conscious, pink-cheeked, and beaming. Dara led her onto the pedestal and Claudia stood staring at herself in the mirror. "I look more like something that goes on top of the cake than someone who walks down the aisle," she said, admiring her image while talking to my reflection.

"You look beautiful," I said. She did. Absolutely beautiful. In an inappropriate-for-her-age kind of way.

If you're wondering about Claudia's wedding I'm surprised, because from what I could tell, she invited every soul on earth. But maybe you were home sick with the flu that day, so here goes:

The big shebang took place on a Saturday evening in an old downtown Chicago hotel that had recently been redone by a trendy designer and was now a hip downtown hotel—with silver-toned ottomans and beige armless sofas scattered throughout the lobby. But the ballroom still retained its original ornate gold, marble, and pillared splendor including *a glass dance floor that changed colors*. Flower arrangements spewed out everywhere. The room felt as lush as one of those MGM movie musicals where the girl tap-dances down a curved staircase while men in top hats and tuxedos sway back and forth leaning on canes. Only this girl was a middle-aged woman in a long white dress and *tiara*. Charlie's older brother was best man. The *matron* of honor—miserable title, but that'd be me—wore a long yellow sheath, the color of daffodils. A black-robed female judge conducted the ceremony.

Charlie and Claudia walked down the aisle arm in arm. She said that if her beloved father weren't alive to escort her, she'd stick with Charlie. Besides, she added, that way she could make sure he showed up in the right place. I liked Charlie. He was short and wiry with a sweet smile and slightly grayed black curly hair. He looked like the kind of guy who'd play the hero in a boxing movie about welterweights. When pronounced man and wife, the kiss went on for so long that one of the guests called out, "Get a room!" Everyone cheered. Claudia was laughing, glowing, winking at me over Charlie's shoulder.

The reception turned into a high-end bacchanal. Aside from Claudia's nonstop guest list, Charlie had invited associates from his wine business, friends and customers from his wine business, connoisseurs and experts and relatives. The guests didn't drink the wine so much as analyze it. *How do you like this varietal character?* a man asked me at the Asian station while sniffing and swirling his cabernet. *How do you know the bride? Where are you from?* I looked across the room at Randy; he was squatting next to a little boy in a tux; he was helping the ring bearer retie his shoe.

"Chicago," I said. "But New York is home."

*   *   *

Marriage has improved my life in many ways, with one notable exception: I've been demoted to the middle seat on airplanes. In my younger days, I preferred a window seat. I liked to keep an eye out for something the pilot might overlook, like an encroaching mountain range. In time, along with diminishing flexibility for crawling over strangers' knees, I became a fan of aisle seats with their easy access to the bathroom. Then I married Randy, a lifelong window guy, and deferred to his boyish delight at pointing out forest preserves, national monuments, and crop circles. I moved to the seat with no redeeming features and often, should an adjacent passenger be an aggressive man or in Randy's case *forgetful,* no arm room.

I tried to make myself comfortable. A lanky young man in a Budweiser T-shirt settled into the aisle seat and zoned out with his iPod. Randy leafed through the airline magazine. He likes the catalog page with the strange travel items. I eyed the passengers still loading onto the plane, dragging luggage and shopping bags and overstuffed totes down the aisle while assessing the people in the rows they passed. I could see the relief in their eyes when they passed the man whose thighs bulged over his seat edge and the joy at passing the mother with the fussy infant. Seats were found. Overhead compartments were slammed shut. The flight attendant demonstrated how to wear an oxygen mask. Nobody paid attention.

As soon as we were airborne Randy opened one of his espionage paperbacks. He popped in his earbuds and turned on his iPod. Men in iPods surrounded me. I don't listen to music on airplanes. I prefer to keep my ears available in case the pilot has to make an important announcement. Randy's presence calmed me, or at least helped cut back on the type of musical associations that did run through my head. Buddy Holly. Otis Redding. John Denver. During the two and a half years of our long-distance courtship, flying back and forth between New York and Chicago, I never told Randy how nervous I felt having thirty-five thousand feet between me and solid ground.

The guy in the aisle seat shifted his position, his shoulder angling into mine. The passenger in front of me lowered the back of his seat into my knees. I thought about the Chicago me, and the New York me. For years I considered New York a foreign country with a bad rate of exchange. But I'd learned to say How-stun Street, not Hue-stun. Soda instead of pop. I'd become more decisive. I no longer held up lines at the deli while debating corned beef versus pastrami. I'd even reached the point where there were New York women who wanted to be friends with me whom I didn't have time for. I was a duck out of water who had learned to navigate the landscape between the Hudson and East rivers. I'd found my nest. I no longer lived in the City of Big Shoulders, but I could lean on Randy and his big shoulders.

I thought how blessed Claudia and I were to find these men to love and then be brave enough to love them. Claudia had let Charlie into her heart; she had finally let down her guard. Or maybe she was just tired of lugging her guard around.

I learned that relying on Randy was a sign of strength, not weakness. After Teddy died, I'd pressed the hold button on my emotions. Randy taught me to trust again, to have faith. He made it easy by being clear and forthright. Was it the New Yorker in him or was it just him? There was no second-guessing, no verbal dodgeball. When he said he loved me, I could believe him. Giving love was one thing. Accepting love, that was the real challenge.

By the time a woman is independent enough to pay her own rent, pop for her own meals, and be able to head out on a Saturday night without a man and still have fun, even get laid when necessary, well, by then all the wrong reasons for getting married don't exist anymore. There's no *we've been going steady since high school, it's time.* There's no social pressure because *all my friends are getting married;* and miraculous old Russian women aside, it's certainly not because *I long to have a baby.* You don't settle for a work in progress, you don't marry someone with *potential,* because if he hasn't developed it by then, he never will; you know what you're getting. You've had so much time to imagine what you're looking for that when it actually shows up it doesn't take years to recognize it. You go in with high hopes but lower expectations. You laugh more. You're not so hard on yourself. When you pledge your love till death do you part, there are fewer decades left to screw it up.

I want to wake up every morning next to Randy. I want to see the world though his eyes. I want to see myself through his eyes. The one reason to get married later in life is the best of all reasons: love.

The plane hit a bump—acknowledged by me with something between a yelp and a muffled shriek. I thought Randy was sleeping. His eyes were closed, his headphones on, but he immediately reached over and held my hand. Bumps are so much easier with him by my side, both of us heading in the same direction.

ONE LAST THING YOU SHOULD KNOW IN BACK

~~~

When I was first adjusting to my life in New York, in constant search of tranquility, I spent time in Central Park, New York's temple to tranquility. I'd sit on a bench and cheer myself on: *I'm grounded. I'm centered. I'm cool.*

Sometimes the bench would be near the boathouse. Other times off the reservoir. Once by the carousel, and another time across from the Marionette Theatre. Long after I stopped retreating to the benches, I'd still find myself pausing to read the plaques that grace so many of them, the small metal labels complete with dedications.

Some of the inscriptions strike me as self-serving: PETER, EDDY, DOROTHY, AND ELIZABETH GIVE THIS BENCH WITH LOVE TO THEIR PARENTS.

Others can break my heart. All those with the date September 11, 2001.

Discovering a plaque for "the joyful life of Jim Henson who loved this walk in the park" saddened me on behalf of Kermit and Miss Piggy—and me.

Around the curve from the entrance at Eighty-First Street and Central Park West a plaque is inscribed: SARAH, WILL YOU MARRY ME? LOVE, DREW.

Did Sarah say yes? Or did Drew just blow a month's pay on a testament to his inability to read a woman's signals?

While I continued reading benches, Randy swore off subways. Maybe it was something he dreamt, or ate, but one morning he woke up, declared he'd had his fill of mass transit, and started walking to work.

He walks from Riverside Drive to Central Park's entrance at Eighty-Fifth, weaves his way past the Delacorte Theater and up to Belvedere Castle.

He walks across the smooth white wood Bow Bridge, always slippery on rainy days, stopping to check out the algae-covered pond below, and all the turtles gathered on a single rock, like they're conducting a co-op board meeting.

The band shell and the long, bench-lined Poets Walk follow Bethesda Fountain, with its circular brick terrace and water-spewing winged angel propping up blasé pigeons. It's a beautiful pathway, Parisian in feeling, with the last great stand of elm trees in America creating a magnificent canopy overhead. Statues of famous poets like Robert Burns and forgotten poets like Fitz-Greene Halleck pop up along the way, ending at a tall bronze of Christopher Columbus in a belted tunic, medallion draped around his neck, and a fur-trimmed cape. He's facing east, and looking outward, like he knows where he's going. Which in his case should have been west.

I knew Randy's route because the ad agency where I worked lost its big account and I lost my job. I began accompanying him—transforming his peaceful, meditative journey into a chatterfest of questions.

"What's so great about the Great Lawn?"

"How come the Sheep Meadow doesn't have any sheep?"

"What's with all these people in paddleboats?"

Randy communes with nature, feels at one with the earth. He can identify trees by their Latin names and recite the entire history of Olmsted and Vaux designing the park. He likes bird-watching, which just goes to prove you can be married to a man for years and still be surprised by him. And then there's me, who won't even watch the Discovery Channel, a woman who feels blessed to live in a city with thirteen thousand taxis.

One morning in late July, I begged off from walking Randy to work. I kissed him good-bye with the kind of kiss designed to embarrass a teenager. As soon as the elevator doors closed behind him, I slipped out of my robe and into a green cotton sundress. I hurried to the subway, stopping only at our corner bodega to buy a dozen long-stemmed pink roses.

I took the subway to Sixty-Third and Broadway, heading Randy off as I walked east and into the park just north of Sixty-Sixth to the base of Poets Walk, right behind the butt of Columbus.

I paid for the bench with my unemployment checks, proud of myself for basically recycling the money back to the city.

I sat and waited, feeling self-conscious as I clutched the bouquet of roses, the skirt of my green dress spread out across my knees. Earnest-looking men and highly focused women wearing suits and carrying briefcases and talking into cell phones rushed past. I must have looked like a jilted lover, some pathetic Mrs. Havisham.

On one side of me a bench was dedicated to Guy Williams, a television star who played Zorro when we were kids. On the other side, a bench in honor of a woman named Inger Fredriksen. I pictured her as a buxom blond Swede.

Maybe some fascinating warbler or noteworthy flicker delayed Randy. It seemed quite some time before I saw him striding down Poets Walk, chin forward, energetic, so wildly dear to me.

Just as he passed Sir Walter Scott he spotted me. He smiled in surprise. I smiled back. He walked over, asked what I was doing there, sat down, and kissed me.

I gave him the roses, then slid to the side.

I didn't expect him to cry. But he's a man capable of a profound depth of feeling.

I told him he'd better stop before he got to the office. That people would think he was crying over the stock market.

He laughed. Then kissed me again.

It's a lovely bench. Randy's bench. With its small silver plaque.

It's the one that says: MY BEAUTIFUL RANDY ARTHUR

If you spend enough time there, you'll feel right at home.

The Thank You Page

Is there anybody out there who didn't read an early draft? Probably not. But Catherine Ventura (who was on *It's Academic* in high school and is still ridiculously smart), Mindy Greenstein (my most patient reader; and shortest), and Mark Burk (the grand master of depth and clarity) read more versions than anyone should humanly bear.

I'm about the eight millionth writer to thank Charles Salzberg on an acknowledgments page. But the only friend who can get him to eat at Bloomingdale's.

Heartfelt thank yous all around go to:

Kathy Sagan. I will say it again. Kathy Sagan. Kathy Sagan. A great editor, kind person, and a credit to mankind in general.

Joyce Hunt. Former archivist for the New York Proust Society and forever dear friend.

Dickie Harris, who first inspired me to write when he told me: "Everyone says what you want them to say and everyone dies when you want them to die."

Professor Sam Apple, who first kicked my butt to write this particular book. You rock, Shmulik.

Carlye Hirsch at the Apple store on Fifth Avenue, who taught me how to format chapters. No relation to Sam Apple.

Jeff and Judy McElnea, who introduced me to David Fisher, my writing guru; Laura Stevens Fisher, cheerleader guru; and Laurie Rosenfield, all-round guru.

Mike Lynn and Steve Brodwolf, my wise and wacky Promo-sapiens.

JoAnn Tansman, my personal paparazzi.

Cynthia Herrli, my Swiss Miss.

And the divine Jody Klein.

A lot of my participles would be dangling and paragraphs rambling if not for: Gail Eisenberg (who first called me a Nose Talker), Jennifer Berman, Bernadette Duncan, Laura Arens Feurstein, Debra L. Eder, Ronnie Weinstock, Robin Horton, and Deb Victoroff.

You too, Eric Weber, but I don't want to risk emasculating you by putting your name in the above paragraph.

A huge cyber thank you to my fabulous right-brain Web designer Suzi Barst and left-brain Web developer Julian Yochum. The perfect brain trust.

If you're a writer looking to find the name of my agent by reading my acknowledgments, you're in luck: Gail Hochman. I love her.

And a mega thank you to Santi Suarez, who fixed up Lynn Crosswaite with Dan Turrett who then fixed up Randy with me.

G GALLERY READERS GROUP GUIDE

THE LAST
BLIND DATE

~~~~~~~~~~~

LINDA YELLIN

DISCUSSION GUIDE

~~~~~~~

1. A big theme in *The Last Blind Date* is the uprooting of one's life—starting over. What does it take to start over? Courage? An adventurous spirit? Desperation? Think about people you know who have uprooted themselves. How do their stories end?

2. Linda waits over two years to meet Randy's children. Do you agree with his decision not to introduce his children to women he dated? What do you think his reasoning was? Do you agree with his decision to not introduce his children to Linda for so long?

3. When Linda is worried that Randy won't make a commitment to her, she's told by a coworker who always speaks in sports metaphors that "Michael Jordan was famous for never thinking about the last game, only focusing on the next one, and how [she] shouldn't dump former losses onto some guy who had just shown up at halftime." Is that good advice? Was it relevant to Linda's situation? Have you ever been wary of a current relationship because of problems in a past relationship?

4. Linda writes, "I used to share every detail of my life with Claudia and now most of my confidences were shared

with Randy. You can't be married to a man and reporting the intimate details of your life to a girlfriend, so as much as we adored each other, the distance between Claudia and me had grown wider than a plane ride." Do relationships change when a close friend falls in love or gets married? In many ways, Linda and Claudia are quite different from one another. What is the glue that holds their friendship together? Why do you think Linda's friendship with Claudia survived her move to New York when several of her other girlfriends drifted away? Are there quirky, unexpected friendships in your life? What are they based upon?

5. In the chapter "Dating for Girlfriends," Linda explores the complexity of making new friends; the feelings associated with missing long-term girlfriends; and the importance of female friendships. She's told that a potential friend "doesn't even have time for the girlfriends she already has." Is it more difficult to make friends later in life?

6. Before Linda meets Randy's children, she asks for advice from two friends who were both second wives and stepmom experts. She's told, "Whatever you do, never get between a little girl and her daddy." And that she must "accept the fact that a man will always put his kids first." Do you agree with that advice? Did you ever have to adjust to stepchildren? A stepparent? What was it like the first time you met them? Were you ever jealous of their relationship

with your partner or your parent? How did you feel about Randy asking Linda to "throw the game" when Phoebe and Benjamin get upset that she's winning at bowling?

7. How does Linda's relationship with Phoebe evolve? Did it seem to be more challenging than her relationship with Benjamin? Why? Do you think it's more difficult for girls to accept a new stepmom than it is for boys? How much did the kids' ages at the time they met Linda factor into their acceptance of her? Did Randy do a good job of maintaining a balance between his relationships with his children and his new wife?

8. Linda is often intimidated by Randy's ex-wife. The night before she first meets Phoebe and Benjamin, Randy's mother tells her "what an excellent mother Susan was, how she was always volunteering for school trips, making organic meals, sewing costumes for school plays." When Linda attends Benjamin's baseball game she observes, "Susan said several hellos. She knew everyone's name. I envied her being the real mother, the involved mother, the Snack Mother." When introduced to another mom, Linda writes, "The fact that Susan and I looked like sisters only complicated matters." What did you think of the relationship between Linda and Susan? Is it atypical? How did you feel about Linda trying to fix Susan up on a blind date? Do you think it is unusual that Randy married two women who looked a lot alike? Do you know anyone who's also done that?

9. How did you feel about the relationships between Randy's parents, Larry and Ruth? And Linda's parents, Bernie and Vivien? How, in different ways, do they exemplify good marriages? Do you think that children of good marriages tend to end up in a good marriage? What did you think about the ways Randy and Linda interact with their parents? Consider Linda's phone calls with her parents and the visit to the retirement home in your discussion.

10. When Linda goes back to Chicago for a visit after settling in New York, she wonders, "Was I a Chicagoan living in New York? Or a New Yorker from Chicago?" How long does it take to feel truly at home in a new location? By the end of the book, do you think Linda considered herself "a New Yorker"?

11. After Claudia's wedding, on the plane home to New York, Linda realizes she's "learned that relying on Randy was a sign of strength, not weakness. After Teddy died, I'd pressed the hold button on my emotions. Randy taught me to trust again, to have faith . . . giving love was one thing. Accepting love, that was the real challenge." Do you agree that accepting love can be more difficult than giving love? What are some of the other things that Linda learned throughout the course of her story?

ENHANCE YOUR BOOK CLUB

1. Visit the author's website at http://lindayellin.com. It includes a timeline and pictures of her life, some of her magazine pieces, and a Q&A with Linda.

2. Have a movie night renting some good old-fashioned New York love stories, such as *An Affair to Remember; Working Girl; When Harry Met Sally; West Side Story; You've Got Mail.*

3. Linda writes about the numerous benches bearing dedications in Central Park and of Randy's enthusiasm for the park's history. Learn more about Central Park at: http://www.centralpark.com/guide/history.html. To find out how to get a personal plaque on one of the park's benches, go to: http://www.centralparknyc.org/donate/honor-someone-special/adopt-a-bench.html.

4. The next time you're in New York, visit Randy's bench. It's just south of Poets Walk, "right behind the butt of Columbus."